GOTHIC ARCHITECTURE

SIMPSON'S HISTORY OF
ARCHITECTURAL DEVELOPMENT
New Edition

———

VOLUME I
ANCIENT AND CLASSICAL
ARCHITECTURE
Hugh Plommer

VOLUME II
EARLY CHRISTIAN, BYZANTINE AND
ROMANESQUE ARCHITECTURE
Cecil Stewart

VOLUME III
GOTHIC ARCHITECTURE
Cecil Stewart

VOLUME IV
RENAISSANCE ARCHITECTURE
J. Quentin Hughes
and
Norbert Lynton

VOLUME V
NINETEENTH AND TWENTIETH
CENTURY ARCHITECTURE
Thomas Howarth

Simpson's History of
Architectural Development
VOL. III

GOTHIC
ARCHITECTURE

BY

Cecil Stewart

DAVID McKAY COMPANY, INC.

Published throughout the world
except the United States, by
LONGMANS, GREEN AND CO LTD

PRINTED IN GREAT BRITAIN
BY JARROLD AND SONS LTD, NORWICH

CONTENTS

PLATES

between pages 128 *and* 129

13 Salisbury Cathedral; cloisters (*Reece Winstone*)
    Wells Cathedral; stairs to chapter house (*Reece Winstone*)
    Wells Cathedral; choir vaulting (*Herbert Felton*)
14 Gloucester Cathedral; choir (*National Buildings Record*)
    Gloucester Cathedral; cloisters (*Albert W. Kerr*)

between pages 144 *and* 145

15 King's College Chapel, Cambridge; nave (*A. F. Kersting*)
    Westminster Abbey, Henry VII Chapel; pendant vault
    (*Herbert Felton*)
16 Cologne Cathedral; from the south-east (*Bildarchiv Foto
    Marburg*)
    Strassburg Cathedral; detail of west front (*Courtauld
    Institute of Art*)

between pages 176 *and* 177

17 S. Elizabeth, Marburg; from the north-west (*Bildarchiv Foto
    Marburg*)
    Braunschweig Town Hall (*Bildarchiv Foto Marburg*)
18 Burgos Cathedral (*A. F. Kersting*)
    Palma, Majorca; south front (*Fox Photos Ltd*)

between pages 192 *and* 193

19 S. Caterina, Pisa; west front (*A. F. Kersting*)
    Siena Cathedral; west front (*Courtauld Institute of Art*)
20 Siena Cathedral; interior (*Alinari*)
    Florence Cathedral; south side (*Alinari*)
21 Milan Cathedral; west front (*A. F. Kersting*)
22 Palazzo Communale, Siena (*Alinari*)
    Doge's Palace, Venice (*Mansell Collection*)

between pages 208 *and* 209

23 Krak des Chevaliers (*A. F. Kersting*)
    Château du Pierrefonds (*Giraudon*)
24 Harlech Castle (*Aero Pictorial Ltd*)
    Moreton Old Hall (*J. Allan Cash*)

EXPLANATORY NOTE TO THIS REVISED EDITION

John Shute, probably the very first English writer on architecture, prefaced his work[1] with the apology: 'For I am but a gatherer and disposer of other men's Stuffs at my best value.' I might well say the same about this particular volume of Simpson's *History*, for it embodies little more than the information I have been able to garner from others. The duty which I have tried to perform, as editor, has been to accept, as a basis, Simpson's original writings, and to expand and modify them in the light of modern historical research. Above all, I have kept in mind that the purpose of this work is to provide information for the student, rather than to present new ideas and discoveries for the specialist.

I cannot say, like Simpson, that 'there are very few churches of importance in France, Germany, or Italy mentioned in this volume which I have not studied', nor that 'my primary interest for over thirty years has been medieval architecture'. But then, I was not a pupil, as he was, of that great Gothic Revivalist, George Frederick Bodley. Nevertheless, I have covered a good deal of the ground. Except for Spain, which I have not yet had the opportunity to visit, I have seen the best that western Europe has to offer to the sum of Gothic architecture, and my appreciation has not been coloured, as was that of Simpson and so many of his contemporaries, by the desire to acquire convenient details which might, when the occasion arose, be applied in architectural practice. The study of architectural history is now, fortunately, freed from such materialistic prejudice. It is enough if one studies Gothic architecture because one likes the look of it. Equally, one will learn more by looking at it than by reading this book. Happily, there is still plenty to see. I dare say there is not a country nor a district in western Europe without some monument to its medieval past. That this book may help towards some understanding of what one may see is its main aim.

I have followed Simpson's method and, like Simpson, have accepted the hackneyed sub-division of English Gothic—Early English, Decorated, and Perpendicular—because, in spite of

[1] *The First and Chiefe Grounds of Architecture used in all the ancient and famous Monyments*, by John Shute, paynter and architecte, 1563.

disadvantages and modern alternatives, they remain most generally understood. I have added new introductory material and a chapter on secular architecture, and have re-written most of the rest. Nearly all the original illustrations have been re-drawn so that they follow the pattern and scale of those in Vol. II, and many more have been added. But it is still Simpson's *History*. The errors of omission and commission are mine.

I wish to thank Dr. J. E. Partington for his guidance on vernacular architecture in the Middle Ages, and Mr. Clifford Pickup for his help in matters concerning the structural significance of the pointed arch. I am grateful, too, to those students who from time to time have helped me in the preparation of the line drawings; to those who provided the photographs, the sources of which are indicated in the list of plates; and to my wife, without whose constant assistance this work would never have been completed.

1960   C. S.

NOTE TO SECOND IMPRESSION

I am grateful to Mr. John H. Harvey for pointing out many errors in the 1960 edition, which I have now been able to correct.

1963   C. S.

CHAPTER I

THE STUDY OF GOTHIC ARCHITECTURE

THE Gothic tradition in the West, like the Byzantine in the East, never died. Not a year passed without the erection of some Gothic building. In France, Germany and England the Gothic style persisted through the Renaissance years, and even in the eighteenth century, when it seemed to have reached its lowest ebb, the antiquarians and the archaeologists found it possessed of an interest that stimulated an astonishing revival, the fruits of which remain among the principal adornments of our nineteenth-century cities. Even Sir Christopher Wren, who described Gothic architecture as a 'fantastical and licentious manner of building', was responsible for several Gothic works, of which Tom Tower at Christ Church, Oxford, is perhaps the most remarkable; at S. Michael's, Cornhill, S. Mary, Aldermanbury, and S. Alban's, Wood Street, he adopted the Gothic mode, though not very successfully. Vanbrugh's house at Blackheath was enlivened by medieval castellations and a fortified tower. Other great architects, like Hawksmoor, Wyatt, Kent and Nash, all used Gothic stylisms. In France, even at Versailles, the Royal Chapel was designed on Gothic principles, complete with flying buttresses, although the details and mouldings were Classical; and Marie Antoinette built for herself in the grounds of the Petit Trianon a retreat from Classical formality, a hermitage that was at once romantic and Gothic. Nor did the Gothic mode disappear even for cathedrals. That of Orleans was built by the greatest French Classical architects through the reigns of the Bourbons from Henry VI to Louis XVI. In Germany, as for instance at the Marienkirche at Wolfenbüttel and the church at Bückeburg, we find buttresses, traceried windows, ribbed vaults and all the characteristics of Gothic architecture persisting well into the seventeenth century. In England, at Liverpool and at Guildford, the style which might have died with Elizabeth I is continuing even now through the reign of Elizabeth II.

It was Goethe who led the western world in a new, romantic attitude towards Gothic. In 1772 he wrote his paean of praise for

I

Erwin of Steinbach, whom he believed to be the designer of Strassburg cathedral:

> When for the first time I went towards the Minster, general notions of Taste filled my head. By hearsay, I honoured the harmony of the masses, the purity of the forms, was a sworn enemy of the tangled arbitrariness of Gothick ornament. Under the Gothick heading, I piled up, like the article in a dictionary, all the synonymous mis-understandings of the confused, the unregulated, the unnatural, the patched-up, the botched, the overladen, which had ever passed through my head. . . . And so, as I walked towards the Minster I shuddered in prospect of some malformed, curly-bristled ogre.
>
> With what unlooked-for emotions did the sight surprise me, when I stepped before it! A sensation of wholeness, greatness, filled my soul; which, composed of a thousand harmonizing details, I could savour and enjoy, yet by no means understand or explain. So it is, men say, with the bliss of Heaven. . . . It [Strassburg cathedral] rises like a most sublime, wide-arching Tree of God, who, with a thousand of boughs, a million of twigs, and leafage like the sands of the sea, tells forth to the neighbourhood the glory of the Lord, his master. . . . As in the works of eternal Nature, down to the minutest fibrel, all is shaped, all purposes to the whole. How the firm-grounded gigantic building lightly rears itself into the air! How filigree'd, all of it, and yet for eternity![1]

The idea of Gothic architecture was thus raised above the merely pretty and fanciful into which it had relapsed. No longer was it to be regarded only as a style that would do very well for a country folly or a summer-house. Gothic architecture was seen to be imbued with a mysterious and wonderful grandeur which deserved study. In 1773, the year after Goethe's visit to Strassburg, the first volumes of Grose's *Antiquities of England and Wales* were published. These, and the succeeding studies of Scotland and Ireland, were amply illustrated by careful engravings of general views and details of ornamental sculpture, fonts, brasses and other ecclesiastical objects. In 1786, Gough's *Sepulchral Monuments of Great Britain* and Hearn's *Antiquities of Great Britain* were published. In 1795 an assistant of James Wyatt, John Carter, published his *Ancient Architecture of England*. This was divided into two parts, the first being entitled 'The Orders of Architecture during the British, Roman, Saxon and Norman Eras', and the second, 'The Orders of Architecture during the Reigns of Henry III, Edward

[1] Translated by Geoffrey Grigson and published in the *Architectural Review*, Vol. 98, pp. 156–9.

III, Richard II, Henry VII and Henry VIII'. Gradually, through the last twenty years of the century, there was accumulating in England and abroad a mass of documentary material, and the study of Gothic architecture had become as acceptable to the dilettanti as had been, fifty years before, the study of the Italian Renaissance.

The study of Gothic involved two problems. First, there was the question of how it originated, and second, the problem of nomenclature of its varied manifestations. Of all the various theories of the origin of Gothic, the most astonishing was that propounded by Sir James Hall in a paper read to the Royal Society of Edinburgh in 1797, which was so well received that for fifteen years he persisted in his researches and produced, in the end, a handsome folio and a most curious structure in his garden. The folio—*The Origin, History and Principles of Gothic Architecture*—set out to prove that not only did Greek architecture have its origin in timber construction (as was commonly accepted), but also Gothic. Nor was the author content merely to theorize. 'The whole of this theory', he wrote, 'has been submitted to an experimental test, by the construction of a wicker fabric now standing in my garden. In it all the peculiar forms of Gothic architecture have been restored to their original state. The facility which has attended this restoration is very satisfactory, and affords, I conceive, no small confirmation of the theory by which it has been accomplished.'

Every feature was carefully considered. The incidence of crockets was justified by the natural burgeoning from the main stems. Their appearance in high places such as steeples, where, in his structure, the branches could have no direct contact with the ground, was explained by the custom of decorating churches on Palm Sunday with fresh twigs. Even the most complex tracery and vaulting were shown to have originated in simple wickerwork. It is all delightfully easy. The transition from Early English to Decorated becomes obvious as each bud unfolds and creates a further crocket, and as each branch is added for reinforcement, to produce a flowing tracery. And when we clear away the thicket and allow for the natural deflection of the arch branches under the load of thatch, we arrive, of course, at the Perpendicular style.

'Where an obvious source presents itself,' Sir James Hall concluded, 'to which all these forms infinitely varied in all other particulars, and agreeing in this alone, can easily be traced, may

we not presume that the genuine origin of the style is discovered?'
But there were some outstanding facts which were more difficult
to explain, the chief being that it was commonly accepted that
Gothic architecture was the successor to Romanesque; and it
would be difficult to suggest that the heavy, round-arched
Romanesque had a timber origin. 'In answering this objection,'
he wrote, 'I must admit that some parts of the subject are involved
in obscurity which I cannot pretend to penetrate.'

 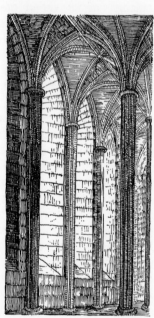

After Sir James Hall.

But Sir James did not hesitate for long. If his theory was
correct, there must be some answer. Are we *sure* that Romanesque
architecture is earlier than Gothic, just because the surviving
Romanesque buildings are older than the surviving Gothic
buildings? 'There is no direct evidence,' he said, 'that the twelfth
century was the period of its [Gothic's] first introduction. Buildings
of this sort may have been erected at far earlier periods, without
having been preserved; or Gothic works may exist at this hour
the antiquity of which is far greater than has been supposed.'
    What is significant is not the fancifulness of Sir James Hall's
theory, but the fact that he was only one among dozens of learned

men who were becoming more and more interested in the study of Gothic archaeology. Britton's *Architectural Antiquities*, Vol. V, mentions no fewer than sixty pamphlets devoted to Gothic studies. There was, however, much confusion of terms and of dates. Norman work was frequently confused with Saxon, and the pointed arch might belong to either. It was not until 1819 that an acceptable glossary of terms and a chronology was provided. Its author was Thomas Rickman, and his *Attempt to Discriminate the Styles of English Architecture* not only gave most convenient labels—Early English, Decorated, Perpendicular and so on—but, by means of hundreds of careful engravings, set recognized models which professional architects could apply in practical design. His titles, though temporarily discarded in the heyday of the Victorian Gothic Revival, remain in common parlance, and in spite of occasional inconvenience seem preferable to a numerical system such as First, Second and Third Pointed, or to the highly complicated titles which Rickman's pupil, Edmund Sharpe, devised, and which led to such extraordinary combinations as 'the early years of the late middle pointed'.

Having acquired the vocabulary, architects now began to explore the grammar, and especially the construction, of Gothic. At once it became evident that Gothic was something much more than the mere application of stylistic trimmings; Gothic was a way of building. The standards of judgment were laid down by Augustus Welby Northmore Pugin in his *True Principles of Pointed or Christian Architecture* (1841), as follows: '1st, that there should be no features about a building which are not necessary for convenience, construction, or propriety; 2nd, that all ornament should consist of enrichment of the essential construction of the building.' Pugin discovered that in Gothic architecture alone these principles applied. To Pugin, Gothic was essentially masonry construction, whereas Greek was no more than wooden construction translated into stone. 'Pointed architecture', he added, 'does not conceal her construction, but beautifies it: Classic architecture seeks to conceal instead of decorating it . . . nothing can be worse.' Nor are the buildings of the Renaissance any better. The key to Gothic architecture is to be observed in the buttresses and flying buttresses:

> Who can stand among the airy arches of Amiens, Cologne, Chartres, Beauvais or Westminster, and not be filled with admiration at the mechanical skill and beautiful combination of form which are united in their construction? But, say the modern critics, they are only props,

After Pugin.

(Left) Section of a pointed church, with the flying buttresses decorated. (Right) Section of St. Paul's, London, a church built in the revived pagan style with flying buttresses concealed by a screen.

and a bungling contrivance. Let us examine this. Are the revived pagan buildings constructed with such superior skill as to dispense with these supports? By no means; the clumsy vaults of St. Paul's, London, mere coffered semi-arches, without ribs or intersections, have their flying buttresses; but as this style of architecture does not admit of the great principle of decorating utility, these buttresses, instead of being made ornamental, are concealed by an enormous screen, going entirely round the building. So that in fact one half of the edifice is built to conceal the other. Miserable expedient! worthy only of the debased style in which it has been resorted to.

A further complication in Pugin's theory arose from his religious beliefs, which were vehemently Roman Catholic. Gothic architecture, he considered, was the architecture of the only true Christian faith. 'Indeed, if we view pointed architecture in its true light as Christian art, as the faith itself is perfect, so are the principles on which it is founded.' The decline in architecture, in fact, coincided with the decline in faith; the Renaissance, with the Reformation. 'In the name of common sense,' he cried, 'whilst we profess the creed of Christians, whilst we glory in being Englishmen, let us have an architecture which will alike remind us of our faith and our country!' Pugin's concern was, of course, less with the Gothic of the past than with the possibility of its adoption in the future; but his writings introduced a remarkable twist to the study of Gothic, for Gothic after Pugin was to be regarded as the 'functional style', into which every feature was logically integrated and in which each stage of development could be traced automatically and practically from the last.

The scientific nature of Gothic structure was expounded in a less excitable way by Alfred Bartholomew in his *Specifications for Practical Architecture* (1840): 'In pointed architecture,' he wrote, 'all is structural, from the boss which confirms the arch ribs (radiating from it as the spokes radiate from the hub of a wheel), to the wall buttresses which receive the energy of the vaulting.'

In vaulting, he went on, the Gothic builders began by reducing the lateral thrust of the work to the smallest limits, by cutting out all the otherwise more level and hazardous parts of the vaulting, so that what remained scarcely left its perpendicular bearing upon the walls. They next greatly reduced the weight of the vaulting, by forming it of small stone ribs, with a mere thin cuticle of lighter materials in short and narrow panels between the ribs. By putting all the strength into the ribs, strutting them across as was necessary, the active force was conducted 'as easily as water is conducted down a pipe'. Then knowing by the laws of the resolution of forces the way in which the united thrusts would move, they counteracted, by the smallest quantity of materials set in the form of flying buttresses, pinnacles and wall buttresses, that force which unrestrained might have endangered the walls. Thus every feature was brought into active service, and they were able to carve and enrich every part of the fabric.

Having described the method by which the active forces of the vaults were conducted to the ground with an absolute minimum of materials, Bartholomew proceeded, in a florid style which I have contracted for ease of reading, to explain the significance of flying buttresses and pinnacles. Having found the precise place where the active force of the vaulting was pressing against the wall, the builders provided the flying buttress, just as a modern carpenter provides temporary shoring against a dangerous wall. Thus the thrust at the point where the flying buttress joined the wall buttress concentrated all the active forces communicated by the vault, 'in the same manner as in wrestling all the force received by the arms becomes concentrated in the spine, pressing its vertebrae close together'. Further to direct the course of the active force, they ran up the head of the wall buttress in the form of a pinnacle, which having only downward gravity so changed the course of the active force that it could be confined within the body of a buttress of comparatively moderate dimensions. The pinnacles, which were vulgarly considered merely as ornaments, became the most refined instruments in the economy and security of buildings. 'In fact, the whole form, position and management of the counter-abutments of Gothic vaultings, were like those of a human skeleton placed in a leaning posture, with the bones of the legs away from the base, those of the hands and arms pressing against the moving part of the vault, with the skull erect to confirm and steady the spine, and the whole strengthened by sufficient flesh and muscle.'

Bartholomew was probably the first to enunciate the principle that good architecture was always intimately associated with clarity of structure. The study of Gothic thereafter was concerned with the development of the style as a logical structural process, in which each new feature was introduced to solve a particular building problem. Usually it began with the vaults, for every

After Alfred Bartholomew.

feature was a consequence of these. Bartholomew said that 'PURE TASTE IN ARCHITECTURE HAS IN PAST AGES BEEN PURELY STRUCTURAL and that a departure from this wisdom is the true cause of the TASTE (or to speak more properly the WANT OF TASTE) in modern architecture.' So, at the outset of Victoria's reign, much of the romance and glamour of Gothic study had departed. Its qualities were evidently concerned with mechanical skill and contrivance rather than with the mystery of religion or subtleties of spatial relationships and proportions. For nearly a century this practical approach to Gothic architecture dominated historical study. If there was wonder in Gothic, it was only in consequence of the application of the proper building technique. One admired Gothic architecture in the same terms as, say, the Great Western Canal or the Clifton Suspension Bridge. They were great structural achievements, no more than that.

It was left to the two dominating figures of the second half of the nineteenth century to formulate this rational, as opposed to mystical, approach to Gothic studies. In England, in 1855, George Gilbert Scott, as Professor of Architecture at the Royal Academy, broke with the established Classical tradition by delivering a course of lectures on medieval architecture. In these lectures he did little more than develop Pugin's Principles, but Scott, being neither a Catholic nor a medievalist, was able to tone down some of Pugin's vehemence. To Scott, the claims of Gothic for especial study were: 'Firstly, that, though we are in the habit of considering it antiquated, it is in fact the architecture of the modern as distinguished from the ancient world. Secondly, that it is the architecture of the Germanic nations, through whose lands the main stream of civilization now runs. And thirdly, that it is the latest original style of architecture which the civilized world has produced.'

To show how that style developed, and to fix precisely the moment when it reached perfection, was his aim. He was able 'to fix the end of the thirteenth century, viz., from 1270 to 1300 A.D., as the period at which the most perfect ecclesiastical architecture is to be found'. The object of Scott's investigation was not purely antiquarian. It was, in the absence of a nineteenth-century style of architecture, to determine the most suitable point from which in practice one should develop an architectural revival. What Scott did not seem to realize was that the logical consequence of the thirteenth century was the fourteenth century, and not the nineteenth; that it was impossible to revive a style without regard to the spirit of the age, a spirit which, in spite of Pugin's exhortations, was singularly remote from medievalism.

Scott's contemporary in France, Eugène Viollet-le-Duc, saw the wonder of Gothic in strictly practical terms. Gothic was simply a sound way of building, given certain material conditions and limitations. 'The adoption of the pointed arch was surely the result of observations which the builders had made upon the dislocation of semi-circular arches. Some had been pleased to see in the use of the pointed arch a symbolical or mystical idea; they had pretended to demonstrate that these arches had a deeper religious meaning than the semi-circular arch. But men were quite as religious at the beginning of the twelfth century as at the end, if not more so, and the pointed arch appears at precisely the moment

when the spirit of analysis, or the study of the exact sciences and
of philosophy, began to spring up in the midst of a society up to
that time almost theocratic.' What Viollet-le-Duc set out to prove
was that Gothic was an intellectually satisfactory way of building.
Its emotional content was not important. So, in his article,
'Construction', in his *Dictionnaire Raisonée* (1854–68), he follows
the course of medieval building technique:

> Logical deductions follow one another with fatal severity. One step
> forward can never be the last, one must always go on; from the moment
> that a principle is the result of reasoning, it at once becomes its slave.
> Such is the spirit of the western nations; it comes out as soon as the
> society of the Middle Ages begins to be conscious and to organize
> itself; it could not be checked, for the first man who founds a principle
> upon a course of reasoning cannot say to Reason 'thou shalt go no
> further'.

It must not be assumed from this that Viollet-le-Duc had arrived
at a conclusive estimate of the Gothic style. Unlike Scott, whose
concern was the discovery of 'the true point of perfection which we
should take as the nucleus of development,' Viollet-le-Duc had
determined to exploit the underlying principles of Gothic in the
terms of the new materials now available. 'Gothic', he says, 'is
primarily a useful study because it establishes true principles to
which we ought to submit today. If the Gothic builders had had
at their disposal cast iron in large pieces, they would have availed
themselves eagerly of this sure means of obtaining supports as
slender as possible yet rigid, and perhaps they would have used
it with more skill than ourselves.'

It will be noticed that both Scott and Viollet-le-Duc are agreed
on the desirability of the study of Gothic on practical grounds.
Scott's aim was simply to revive the old style and in some way
fit it to the needs of the nineteenth century; Viollet-le-Duc was
determined logically to follow the structural principles of Gothic,
but at the same time to take advantage of the possibilities of new
materials and especially of cast iron. As he put it, the problem to
be solved was 'to improve on the system of equilibrium adopted
by the medieval architects by means of iron, but with due regard
to the qualities of that material'. It must be admitted that the
architectural products of both men were disappointing. Scott's
churches do not even remotely resemble those of the Middle Ages
he so much admired; Viollet-le-Duc's essays in original design,
as illustrated in the *Entretiens*, seem remarkable for their oddity

After Viollet-le-Duc.

Design for a concert hall in stone, iron and brick.

rather than their rationality. He did not, however, pretend, as I am afraid Scott did, that he was producing masterpieces. All he claimed to do was to establish a reasonable principle of design which he thought might be 'capable of possessing style'.

There can, I think, be little doubt that the study of Gothic architecture was befogged by its practical possibilities. One studied Gothic in order to acquire not only the vocabulary but also the details which could be applied in architectural practice. It was a natural consequence that the Royal Institute of British Architects instituted 'Gothic' as an examination subject for those intending to specialize in Gothic architecture. Other candidates might choose Classical or Renaissance. There was no other choice; but then, the modern movement at the beginning of the twentieth century had not begun or, if it had, was unrecognized. The twentieth-century student of Gothic was therefore largely dependent upon the writings and thoughts of the nineteenth century, and the writers of text-books, Banister Fletcher, Statham, Simpson, and the rest, followed the Victorian lead in emphasizing the essentially practical nature of Gothic, by tracing the logical sequence of its development.

During the last twenty years, a new and different approach has been made towards the study of Gothic. It has become obvious that nineteenth-century realism could not explain the wonder of Gothic. It is not enough to say that the medieval builders wished, on grounds of permanence, to erect a structure with a stone ceiling and that the pointed arch, together with the rib system of vaulting, was a consequent statical convenience. It would have been possible, with a little extra masonry, to develop a round-arched system. While the Victorian writers explained how the forces of vaults were carried by flying buttresses over the roofs of the aisles and down to the ground by carefully stepped wall buttresses, they did not explain why, in the first place, the Gothic builders wanted to erect such lofty vaults, why they set themselves such a formidable task. It was not necessary on purely practical grounds. The cathedrals of France, to function as places of assembly and worship, could have been as materialistically efficient boxes had they been half the height. Their loftiness must have sprung from some aesthetic concept. But the nineteenth century, enthralled by Darwin's theories of selection, saw Gothic architecture as little more than the logical development of an architectural species. It was the rational answer. Romanesque, Early English, Decorated, and

Perpendicular were simply evolutionary stages. The twentieth century, on the other hand, enthralled by Freudian theories, is more introspective and more concerned with metaphysics and psychological response.

Certainly the Victorian explanation of Gothic is easier to follow. It explains how the structural problem was solved; what it does not explain is why the problem was made so difficult. Nor does it explain many features of Gothic—rose windows and the multiplicity of towers and steeples, for instance—which cannot be ascribed to structural necessity.

It is likely that the only age which properly understood Gothic architecture was the Gothic age, and that succeeding generations can only interpret Gothic in the terms of their own ages. To illustrate the new approach to Gothic study, it is only necessary to turn to the writings of three men: Otto von Simson,[1] John Harvey,[2] and John Summerson.[3] All agree that Gothic is much more than rational architecture. To von Simson, Gothic is a representation of supernatural reality and the church a symbol of God on earth. To Harvey, Gothic is the outcome of a way of thought, the result of a special kind of spiritually inspired design. To Summerson, the essence of Gothic is the pointed arch, used because it struck that note of fantasy which the mind of the age desired and which, as applied in the thirteenth century to every part of the cathedral, resulted in a multiplicity of shrines—or aedicules, as he calls them—descending from the bay unit canopied by the vault to the smallest wall niche. Each writer is concerned with the aesthetic values, and unfortunately all are faced with this difficulty: that the views of the Gothic builders on matters of aesthetic appreciation, if they ever expressed them, have not been preserved. Nor do there seem to be many records on the symbolic significance of their works. Von Simson suggests that geometry was the basis of their art; that in the first Gothic buildings, as at S. Denis and Chartres, efforts were made to apply principles of proportion on a geometrical basis. Certainly there is evidence in the surviving architectural drawings that the designers were concerned with geometrical canons and that they were aware of the peculiar properties of the Golden Section. This ratio, in which the lesser dimension is to the greater as the greater is to the whole

[1] *The Gothic Cathedral*, 1956.
[2] *The Gothic World*, 1950.
[3] *Heavenly Mansions*, 1949.

(or, A:B :: B:A+B) has had its devotees in all ages. It is related to the ratios of musical consonance, to the proportions of the human body and to the growth of plants. Geometrically it is expressed in the pentagon and the pentacle. Von Simson examined the dimensions of the nave of Chartres and discovered a remarkable affinity with Golden Section proportions. The height from the base of the plinth to the springing of the nave arcade is 8.61 metres; the height of the shafts above is 13.85 metres; the whole height to the springing of the vaults is thus 22.46 metres, and the total height from the floor to the crown of the vault is 36.5 metres. Now these figures, 8.61, 13.85, 22.46 and 36.5, seem too close to the sequence of the Golden Section to be accidental, but this alone cannot account for the wonder of Gothic.

To Harvey, the most important feature is the aspiring character which distinguishes Gothic from all other architecture, the sense of vertical space, 'jagged, leaping like a flame'. To Summerson, the aim is 'a desire to dissolve the heavy prose of building into religious poetry; a desire to transform the heavy, man-made temple into a multiple, imponderable pile of heavenly mansions'.

None of these views seriously conflicts, except perhaps in emphasis. All agree that there was an aesthetic idea behind Gothic design, and that Gothic architecture was quite different in spirit from Romanesque. Much still remains to be studied and explained, especially about the dynamic nature of the style—for at no point do the designers appear to have been convinced that a completely satisfying solution had been found. Always they seem to have built in the style of the moment; to restore old work, or to complete a work in the forms and stylisms of a previous generation, does not seem to have occurred to them. Equally inexplicable to our age is the passion for intricate and often exquisite carving in places far out of reach of ordinary vision, as, for instance, in the bosses which adorn the high vaults at Exeter Cathedral, or in the complex gargoyles of Notre-Dame. We can guess that when one was building for God only the best would be good enough, that the current fashion in building was believed to be superior to what had gone before, and that every detail, however remote, deserved the same care and attention. But that is altogether too prosaic an interpretation. There can be no doubt that there does exist in the finest achitecture an apparent unity of design and a wonderful harmony of line and light which suggest matters spiritual rather than temporal. It is this transcendental quality which imbues the finest Gothic. 'It has', wrote Lethaby, 'the mystery of the great forests behind it.' Therein lies a part of the answer. Gothic possesses a mystery and a magic that seem inexplicable. An explanation would destroy the magic. Of all architecture, Gothic is the most exactly attuned to the mystery of the western faith, and the Gothic age was, we are led to believe, the age in which the fervour of faith was strongest. The Gothic cathedrals are a natural consequence.

CHAPTER II

THE GOTHIC WORLD

THE limits of the Middle Ages cannot be clearly separated from earlier and later phases of history. They encompass a stage in the growth of western society, which had its formative period, its age of maturity, and its long decline. To some extent the formative period coincided with the decline of the Roman world, and the decline of the medieval world coincided with the beginnings of the Renaissance. Every age is, in fact, the result of an infinite series of causes and the beginning of an infinite series of effects. Any age, therefore, is an age of transition, and this is particularly true of the medieval period, not only in its social and political development, but also in its architecture. Nevertheless, it is desirable in a work of this nature to place some limits upon the field of study, and in this volume it is proposed to consider the Gothic period as extending approximately from the middle of the twelfth to the middle of the fifteenth century.

By the twelfth century a degree of social stability had been reached. We may call it feudal in complexion. Christianity had long since conquered the western world and individual nations had been established. A system of farming had been developed which was adequate to maintain not only the farmers but also a growing urban population. It is important to appreciate that in spite of the many splendours of the age—the craft guilds, the pilgrimages and the Crusades, the cathedrals and the castles, the chivalry and all the poetry and romance which are associated with medievalism—society drew its lifeblood from the soil, and the bulk of the population was a peasantry. The basic unit of society was the village.

Feudalism. Feudal society is difficult to define. It varied so much in different countries and at different times that many writers have denied that there was any system in it at all. Yet at the very least it consisted of a collection of customs which had some characteristics in common, even if the perfect feudal State was never realized. The basis of feudal society was land and protection. All land was held from the king, who was the nation's landlord. Around him were the tenants-in-chief—counts, dukes and bishops. They were in duty bound to perform services in return for their lands. Below them were sub-tenants—knights, squires and abbots—who were bound by similar contracts to their immediate superiors; and at the bottom of the scale were those villagers who gave a proportion of their working days to the cultivation of the lord's demesne, and might on occasion be called up for military service. This leaves out of account large elements of society, including villagers, that stood quite outside the feudal bond however conceived. It has been estimated that in Italy, France, and England from about 1280 to 1380, ninety per cent. of the people were villagers and that the population of the villages ranged from two hundred to four hundred. They were thus very small units, but they were also astonishingly self-sufficient. Normally the village supplied everything: home-grown food, clothes of homespun, home-made tools and locally constructed cottages and carts. Architecturally, the only significant buildings were the manor house and the parish church, which would be built by travelling masons in the style of the country and the period. Life was often hard. The villager was frequently a serf; he and his dependents were bound to the soil and could not leave the domain. They could be bought and sold with the estate, and had little redress for wrongs, beyond what private justice allowed. There were very few possibilities of escape from serfdom; the most attractive was certainly the freedom which might be acquired by the serf who had been able to spend a certain period in a chartered town, or who, by good fortune, lived and worked in a village which grew to become a town and acquired municipal rights.

The Growth of Towns. The process by which agricultural communities became urban varied considerably. Sometimes they grew at that point where an important road crossed the stretch of a river which was fordable and had, at the same time, reached the limits of its navigable length. Inevitably traders settled there. Or it might be that a village would grow at an important road junction, or at a point commanding a pass between hills, or at the gate of a castle or monastery. Then there were towns which were deliberately planned as colonial centres and which were called *bastides*. The *bastide* was an astute piece of estate development and a part of military strategy. It paid a lord to attract settlers and traders to his own town and thereby receive in rent far more than he could ever obtain from agriculture. The establishment of a town near a frontier ensured a fighting population which could defend the district. Such towns are to be found most frequently in the valley of the Dordogne in France and in North Wales. They all conform to a pattern of narrow streets at right angles, having near the centre a market square and a church. Nearly all were fortified with impressive walls, as at Montpazier and Ste. Foy-la-Grande, and some, like Rhuddlan, Flint and Caernarvon, were planned in conjunction with a castle.

Ste. Foy-la-Grande. A planned medieval city.

The ordinary medieval towns, in contrast, were of organic growth, and while it may be dangerous to generalize about their character, it is possible at least to refer to their common characteristics. Most towns had a market place and many had city walls; a few were the seats of a bishop, and some were dominated by the lord's castle. The market place and the fortified wall were the most important elements. Indeed, the market place provided the *raison d'être* of the town and the wall gave it the necessary protection. Around the market place, but within the wall, there was the intricate labyrinth of footways between the houses, while beyond lay the countryside. The distinction between town and country was clear and precise. There was no suburban sprawl or scattered expansion, but instead a deliberate physical break between the landscape and the townscape. It was the wall which gave protection, and within its confines there was security for trade and social life. The first burgesses were still farmers, with their shares in the open fields which surrounded the borough, and only gradually did the commercial and industrial aspects of the town become important. The agricultural side came first, and with increasing consequence as a marketing centre the town developed ancillary trade and industry. But the towns of Italy, Germany, France and England would have made little headway if they had depended entirely on the country-people for the purchase of their manufactured goods, for, as has been said, the village was almost self-sufficient. The town merchants, then, found a market for their luxury goods in the nobleman's castle and the bishop's palace. To meet the needs of the feudal courts the mercantile classes supplied the spices and oils, the embroidered costumes and tapestries, the coats of mail and engraved armour, and all the fashionable trappings which are depicted so exquisitely in medieval manuscripts. The development of luxury trade was the natural result of the security that had grown with feudalism; but the town, with its own system of local government, had a degree of independence.

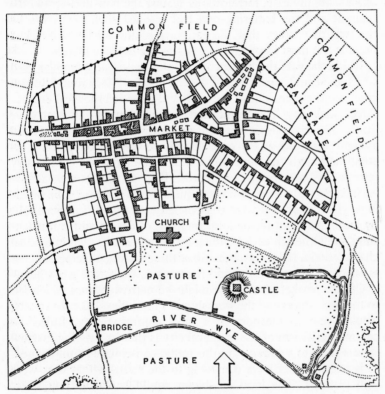

Hereford. An organic medieval city.

It provided the enterprising citizen with opportunities for self-advancement which were entirely absent from the rural world outside.

The medieval town was a compact oasis of urbanism in a country setting, its bastioned walls towering up some thirty feet above the large open fields. The approaches to the city were little more than irregular cart-tracks, designed for the pedestrian and the pack-horse, rather than for the vehicle. They led to imposing and monumental gateways, emblazoned with heraldic symbols, the whole design being so complicated with projecting machicolations, intricate crenellations and fancy turreted peepholes that one cannot help thinking that a great deal of the architectural detail was simply there to give an overwhelming effect of concentrated military strength, rather than to provide purely utilitarian fortifications. In any case, fortifications against the bow-and-arrow, the catapult and the battering-ram had reached such perfection by the twelfth century that the gateways of the medieval city had become the most impregnable units in the defence system.

Inside the gate there branched off the *pomerium*, a circular road which ran continuously round the city (as previously round Roman cities) on the inner side of the walls and provided the local defence forces with easy communication to any part of the protective girdle. The main street from the gate led, with perhaps a twist and a slight widening at the end, directly to the market place. This street, although the most important in the city, was exceedingly narrow by present-day standards, but, as traffic was almost exclusively pedestrian, it was adequate for its purpose. The buildings which flanked it were constructed entirely of local materials, by local craftsmen in the local tradition of design and craftsmanship; and although each building might possess its own individual characteristics there was, because of these common factors, a most satisfactory sense of unity and harmony in the street as a whole.

Off the market place there might be narrower lanes which led to the back stores and the workshops. These alleys, like the streets, would seem to meander in a most confusing way. Indeed, a common criticism of the medieval city is that its twisting, narrow streets seem to a stranger, in this traffic-conscious age, unplanned. It is because they were confusing to the stranger that they were well planned. The local inhabitant would know his way about this labyrinth, but the stranger, or the enemy who had breached the walls, would find himself at a distinct disadvantage. Further, it is important to realize that glass was an unusual and valuable commodity which was used in windows only for the House of God and the houses of the wealthier burgesses. The winding lanes provided a most useful windbreak to protect the great mass of dwellings, with their small, shuttered openings.

The market square was at the centre of the town; it was a large, irregularly shaped place surrounded by the most important civic buildings. It acted not only as a trading centre, but also as a mustering ground for the home guard. The west porch of the church was at one side, the tower still wreathed in scaffolding and with considerable building operations still in progress. The medieval church was never really finished; each generation added to its grandeur until the Reformation came and the impetus to build for the greater glory of God was gone.

This, then, was the medieval city, a city walled for defence with an irregular organic pattern of alleys leading to a central market place, and the whole dominated by the church. It functioned satisfactorily for nearly half a millennium, before a series of dramatic events transformed the whole pattern of the lives and thoughts of men. It was not, as people of later centuries imagined, a city of squalor, filth and huddled slums. Its houses still had gardens and were still close to the countryside. In it there developed a pride of citizenship that has never been surpassed. The citizens' constant preoccupation with the privileges they had obtained for self-government and trade monopoly resulted in a civic patriotism which involved obligations that were not regarded as servile tasks, but as reasonable duties which citizens were proud to perform for the common weal.

The Guild System. The medieval towns were at once the creation and the creators of trade. The basis of organization was the guild system of merchant and craftsman. In all the important trading cities, large and small, guilds, or associations of merchants, were established for the sake of companionship and protection as well as for the purpose of extending and regulating trade. Craft guilds appeared a little later, and were concerned with the maintenance of standards of craftsmanship and with the development of a system of training by apprenticeship. The guild was a fraternity with charitable as well as economic functions. Regulations were made for mutual assistance, for arbitration in disputes; and some guilds founded schools, almshouses and hospitals. The guild system produced an intelligent oligarchy, upholding municipal autonomy against outside power, and devising machinery of local government which worked successfully as long as there remained a stable market and an approximate equality of wealth among the masters. It failed only in those larger towns where the subordinate crafts were swallowed up by the merchants, and where production and distribution of goods were so separated that the artisan became a wage-earner under the merchant. Another cause of disruption, particularly on the Continent, was the coming of journeyman workers, who had served no apprenticeship but were prepared to travel from town to town and hire out their services. Except among the masons, this practice was unusual in England.

The chief medium of international and national commerce was the fair. Every European country had its fair to which the merchants came along the caravan routes with their pepper, cloves and spices from the East, copper goods from Dinant, Flemish cloth, wine from the Rhineland, leather work from Cordova, and furs from Russia. While the fair was generally held in the fair-field and was to the lord a source of considerable profit out of stall rents and entry tolls, and therefore involved no architecture, there can be no doubt of the importance of the periodic influx of widely travelled men in spreading ideas. Medieval architecture could not have developed as it did under the intense localism of feudal life; it received its stimulus more from the town than from the manor or the monastery. The merchants required, quite apart from religious buildings, their guildhalls and their trade halls, which in Italy, Flanders and Champagne are equal, in size at least, to many cathedrals.

The Crusades. Throughout the period with which this volume is concerned, the greatest international movements were the Crusades. Their influence upon architecture, religious and secular, was profound. The Crusading movement began as an enterprise against Muslim power in defence of the eastern Christian empire, and ended with the destruction of that empire. It began as a manifestation of the religious devotion and pilgrim spirit of the Middle Ages, and ended as a political and commercial exploit in the interests of trade. It did not succeed in its professed aims, for the whole of eastern Christendom came under Muslim rule; but it did succeed, indirectly, in fostering the development and progress of western Christendom. It provided a very necessary distraction for the bellicose barons who might otherwise have spent their energies in civil wars at home. It united the West under the Papacy; it encouraged the growth of chivalry, and introduced, to some Crusaders at least, the learning and art and science of the East. Without this stimulus the rapid development of Gothic art would not have been possible.

The early Crusades—primarily pilgrimages under arms with the avowed object of conquering holy places in Palestine—led to the establishment of the Latin Kingdom in Jerusalem, the restoration of the Church of the Holy Sepulchre, and the creation of the

Knights Templar and Hospitaller. The fourth Crusade (1203-4), on the other hand, was less creditable, for it was directed against the eastern Christian empire, not against the Muslims. It resulted in the conquest and pillage of Constantinople and, subsequently, in the diffusion of relics, manuscripts, and works of art of all kinds throughout the western world.

The permanent effects of the Crusades were considerable. In England the Templar churches at London, Cambridge and Northampton were constructed after the model of the Church of the Holy Sepulchre. La Sainte-Chapelle was built in Paris by Louis IX to contain the relics which he had acquired as a Crusader. At Carcassonne and elsewhere, fortifications and castles were built after the fashion which had first been developed in the Near East. In the sculptures of the western portals of Chartres and the illustrated manuscripts of the thirteenth century, one can see how art had been inspired anew; in Venice, the two marble pillars which now stand in the Piazzetta were brought from Syria, and the four magnificent bronze horses which stand over the portal of S. Mark's were shipped from Constantinople. Stolen relics and treasure trove poured into western Europe. Wealth and trade came under the control of the western States. The commercial axis of the world returned, after an interval of a thousand years, to Italy.

The most successful religious wars of the Middle Ages were fought, not in the eastern Mediterranean, but in Spain. The invasion of the peninsula in 711 by the Arabs and Berber tribes met with little opposition, but for five hundred years there was intermittent reconquest of lost ground. Then, in 1232, the Christian reconquest began. Cordova fell in 1236, Seville in 1244, Cadiz in 1250. Armies of volunteers from Normandy, Burgundy and Aquitaine fought for the Cross against the Crescent, and each new enterprise was officially recognized as a service to the Church. The wars did not end until 1492, with the fall of Granada and the final expulsion of Muslim power from western Europe. In that same year, Columbus sighted the New World and the medieval age was over. To architecture, the wars of Spain contributed only a little. It is true that considerable knowledge of Arab science and philosophy filtered into Europe, but in the arts, except in Spain itself, the effects were slight.

Chivalry. It is possible that the most important effect of the wars with the infidel lay in the growth of chivalry, that high ideal which united the medieval knight and the Christian soldier. The idea of chivalry seems to have spread from Spain to Provence and northwards through France. 'It was influenced', wrote C. G. Coulton, 'to a very real extent by the Muslim civilization of Spain.' The code of chivalry did much towards raising the status of women in society, and Coulton even suggests that this 'was probably connected in some degree with the worship of the Virgin Mary, which received such impetus from the Normans'. It is certain that chivalry was responsible for much that was good and new in medieval society. The monk and the priest might serve God and man, but they would not fight. Their services to civilization were inestimable. They preserved learning and were responsible, if only indirectly, for the greatest architecture of the age. Without the soldiers, however, the achievements of the monks might have been negligible.

Chivalry was much more than superficial good manners and picturesque mummery; it represented a remarkable social advance. It involved service of the strong for the weak without thought of remuneration. It represented a genuine endeavour to provide a practical code of behaviour. The great military Orders, the Hospitallers and the Templars and the Knights of S. James of Compostela, formed the standing army of the Crusading movement, maintained almshouses and hospitals for pilgrims, and constructed great barracks and castles. Many architectural memorials of the Knights of Chivalry survive, not only in the Middle East but in western Europe also. The orders of chivalry were second only to the Church in standing for all that was best in medieval life.

The Church. The part played by the Church in medieval times was of incalculable importance. In a world which was intensely local in outlook, there was, at the same time, the supreme unifying force of the Church Militant. It provided that sense of universality which might have been absent within the limited regions of feudal rights and loyalties. The Church was a great bureaucracy, with the Pope at its head, ruling from Rome. Under him were the Cardinals, who elected the Pope; then came the Archbishops and the Bishops, and, finally, the host of parish priests and clerks who were normally appointed by the landowners and were chiefly maintained by tithes. All was organized into an elaborate system, serving not only the spiritual needs of the people but also the functions of a welfare State. The Church preserved, in Latin, a common tongue which fostered means of intellectual exchange throughout Europe. It is to the clerical scholar that we owe all of that learning and philosophy which survived the Dark Ages after the fall of Rome. The monastic schools offered an escape for the studious youth from the brawling life around him. The Church provided medical and educational services, and was a stimulus to art and craftsmanship. It was physically in the heart of the city and mentally in the hearts of the citizens. The parish church was the community centre from the time the citizen was baptized at the font until the day he was buried in the churchyard. The business of the church was an everyday business, not sacred to Sunday. It was a public building in constant use, and it is natural, therefore, that it should be the chief building in the village and in the city, and represent in its workmanship the enduring faith of the people. But this workmanship and skill, which are evident in the meanest of our parish churches, are not purely local achievements. They exemplify in all their important details a common style of architecture that can be paralleled from Avignon to Kirkwall, from Dublin to Pisa. It is this extraordinary unity of purpose and design which makes it so easy to date, with astonishing certainty, the craftsmanship of so many different countries.

Monasteries. Monasticism was probably the greatest civilizing force of the Middle Ages. There has always been a small minority of men who find seclusion and contemplation most suited to their natures, but S. Benedict, in the sixth century, developed a rule of monastic life which was to sweep the western world in the Middle Ages. Under this rule the individual monk was sunk in a community, whose corporate life he had to live. S. Benedict conceived the monastery as a self-sufficient community, in which each monk took part in the celebration of daily Masses, in meditation and in manual work. The buildings were so arranged as to include all the necessary offices, stores and workshops. Poverty, from the personal point of view, was absolute. Collectively, however, the monasteries were soon very richly endowed. In the tenth and eleventh centuries there was a great development of monasticism led by the House of Cluny, in Burgundy. By 1100 this abbey had twelve hundred dependent monasteries, and the Abbot of Cluny was the most powerful ecclesiastic next to the Pope, to whom alone he was answerable. About this time certain monks, appalled by the luxury and laxity which had developed, broke away and established a new and more austere Order, centred at Cîteaux, which claimed to follow more literally the rule of S. Benedict.

These were called Cistercians, and it was not long before they, too, had acquired wealth and power and were exceeding the Benedictines in the grandeur of their buildings. In spite of the criticisms levelled against the medieval monks, the material gains and worldly honour which flowed upon them were, on the whole, well deserved. The often quoted statement of Thorold Rogers is essentially true: 'The monks were the men of letters of the Middle Ages, the historians, the jurists, the philosophers, the physicians, the students of nature.' They were also the instigators of some of the greatest art and architecture of the period.

The Gothic Style. The style of architecture which developed about the middle of the twelfth century was quite different from the Romanesque which had preceded it, even though the relationship between the plan and the section is very close in both. The cathedral of Amiens is as different from the cathedral of S. Albans as is the Parthenon from Stonehenge.

Gothic was an aspiring architecture, and did not depend for its effect, as did the Romanesque, upon the massive and ponderous distribution of its parts. The Gothic builders used the cross vault, the pointed arch and the flying buttress, as had, on occasion, the Romanesque builders; but they developed these as artistic ends, not merely as constructive means. They evolved an articulated, organic style, in which vertical emphasis is the outstanding feature. The walls and the piers which supported the Romanesque vaults were replaced, in Gothic, by an enveloping translucent screen of coloured glass and slender clustered shafts, which carry the eye upward to the system of ribs arching across the nave and aisles.

The Gothic cathedral was a representation of the reality of the supernatural, a manifestation of heaven on earth. It was functional, not only in the practical sense, but also in its spiritual symbolism. It was a vital architecture, ever aspiring towards greater achievement. John Harvey, in his *The Gothic World*, says that when the Chapter of Seville began the building of its cathedral, it resolved 'to build so great a church to the glory of God that those who come after us will think us mad even to have attempted it'.

Throughout the medieval period, the builders persisted in developing the style until it became almost an arrangement of vertical lines of stone, linked by a diaphanous screen and carrying a vault of unbelievable delicacy. The builders never looked back to past stylisms, but always built in the most advanced style of the day. It was, therefore, a progressive architecture, and until matters spiritual were divided by the Reformation and matters material were altered by the Renaissance, this Gothic style prevailed.

The End of the Period. The medieval age reached its zenith in the thirteenth century. Under Innocent III the Papacy was at its most brilliant; all that was loveliest in the Faith was embodied in the life of S. Francis; all that was finest in philosophy and scholarship was defined in the writings of S. Thomas Aquinas. Louis IX had given chivalry its perfected type. The greatest cathedrals had been, or were being, built. And, in the face of Muslim opposition, the western world had united as a stable society.

In the two centuries that followed, medievalism just lost its ideals. A series of events and circumstances led to its dissolution. Out of the Crusading idea was born a new nationalism and patriotism, which replaced the local feudal loyalties. In Germany there was a war between Frederick of Hapsburg and Lewis of Bavaria, Hungary claimed and fought for the throne of Poland, and a league of cantons was formed in southern Germany which, in 1389, became an independent Swiss nation. In Italy the cities of Venice, Florence and Genoa became self-supporting republics. The English united in 1346 to wage a war with France which lasted over a hundred years, and ended in 1453 with the expulsion of the English from French soil. In the same year, Constantinople fell to the Turks and with it all the hopes of the Crusaders.

There were other equally important events which changed the Gothic world. In 1346–9 the Black Death swept across Europe, causing a scarcity of labour and economic problems with which feudalism could not cope. Landlords found themselves compelled to accept money payment in lieu of service; and, in England, much land which had been cultivated reverted to sheep pasturage, with a resultant development of trade in wool. The whole economy of the western world was changing towards capitalism.

At Agincourt, in 1415, a new war machine, the cannon, supported the archers and the cavalry, and the cannon meant the end of the medieval wall as a secure defence against an aggressor. No longer could the monks and the citizens isolate themselves from the turmoil of the outside world. The mendicant friars did what they could, but were powerless against the Plague and the growing nationalism. The wars over Europe had killed the last remnants of feudal pageantry, and a new intellectual and material realism was taking the place of the medieval mystical outlook.

About the middle of the fifteenth century, Johann Gutenberg began printing from movable type. In 1456 he issued the first printed edition of the Bible, which led inevitably to a reformation of men's ideas, and especially of their religious ideas. In 1492, Christopher Columbus set out on his memorable voyage to the Indies, and discovered, inadvertently, America. The world changed rapidly, and medieval society, with its pomp and pageantry, its religious devotion and intimate local outlook, could not survive the changes. By the end of the fifteenth century the medieval world was dead, and a renaissance, intellectual, economic, social, and architectural, had taken its place.

CHAPTER III

GOTHIC STRUCTURE

*T*HE *Pointed Arch.* One of the distinguishing features of Gothic architecture is the almost universal use of the pointed arch in place of the semi-circular arch which we associate with the Romanesque. The fact that the introduction was gradual, and at first limited to those parts of the structure where great weights, and consequently considerable thrusts, were involved, suggests that its use was more probably due to constructional necessities than to aesthetic fancies. The pointed arch was first used for the main arches across the nave vaults and under the towers, where the superimposed load was greatest. The pointed arch allowed a flexibility of design which had never been possible with the semi-circular arch. It made it practicable to determine at will the height of an arch, irrespective of its span, and at the same time to bring together arches of different spans which nevertheless demanded, if only for the sake of unity of appearance, an equal height. Above all, the advantage of the pointed arch was statical in that it made possible the carrying of considerable loads with the minimum of abutment.

Gothic architecture solved in an economical way the problem of spanning space by stone. The two obvious ways of doing this are by a beam, and by an arch; in both cases the fundamental problem is to carry the vertical loads of the beam or arch itself, and of any walling above, across to the side supports. This process sets up, within the member, horizontal forces which in the case of a beam are resisted within the beam itself, and the side supports are called upon to carry only vertical loads. But stone can be used as a beam only over relatively small openings, the sizes of which are limited by the availability of sizeable monoliths, problems of erection and the natural weakness of stone in resisting tensile stresses. The arch, on the other hand, has a great advantage in that it transfers the horizontal forces, together with the vertical loads, directly on to the supports, and if perfectly designed ensures that all the voussoirs are subject to compression only.

It is found, in an arch, that the combination of vertical and horizontal forces forms a curve or line of thrust. If the shape of the arch conforms to this line of thrust, then it will act wholly in compression. Theoretically, it is possible to design an arch for any system of loading so that all its members act in compression; and conversely, it is possible to ascertain the best system of loading

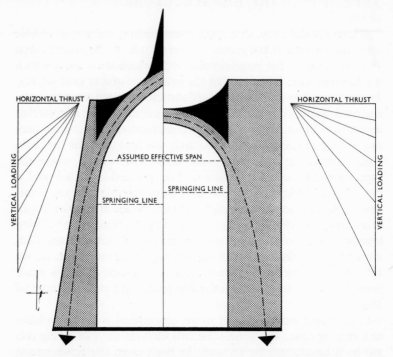

for a particular shape of arch. The diagram shows an analysis of a pointed arch and a semi-circular arch of the same span, carrying the same vertical loads (shown in black). The system of loading is the most appropriate for each case, so that the lines of thrust coincide with the centres of the voussoirs. Theoretically these present perfect solutions to each problem—a condition rarely achieved in practice.

A comparison reveals that the loading required for the pointed arch is more clearly defined and more easily expressed in practice than in the case of the semi-circular arch. A concentration of load at the haunches and a heavy concentration at the crown provided the builders with a more precise problem to solve, one which strongly dictated the general form of the structure and is expressed very clearly in Gothic architecture. The system of loading required for the semi-circular arch, on the other hand, is not so clearly defined, and for the same loading causes a greater horizontal thrust. The horizontal thrust from the semi-circular arch is some forty per cent. greater than that from the pointed arch. This is, of course, one of the prime factors in dictating the size of buttresses.

The polar diagrams shown on either side of the arches provide a method of analysing the thrust in each arch. By plotting the vertical loads and the horizontal thrust, it is possible to ascertain the direction and magnitude of the thrust at any point along the span. In practice, it is not possible to make an accurate analysis of a masonry arch, because many important factors are difficult to assess; for instance, it is difficult to ascertain the extent to which the walling above an arch may direct the loads. In the case of a small opening in a well-bonded wall, the form of the arch is not important; but when there is a large span, and it is desirable to reduce to a minimum the amount of stone abutment, and at the same time ensure that foundation loads are as little as possible, then special consideration is necessary. The Gothic system of construction provided an admirable solution. It produced a framed structure in which the principal stresses were compressive and therefore most appropriate to masonry. The pointed arch, which was the most influential member in the framework, offered many advantages over the semi-circular form, advantages which were essentially practical. For instance, it was possible to refine the arch outline and reduce the amount of material employed, while discerning more precisely the position and direction of the line of thrust. This resulted in a more accurate placing of buttresses, so that their shape and weight would be most efficiently employed. It led to the superimposition of pinnacles, which by their additional weight further deflected the thrust. It led to the abandonment of the wall as the principal means of support, and thus made possible the development of the traceried window which, by the end of the Gothic period, almost filled the spaces between the buttresses. All these—the pointed arch, the buttress, the pinnacle, the traceried window and the ribbed vault (which will be considered presently)—combined to produce a triumph of masonry and a unity of structure and design rarely surpassed. The pointed arch was superior structurally and economically to the round arch of the Romans and their successors. It was not, let it be understood, the result of precise calculation. The Gothic artifact was achieved only by a process of trial and error. The successes are evident from the structures which have withstood the test of centuries; the errors, of which there were many, can be ascertained only from the manuscript records of building disasters.

The pointed arch was not, of course, an invention of the Gothic builders. Its constructional value was recognized by the Assyrians and the Sassanid Persians. It was adopted by the Saracens and found its way to Sicily, where it was used by the Normans early in the eleventh century. In southern France, especially in Provence, there are continuous pointed vaults reinforced by pointed transverse arches which belong to the Romanesque period. The date when the pointed arch was first introduced varies in different countries. In northern France it first appears between 1100 and 1120; in England it was not used constructionally before 1140, the approximate date of Fountains, Malmesbury and Buildwas Abbey churches. It occurred 'accidentally', so to speak, in arcading formed by intersecting semi-circular arches, both in England and abroad, about the middle of the eleventh century, and hence arose the idea that builders obtained the suggestion of the form from these arcades. But this theory has little to substantiate it. Even if the pointed arch had not been used long before this interlaced arcading was introduced, the fact remains that the builders would be unlikely to abandon a form which had behind it centuries of tradition merely from a hint conveyed accidentally. The pointed form was adopted because it proved a most valuable structural asset, and also for aesthetic reasons. In Germany its introduction was late, and in the greater part of Italy later still—in fact it never entirely superseded the Classical form. In the little Loggi del Bigallo, Florence (c. 1360), and in many contemporary Italian buildings, all the arches are semi-circular.

The steeper the pointed arch, the less its lateral thrust. Many of the early medieval examples are also the most acute, as though the workmen were determined to make the most of its statical advantages. But this is not always the case. Some of the earliest are among the flattest, having a rise only a trifle more than a semi-circular arch affords, especially where used in vaults, and suggest that the new form was used reluctantly, and with grave doubts about its appearance. It is easy to design a pointed arch so acute that it exercises virtually no side thrust at all, but only vertical pressure. Arches of such excessive steepness were not uncommon in blind arcading flanking windows in early thirteenth-century churches in England, but such extremes were rarely resorted to in arches over openings. An arch enclosing a space approximating to an equilateral triangle was the general favourite until the middle of the fourteenth century, and was by no means discarded entirely then. After that date, in England especially, the four-centred form, commonly called the Tudor arch, and in France the three-centred, were the most characteristic. Both forms are structurally weaker and are often considered to be evidence of the decreasing vitality which marks the later work in both countries. In England this is attributed to the Black Death, the great plague of 1349 which swept away one half of the artisans of the country; and in France, in great measure, to the Hundred Years War, which lasted from 1346 to 1453 and seriously interfered with all building.

That the pointed arch was adopted for constructional rather than aesthetic reasons is evident from the fact that, where both forms occur in one structure, it is the pointed arch which is used where there are great loads to sustain or where abutment is strictly limited. It was not, therefore, simply a matter of fashion. The transition to, and universal adoption of, the pointed arch as a matter of taste was rapid, especially in France and England, and once the advantages of the pointed arch were appreciated the builders never looked back or reverted to the semi-circular form.

The Mouldings of the Arch. The building of arches in a series of rings, each forming a centre on which the next is built and each projecting beyond the last, was an innovation of Romanesque times which persisted through the Gothic period; but, as the style developed, the scale and contour of the arch mouldings underwent considerable change. In the earliest Norman arches, as, for instance, at Jumièges and St. Albans, the arches were square-edged. The first step towards the moulded arch was to chamfer this edge or to transform it into a roll. In section the outline followed to a great extent the shape of the arch. Thus, when the arch was semi-circular the mouldings were semi-circular; when the pointed arch made its appearance, the mouldings were pointed. As the structure grew lighter and more delicate, the mouldings became smaller and more intricate. The change is especially noticeable about the middle of the twelfth century in England, owing largely to the general employment of soft, easily worked stone from Caen, Beer, Ancaster, Bath, etc. The mouldings became a series of bold projections and deep hollows, alternating to produce marked

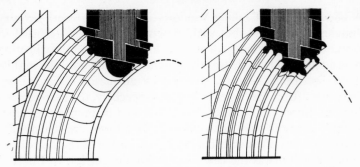

(Left) Norman arch mouldings; (right) Early English arch mouldings.

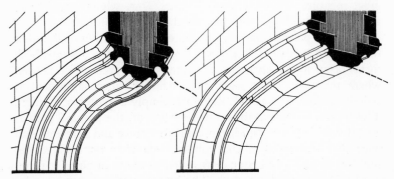

(Left) Decorated arch mouldings; (right) Perpendicular arch mouldings.

contrasts of dark shadows and strong highlights. Only in those parts of the country where stone was hard and difficult to work, as in parts of Yorkshire, did simple chamfers persist. From 1250 to 1350 the mouldings were flatter and the wave and ogee were the common forms. These were generally grouped, two or more together, each group being separated from the next by a deep hollow where the stones of two arches or orders met. The ogee did not appear in English work until the middle of the thirteenth century, though it occurred much earlier abroad. In the twelfth century, in the south of France and in Burgundy, most of the mouldings were of this section, and the contours had a delicacy far greater than in northern France or England.

When, in the fifteenth century, the flat, four-centred arch supplanted, to some extent, the more acutely pointed arch, some of the mouldings became wide and shallow. As a rule they are distinguishable from earlier mouldings by a certain angularity and hardness of outline. There seems always to have been a remarkable affinity between the general character of the architecture, the profile of the arch and the outline of the mouldings. Indeed, it may be said that the mouldings in Gothic times are as sure an index of the period of architecture as are the more obvious structural parts. By the mouldings the date of any work in England or northern France can often be determined where other evidence is conflicting or unreliable.

Less attention was paid to mouldings in Italy. There, relief from too great simplicity was achieved by colour decoration, by mosaic and variegated marbles. In this the builders were only following the tradition which had existed since Early Christian times; the arches inside many Italian Gothic churches are unmoulded. Where there are mouldings, they are few and slight, and little difference is discernible between early and late examples.

In France, as much as, or even more than, in England, the mason's rather than the decorator's art was the first consideration. On the whole, however, French mouldings are simpler and fewer than those in England, and less change is obvious from century to century. The French clung to the rounded *bowtell* long after it had been discarded in England. The deep hollows and pointed rounds, so characteristic in England, are rarely found in France, except in Normandy, where the softer, finer grain stone was available. After the Hundred Years War, French mouldings became attenuated and weak, and probably the only significant contribution was that of interpenetration, of the carrying of one moulding through another, in a lacy, tracery-like manner as in S. Maclou at Rouen.

Arch Labels. Labels, or hood mouldings, over arches throw the wet to the sides and prevent it from running down and injuring the mouldings below. There is, therefore, an excellent reason for their occurrence on the outside of buildings. On the inside, however, their justification, except to frame sculpture as in Lincoln Cathedral, or diaper work as in Westminster Abbey, is less obvious. There are no labels over the arches inside the majority of the greater French churches, but in England they are seldom absent.

The mouldings of labels, as of the string courses and other minor details, were always characteristic of their period, so that unity in every part was preserved. While the mouldings of different

countries possess their own peculiarities, the resemblances between those of the same date in different countries are remarkable.
It is true that there are often localisms distinguishing the work of
one district from that of another, but these are, as often as not, the
result of the material available. Thus in Cornwall, and also in
Brittany, where churches were built of granite, the mouldings are
naturally simpler and bigger than in those parts where a soft lime-
stone was employed; but local differences apart, a freemasonry
undoubtedly existed. Workmen travelled from building to building,
from town to town; and wherever they went they carried with
them, if not the actual templates they had used, at least a keen
recollection of the mouldings they had worked. In no other way
can the strong likeness pervading contemporary work be accounted
for. This is more marked, perhaps, in England than elsewhere,
since the country is small and it was united; whereas France and
Italy, besides being larger, were split up into different Duchies
and Kingdoms. In England, a change in detail introduced in one
locality generally found its way into another within a short lapse
of time.

The Pointed Ribbed Vault. The Romanesque builders never
satisfactorily solved the problem of stone vaulting. They did, it
is true, occasionally use the pointed arch and they did invent the
ribbed vault; they did not succeed in their efforts to combine the two. They adopted many rough and ready devices to vault
the aisles, but these were generally unsuitable for the wide spans of
the nave, which called for more scientific treatment. The remedy
was, of course, to use the pointed arch in the construction of the
vault. No longer was there any need to stilt arches or introduce
weak diagonal ribs of semi-elliptical outline in order to reach a
common height. By making the transverse ribs and the longitudinal
arches pointed, all could be of the same height, no matter what the
shape of the vault might be or how wide its span.

In most French vaults the system was complete by 1140; the
diagonal ribs remained semi-circular (having the greatest span)
and the radius of these dictated the height and consequently the
form of the other arches. In England, however, even the diagonals
were slightly pointed. The transition was gradual. The vaults over
the aisles in Malmesbury Abbey Church (*c.* 1140–50) are among
the earliest ribbed vaults in this country in which the transverse
arches and the arches of the nave arcade alongside them are pointed.
The diagonal ribs are semi-circular. In the nave of Durham the

transverse arches are also pointed and, if Bilson's[1] dates are correct (1128–33) these arches are even earlier. But these vaults have no wall ribs.

In France the pointed arch seems to have been employed in vaults almost as early as were diagonal ribs. Many small churches around Amiens, Beauvais, Soissons, etc., have pointed ribbed vaults, which are attributed to 1120–30 but are probably later. The first large structure with such vaults of which the date is known is the choir of S. Denis (Pl. 1), which was finished in 1144. In S. Maurice, Angers (the cathedral) the magnificent vault of 54 feet span is pointed throughout and cannot be later than 1150–53.

The dates of the above examples show that the pointed arch was used for vaulting almost simultaneously in France and England, although the French may have an advantage of a few years. What is more important, however, is that the French, having achieved what seemed to be a satisfactory solution, saw no need for further advance. Even in their fifteenth-century churches the vaults are simply quadripartite, the only ribs being the transverse, diagonal and wall ribs, with very occasionally a ridge rib. The English were different. Step by step, more and more innovations and complications were introduced, each logically arising from the last.

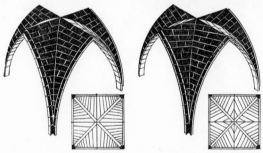

Pointed ribbed vault, showing: (left) French method of infilling, and (right) English method.

The Web. The reason for the differences between French and English vaults may be seen in the method of constructing the web, or infilling panels between the ribs. In early vaults this web was often little more than rubble, plastered on the underside, but later it was coursed stone. In France the stones were usually built parallel to the ridge, so that each lay on a truly horizontal bed. In

[1] *Journal of the Royal Institute of British Architects*; March and April 1899 and May 1902: 'The Beginnings of Gothic Architecture'.

England the stones were laid either at right angles to the diagonal ribs or along the shortest line between the diagonals and the transverse or wall ribs. The so-called French method is, it is true, general in northern France; but it is also not uncommon in England. The so-called English method is general in England, but also occurs in the semi-English work of southern France. The two methods occur side by side in the vault over the cloister of the north side of Westminster Abbey, where there may be strong suspicion of French influence; but there can be no such suspicion in the Lady Chapel of Chichester, or at Fountains Abbey. The truth is that in nearly all the examples, the French as well as the English, the web is by no means built throughout in accordance with any hard-and-fast rule, but it is convenient to associate the one method with France, where little advance in vault design was made, and the other with England, where the most remarkable changes occurred.

The Ridge Rib. The English method of infilling produced an ugly herringbone joint along the summit of the vault, and this

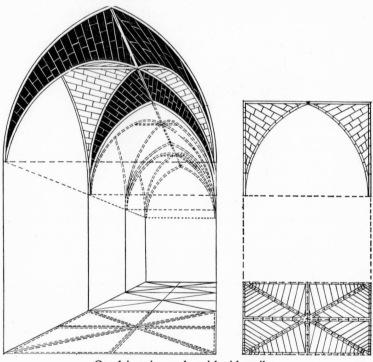

Quadripartite vault, with ridge ribs.

may in part have led to the introduction of a ridge rib. When vaults are constructed with semi-circular arches, there is no ridge line; with the pointed arch, there is. The need to emphasize this line is evident, irrespective of how the stones of the web are laid. It is also important structurally, because it provides in effect a continuous keystone along the axes of the vault. Early examples in England are to be found in Lincoln, Chester and Westminster. In southern France it was common in the vaulted churches of the end of the twelfth century, such as S. Pierre, Saumur; S. Radigonde, Poitiers; and Poitiers Cathedral. The three great bays of the nave of Angers Cathedral (*c.* 1150) are without ridge ribs, but the later choir vaults have them. In the above-mentioned foreign examples the ridge ribs (like the diagonals) are extremely slender and were probably made so because they would otherwise have emphasized disagreeably the domical form of the vaults. In England this problem did not arise, since the ridges were usually level, the exceptions being mainly those which sloped upwards from the centre of the sides in order to provide greater height for the clerestory windows. The architects of northern France rarely used ridge ribs, and to the last seem to have regarded them as absolutely unnecessary. In England the addition of the ridge rib, especially the longitudinal one running uninterruptedly from east to west, is important because it ties together the otherwise disconnected bays of the cathedral, and gives a unity and direction to the design which could never be achieved by string courses along the walls. It becomes, in effect, the spine of the whole vertebrate structure.

Tierceron Ribs. The next important development was the introduction of additional pairs of ribs to subdivide the infilling panels and so reduce their span. In oblong bays one pair is usually introduced in the central compartment, and two or more in the sides. These ribs spring from the same capitals as the diagonals, and join the ridge at a point between the centre of the vault and the outer arches (see p. 40). While there can be no doubt that these ribs greatly facilitated the construction of the vault, they introduced at least two new problems and two new features: the *tas-de-charge* and the boss.

The Tas-de-charge. In a simple tierceron vault there may be as many as eleven, often many more, ribs arising from one capital. It would be impossible at the springing to find room for so many separate arches. Consequently, the lower courses were merged into large single stones upon which the mouldings were carved, and mitred so that the capital could be of minimum dimensions. These lower courses were constructed with horizontal instead of radiating joints up to a point from which the independent ribs could spring. In other words, the pier was continued up above the capital, but was moulded in the form of arched ribs. The merits

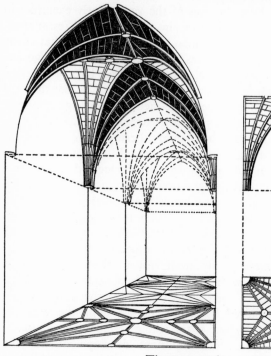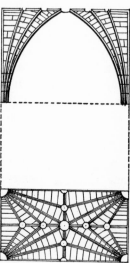

Tierceron vault.

of the *tas-de-charge* were (1) that it united all the thrusts, (2) that it lessened both the span and the rise of the active portion of the vault, and (3) that it brought the thrusts well within the wall, the *tas-de-charge* itself acting as an abutment and taking a good deal of the thrust. The use of the *tas-de-charge* occurred in England about the end of the twelfth century at Glastonbury and in the central pillar of the guard room at Newcastle. In France, where it was less necessary because there were fewer ribs, it did not occur until the thirteenth century, and the first example was in the choir at Soissons, which was finished in 1212.

The Boss. The junction of the various arched ribs with the ridge presented another problem. It was not entirely new, for the difficulty at once occurs whenever diagonal arches cross, because each arch cannot have a keystone of its own. In the crypt at Gloucester and the eastern apse of the south transept at Tewkesbury, the builders simply set up one complete diagonal arch and

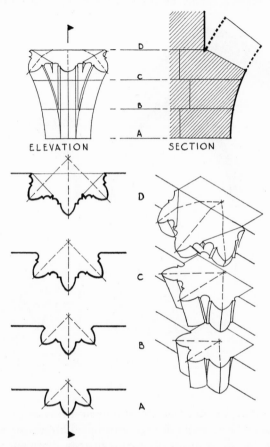

ELEVATION   SECTION

Diagram illustrating the construction of the *tas-de-charge*.

abutted the two halves of the other awkwardly and obliquely against the first. In the transept at Winchester there is one common keystone, shouldered to receive the ribs. The problem was increased with the introduction of tierceron and ridge ribs, for then the arches met the ridge obliquely and it was exceedingly difficult to mitre them successfully at the junction. By carving the meeting stone with foliage, the builders were able to mask effectively any irregularities and at the same time emphasize a feature which was important structurally as a keystone.

Lierne Ribs. The next innovation was largely ornamental, though it may originally have had a constructional basis. It will

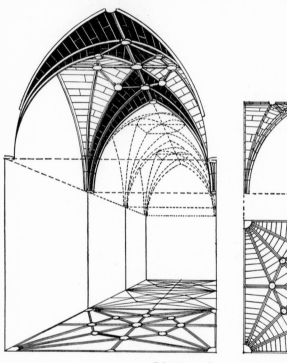
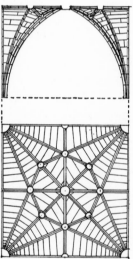

Lierne vault.

be noticed that the intermediate or tierceron ribs are not upright arches, but lie at an angle. By introducing additional struts which linked the tiercerons to the diagonals, further abutment was provided and the vault became a network of forces. At the same time, it produced a rich and star-like pattern, and very soon all sorts of lierne ribs were introduced, many having obviously no constructional value and adding only to the prettiness of the vault. As a result, the spaces between the ribs were often so small that each could be filled by two or three pieces of stone, as in the nave at Norwich. The original idea of a vault as consisting of a framework and an infilling of small, light stones was soon lost in a web of

liernes which covered the whole surface of the vault, no one rib
being any stronger than its neighbour, as can be seen, for instance,
in the choirs of Gloucester and Tewkesbury. The logical consequence was that before long it proved easier to construct a simple
ashlar vault in which rib and panel were worked on the same stone,
the ribs being no more than surface decoration. One result of the
change was that the vault once more became of one substance.
It had not the homogeneity of the Roman concrete vault, but it
exerted far less thrust than the strongly ribbed vaults of the
thirteenth and fourteenth centuries, and consequently required
less abutment. Abroad, the story was carried even further. The
designers, certain of their skill, were attracted by virtuosity. In
France at S. Riquier, and in Spain at Segovia, Salamanca and
Toledo, the liernes no longer followed even decoratively the main
structural lines of the church. Instead we are confronted by a
labyrinth of flame-like curves punctuated by keystones hanging
like stalactites.

Fan Vaults. The introduction of more and more tierceron ribs
presented a further constructional problem, for the span of each
from the transverse or wall rib to the diagonal rib was different.
The transverse rib had the least distance to cover, the diagonal
the greatest, and the tierceron came somewhere in between. The
amount of centering required, therefore, was almost as great as for
an ordinary groined vault. Now it was proposed to make all the
ribs of precisely the same curve. The result was a sheaf of ribs,
semi-circular on plan and shaped like a trumpet, or conoid. The
earliest surviving example of importance is to be found in the
cloister of Gloucester (*c.* 1370) and is associated with the Perpendicular style (Pl. 14). It is now fairly certain, however, that many
of the features of the new style did not originate there but in
London, and that this style was developed by the king's masons
as early as 1292, at S. Stephen's Chapel, Westminster (demolished
1834), and again in the Chapter House of Old S. Paul's, which
was built in 1332.

It has been suggested that the idea of the fan vault was arrived
at almost accidentally from early tomb design, where it was the
custom to suspend over the sarcophagus, or coffin, a pall supported
on four posts. This was translated into wood over the tomb of the
Black Prince at Canterbury, and into stone over the tomb of Sir
Hugh Despenser, who died in 1349, at Tewkesbury. The underside of these canopies was carved in imitation of vaulting, and

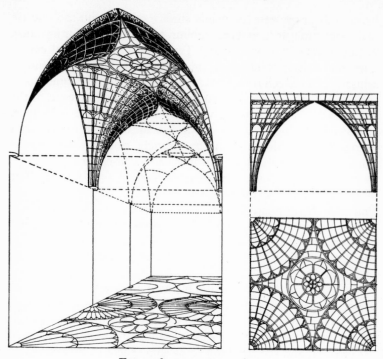

Fan vault over a square bay.

following these miniature examples of sumptuous tombs and tabernacles, the masons evolved the remarkable new system.

The earliest fan vaults, as in the cloister at Gloucester, did not,
being small, involve great engineering skill. They did, however,
introduce two further design problems. The first was that the
central area of the vault, being flat, had to be constructed in a
special way; and the second was that the system of semi-circular
conoids only seemed to work satisfactorily over square bays. The
solution to the first problem was to build the flat area in a series of
wedge-shaped rings of stone, so that in section they constituted a
flat arch, in which the central stone was the keystone and might
be enlarged into a long pendant which weighted and steadied the
vault, as in Bishop Alcock's chantry at Ely. At King's College
Chapel, Cambridge (Pl. 15), and in the nave of Sherborne, a
partial solution to the second problem was achieved. Here strong
transverse ribs mark each rectangular bay, and the conoids are
allowed to continue up to the centre and are mitred at the sides.

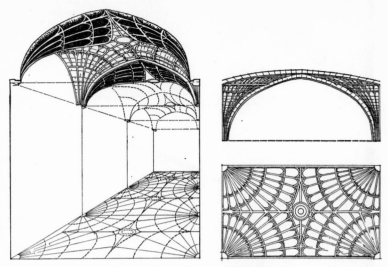

Fan vault over a rectangular bay.

The idea of pendants, however, suggested another more exciting solution, and at the same time produced yet another form of vault.

Pendant Vaults. In the choir of Oxford Cathedral (1478–1503), the pendants from the transverse arches were, in effect, elongated voussoirs. These pendants defined a square space, and from them sprang a rib and panel vault. The distance between the pendants and the side walls was filled with transverse barrel vaults. It was a solution of a kind, but was to be far surpassed by William Vertue in the construction of the Henry VII Chapel (1500–12) at Westminster (Pl. 15). Here again there are great transverse arches and pendants, but they are used in conjunction with fully-developed fan vaults. The infilling panels are omitted, so that one is left with only an elaborate lacework of masonry, and one can glimpse the great transverse arches through the vault.

The story of vaulting is complete. The earliest vaults were all infilling and no ribs. Then at Durham diagonal ribs were added; at Lincoln, ridge ribs and tiercerons; at Tewkesbury and Winchester, liernes were introduced, until a single stone was often enough to fill the spaces between the ribs; then in the cloister of Gloucester, the rib and panel became one. Finally, at Westminster, the panel disappeared and the vault became no more than an intricate network of stone. Beyond this the medieval architects

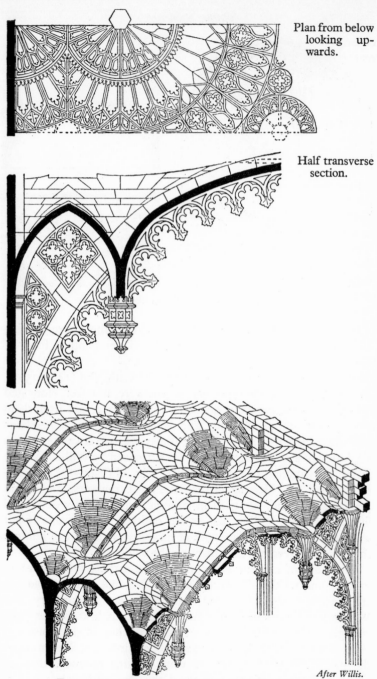

Plan from below looking upwards.

Half transverse section.

After Willis.

Fan vaulting from Henry VII Chapel, Westminster.

could not go. The limit of their constructional skill had been reached.

The Flying Buttress. The development of the ribbed vault and the introduction of the *tas-de-charge* had located the position and line of thrust of the vaults. This necessitated a system of support and abutment. There had been no problem in the case of barrel vaults, for there the thrust was continuous along its length, and all that was necessary was that the supporting wall should be sufficiently thick. With the ribbed vault, the thrusts are concentrated at given points, and the wall in between these points is of little value. This was recognized so thoroughly after the twelfth century that, in France especially, the wall became a window, and a series of supports was substituted for continuous abutment. These supports stretched across from the outside of the nave wall to the inside face of the aisle or triforium wall. They were not simply solid walls at right angles to the nave, for these would have weighted unnecessarily the arches over the aisles and interfered with free passage in the triforium, but were, as a rule, quadrant arches. They were, in fact, flying buttresses, although they might be hidden by the roof of the triforium. Such a system occurred along the nave triforium at Durham (1133) and also at Abbaye-aux-Dames (mid-twelfth century). They possessed the advantage over exposed buttresses of being less liable to decay, and as long as the nave was comparatively low or the triforium relatively high, the solution was satisfactory. But if it was wished to omit the triforium gallery, or to increase the height of the clerestory, it became necessary to

Malmesbury Abbey Church; flying buttress and pinnacle.

introduce these buttresses above, and independent of, the aisle below. This step was apparently taken first in France. In England it did not occur until the Canterbury choir was rebuilt by William the Frenchman (from Sens), 1175–8. But even there they only just appear a little distance above the side roof, and the builders seem to have suspected their efficiency, because they introduced a subsidiary arch underneath. The original flying buttresses of S. Denis (1140) have disappeared, but the construction is so delicate that it is almost certain that they were there. By the thirteenth century flying buttresses had become the hallmark of French Gothic, and no church of the Royal demesne was complete without them. In this country, where our cathedrals are more modest in height, the hidden buttress usually sufficed, and where flying buttresses did occur they were often later additions, as, for instance, in the choir of Lincoln.

Flying buttresses transmit, rather than resist, thrusts. Starting from the upper part of the nave wall—as a rule from slightly projecting buttresses—they conduct the thrusts to buttresses built out from the aisle wall. In Notre-Dame, Paris, which has double aisles, the principal flying buttresses are in single spans. As a rule, however, in double-aisled churches, the portion of the wall over each pier between the aisles is carried up to form an intermediate buttress, so that each flying buttress consists of two arches. The first arch transmits the thrust of the vault from the nave wall to the intermediate buttress, and the second carries it over to the outer buttress. This last has to be sufficiently strong to resist the thrust of the flying buttress itself and such transmitted vault thrusts as have not been neutralized on the way. A similar problem and solution occurs at Westminster, where the continental method of flying buttresses in two tiers was adopted in order to bridge over the cloisters as well as the aisles; but this is exceptional.

There was evidently no hard-and-fast rule to determine the relative position of the flying buttress to the vault. This differs considerably in the various examples. The builders clearly did not make careful calculations to ascertain the amount of pressure exercised, the exact direction it took, or the precise point from which it started. They judged from experience, from failures and from successes. It is a question whether such calculations, if made now, would be of any use, because given one single instance of bad workmanship or of defective material, the calculations would be upset, unless an enormous margin of safety were allowed.

In the majority of examples, the top of the intrados of the arch of the flying buttress—or of the most important one where there are several—butts against the nave or choir wall approximately on a line with the top of the *tas-de-charge*. Sometimes, however, it is above the *tas-de-charge* and at other times below, usually the latter in early examples. The pitch of the vault (the thrust of a steep vault is nearer vertical than is that of a flatter one), the height of the *tas-de-charge*, and the weight of the wall above the springing line of the vault, must all be taken into account in determining the exact position of the flying buttress. Again, the depth of the buttress from soffit to the top of the coping, and the slope of the coping, make a considerable difference. In early buttresses the bottom curve was often a quadrant, and the top slope of low pitch; the mass of masonry against the wall which offered resistance to the vault thrust was consequently small. This was most unsatisfactory when the flying buttress was low down; for then, if the upper part of the wall ceased to be perpendicular, owing to the thrust of the vault or other causes, the top of the flying buttress dropped and began to press hard against the wall, which soon collapsed because it was subjected to an outward thrust above and an inward thrust below. The later buttresses were usually of a steeper pitch, having an underside curve the equivalent of a half-pointed arch. There was often a considerable space between the top of the voussoirs composing the soffit curve and the bottom of the coping. This space might be solid, and either plain or with sunken panels on its face; or it might be pierced. Such a buttress provides a considerable margin when any uncertainty exists as to the exact direction of the vault thrusts. Moreover, it acts over a large surface, and consequently affords greater support to the wall.

Flying buttresses are not used merely to resist or transmit vault thrusts. In the lofty cathedrals of northern France, such as Reims, and Amiens, where two flying buttresses come one above the other, the upper one has no relation whatsoever to the vault. Its function is simply to aid in supporting the high wall of the clerestory and to take the thrust of the timber roof above the vault, which is often considerable. At Beauvais, where there are three tiers of buttresses, the lowest is far below the vault, the middle one slightly above the *tas-de-charge*, and the highest close under the top parapet. The first and last have nothing to do with the vault; they are merely stiffeners to the wall.

It must not be supposed that the builders, when they adopted flying buttresses, dispensed with other methods of counteracting thrusts. On the contrary, they developed them. The side walls of the nave were still carried up above the vault, in many cases far higher than before. In Reims Cathedral there are several feet between the top of the vault and the bottom of the tie beam, and consequently the same amount of extra walls at the sides and a large increase in the weight pressing on the vault thrusts.

The Wall Buttress. Of all the methods of controlling and stabilizing the thrusts of arches and vaults, the most common is the wall buttress and pinnacle. The change from the wide, shallow, Romanesque buttress to the narrow, but deeply projecting, Gothic buttress was gradual. The statical fault of the Romanesque buttress was that the projection at the base was altogether too slight. It was no more than a pilaster strip, with little or no constructional value, which served only to give periodic relief to the exterior. The general adoption of ribbed vaulting led logically to a system of piers and panel infillings along the supporting walls. The distinguishing features of the Gothic buttress are that they are usually divided into stages, each set back by short slopes from the one below, and that they terminate either in a chamfer, or slope, against the wall, or in a gable, which may be topped by a pinnacle. All these features are significant aesthetically and structurally. The setting back by stages ensures that while the minimum of material is used the line of thrust still falls within the buttress, and the pinnacle provides a useful counterweight. Reference to the diagram on page 30 shows the relative efficiency between this trapezoidal form of buttress and the rectangular buttress of the Romans. The former is more efficient, because its centre of gravity is nearer to the source of thrust. By comparison, the amount of material required to restrain the greater thrust of the semi-circular arch is more than twice that required in the case of the pointed arch, with its trapezoidal buttress and lesser thrust.

When a buttress is in different stages, these are separated from one another by sloping weatherings or set-offs, or else by steep-pitched gables which lie against the face of the stage above. There does not seem to be any rule for the number of stages or the slope of the set-offs. It has been suggested that the top slopes should be steeper than those below, because, being higher, they would appear more foreshortened. Occasionally they are made so, but by no means universally. In some, the top slopes are the flattest. When the top is crowned by a gable, this may be below, level with, or carried considerably above, the parapet. When it rises above, it has the advantage of providing a mass of masonry which, by exercising a vertical pressure, considerably neutralizes the side thrusts. This is also the function of pinnacles, which play so important a part in Gothic architecture. They are not merely ornaments; in some cases they are absolute necessities upon which the

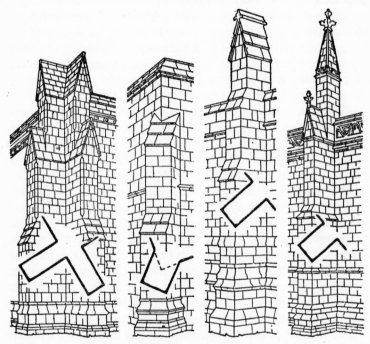

Buttresses *c.* 1250–1400.

stability of the structure depends. It is true that they were sometimes introduced, in fifteenth-century English work, when the need for them did not exist (for instance, in churches with flat timber roofs, which exert little or no lateral thrust). Sometimes, too, they occur in greater churches, as, for instance, in the Selby choir and the nave of York, where there are no stone vaults to sustain. There they are evidence of an intention to construct a stone vault which was never carried out, for in both these cases the vaults are of wood.

In the middle of the thirteenth century, the method was introduced of making one buttress do the work of two at the outside corners. This was placed diagonally, and was logical, for the resultant thrust at the corners is diagonal. But diagonal buttresses never became universal, and two buttresses at right angles to the wall and to each other were used up to the end of the Gothic period.

The buttress, like so many structural features of Gothic architecture, was soon utilized for ornamental carving or to provide settings for sculpture. Not content with the opportunities already available in the jambs and heads of doorways, in the bosses in the vaults and the capitals of the columns, the sculptor claimed the buttress also. Beautiful examples of niches with delicately cusped canopies over them, to give protection to the sculpture, are to be found in the east end of Ely and the west front of Wells. At Wells the niches are on all sides, and with their figures produce a richness of effect unsurpassed elsewhere in Europe. During the thirteenth and fourteenth centuries it was customary to enrich both walls and buttresses with panelling. The result was that the buttresses no longer stood out so obviously as before, since their outline was lost in the general scheme of rich elaboration. Partly perhaps as a corrective to this, the upper stages were often different in plan from those below. They were octagonal, hexagonal, or square placed cornerwise; the different faces were commonly crowned by canopies from which arose a crocketed pinnacle. In the fifteenth century, and especially at the angles of towers, buttresses were often octagonal from top to bottom, and so richly panelled in harmony with the walls and the windows that their function as abutment to the vault was no longer obvious.

The Window. That the pointed arch was primarily a structural device, rather than an aesthetic fancy, is to some extent proved by the fact that there was evidently a considerable reluctance to abandon the semi-circular arch over such minor openings as windows or doorways. At Fountains, Ripon and New Shoreham, for instance, the pier arcades are pointed to facilitate the vaulting, but the windows remain semi-circular. At Glastonbury, although the window is pointed, the inner arch is semi-circular. According to Bond,[1] the lancet window did not come into general use in England until 1170. In France it was earlier, but there, too, there was a considerable gap in time before the pointed arch was adopted for windows and subsidiary openings.

When the pointed arch supplanted the semi-circular for windows,

---

[1] Francis Bond: *Gothic Architecture in England,* 1905.

After Brandon.

Oundle Church, Northants. The west window of
south aisle, showing lancets under one arch.

the lights were elongated considerably and to some extent made
narrower also. In England the tendency towards loftiness was
especially marked, while in France the lights were much wider in
proportion. In England the designers composed groups of lancets
under one arch, whereas France moved more quickly towards a
system of tracery. Usually, in England, an odd number of windows,
three, five or seven, were grouped together, and occasionally they
were graded in height, the better to fill the space under the wall
arch. In the jambs outside and on the splays inside there was often
much enrichment of mouldings and ornament. Sometimes the
lights were so close together that they were separated merely by
wide ashlar mullions, and in effect formed one window. For nearly
a century the English persisted in using simple lancet windows, and
were mainly concerned with perfecting proportions, while the
French were developing tracery. Most of the early French tracery

Lindfield Church, Sussex. Plate tracery, window in north transept.

is of the kind known as 'plate', and consists of circles, quatre-foils and other geometrical figures pierced through the masonry which fills the heads of the windows. At Chartres, Laon, Notre-Dame in Paris and others, there were many such windows before the end of the twelfth century.

The development from 'plate' to 'bar' tracery followed natur-ally when the stones were worked and moulded to the re-quired shape, instead of being cut out like fretwork. Bar tracery is found at Orbais (1200) and in the eastern chapel of Reims

Cathedral (1212), but it did not occur in England until much later. The Westminster choir, begun 1245, is commonly cited as the earliest example, and that was probably of direct French origin, for the resemblance to Reims is very close. Earlier still, however, is the large west win-dow of Binham Abbey, which was constructed by Richard de Parco, who was Prior from 1226 to 1240. Another important example mentioned by Bond is at Netley, which he dates at 1239. Indeed, it is not necessary to assume that bar tracery was intro-duced to England from abroad. The germ of it had certainly

After Viollet-le-Duc.

Chartres   Cathedral.   Plate tracery.

existed even in Romanesque times, when windows were moulded and grouped under one hood moulding. An interesting transitional example occurs in the north aisle of Stone Church, Kent (1240). Here there are three windows, side by side. They are all alike, each consisting of two lights with a quatrefoil above enclosed by a hood moulding. The arches are all moulded. It is partially plate tracery, but the mouldings intersect, and if the spandrels had been pierced the window could have been formed entirely of bars of stone.

One characteristic trait of French traceried windows, which does not occur in England, is that the arches of the window-heads, especially those in the clerestories, are much stilted; or, in other words, the tracery comes down far below the springing line. The whole of the window-head may be filled with a large circle, either cusped or plain, which is the full width of the lights below. Such windows, generally of two lights, occur most frequently around the eastern apses, where the available window space is much narrower than elsewhere. Apart from this, there is very little difference between English and French tracery from 1250 to 1300. The designs always consist of geometrical figures, circles, quatrefoils, trefoils, spherical triangles, etc. Early in the following century, however, English tracery lost all its stiffness and became extremely complicated. While the French persisted in using the earlier and simpler forms, English tracery became sinuous and flowing. There can be no doubt that the credit for this departure belongs to England, and it is likely that its later appearance in France was the direct consequence of the English occupation during the Hundred Years War.

After Viollet-le-Duc.
Reims Cathedral.
Stilted arch
window.

Curvilinear tracery provided far greater variety and a much better setting for stained glass. It made possible a continuity of design in the windows that was much superior to any of the more obvious geometry of the thirteenth century. Suddenly, about 1350, the graceful tangles were abandoned. The tracery bars were

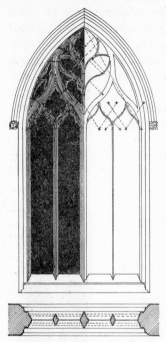

After Brandon.
Sleaford Church, Lincolnshire.
Curvilinear tracery.

straightened and the windows were filled with a series of long, straight-sided panels reaching from sill to window-head. The reason for the change has been attributed to the Black Death and the consequent shortage of labour; for this new tracery was much easier to build and more economical of material. But there was also a change in glass. Before, it had been thick and relatively opaque; now it was thin and translucent. Before, it had been heavy with colour; now, it was possible to build a church that was a lantern of light. In the great east window of Gloucester, the area of a tennis court, nearly all is white and only a quarter of the glass is coloured (Pl. 14). In most of the large fifteenth-century windows the lights were divided horizontally by transoms, forming a grid, so that each figure or heraldic device could be completely framed. The window thus became a portrait gallery, and the beauty of the tracery was subsidiary to the beauty of the glass. Architecturally the window was in harmony with the wall, and the same panelling system covered both; but now window predominated over wall. Indeed, in John Wastell's King's College Chapel the system is perfected. There the windows stretch from one end of the chapel to the other, only interrupted by the great, deep buttresses.

The traceried window, like the vault and the buttress, may be regarded simply as part of a wonderful aesthetic composition, or it may be considered as a purely functional and constructional feature of Gothic architecture. Certainly, in much early work the structural scheme could be complete without the introduction of tracery bars, for the weight of the superincumbent wall could easily be carried by the window arch. The structural problem only arose when the window was wide and was to be filled with glass. Then tracery subdivided the area so that the leaded lights could, with the aid of iron cross-bars, withstand wind pressure. Later, when arches in the weaker form of the ogee or four-centred kind were used, then tracery became of real value in strengthening and cross-bracing the arched opening.

Much of the beauty of traceried windows is due to the emphasis given to certain parts of the design. Some bars are wider than others and have a greater number of mouldings worked on them. The lights at the heads may be similarly grouped. There is no inflexible rule, but in four- and six-light windows the central mullion is generally thicker than the others. In a five-light window the two central mullions are similarly emphasized by extra mouldings. The same scheme of subdivision is

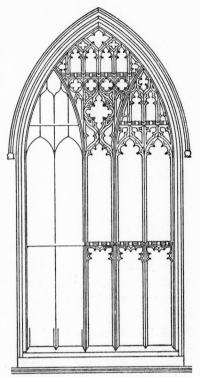

Claypole, Lincolnshire. Perpendicular tracery.

generally carried through in the tracery at the window-heads. The main divisions are emphasized, and great delicacy is often given by the slightness of the intermediary bars. A further refinement in most large windows is the greater width of the central light compared with those at the sides.

There is an enormous difference in proportion and in detail between mullions and bars of early and late traceried windows. Early mullions were very wide, but had little projection from the glass; later examples were deeper and thinner. The mouldings, too, as in every other part of the structure, changed through the centuries. When the windows followed a simple geometric pattern, the mouldings followed suit; when the lines of tracery were flowing, the mouldings were mainly ogees, and in the last phase the mouldings were usually slight and shallow.

Most windows are enriched at the heads by cusping, so that in

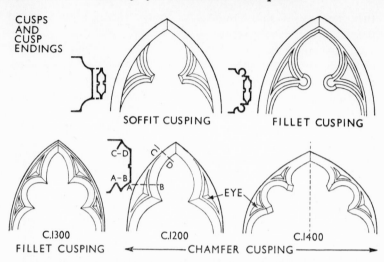

CUSPS
AND
CUSP
ENDINGS

SOFFIT CUSPING   FILLET CUSPING

C.1300   C.1200   C.1400
FILLET CUSPING   ◄———— CHAMFER CUSPING ————►

place of a simple lancet the opening becomes a trefoil or,
occasionally, a cinquefoil. It has been suggested that the constructional purpose of the cusps is to strengthen the arch at its weakest
point, but this is unlikely. Cusping is found earlier than bar
tracery; it occurs in simple lancet windows and in early plate
tracery. Usually, in these cases, the cusps spring from the flat
soffit alone and are either worked out of the voussoirs or else are

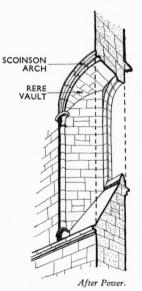

SCOINSON
ARCH

RERE
VAULT

After Power.

tenoned in to the opening. Many such have
dropped out and have not been reinstated in
'restoration'. This 'soffit' cusping, as it is
called, disappeared as bar tracery developed,
though it occurs in the heads of the triforium
openings of the Angel Choir at Lincoln, *c.* 1260
(Pl. 9), and Westminster Abbey; and it is found
even as late as the fourteenth century in the
highly enriched windows of Leominster Church.
Generally, however, in most windows from
about 1250 onwards the cusping starts from
a fillet which is carried up from the jamb,
and the back of the cusp is usually chamfered
so as to form an 'eye' which is sometimes
pierced and glazed. The cusp terminations
in the different centuries vary considerably.
In the thirteenth century they finished square,
or with a knob; in the fourteenth century,

they came to a sharp point and in the fifteenth to a broad point.

In the windows of the eleventh, twelfth and early thirteenth centuries, the arch on the inside face of the wall over each light is generally concentric with the window-head, but, because of the wide splaying of the jambs, is wider and rises higher. When many lights are grouped together to form one window, the treatment of the inside is often different. Sometimes, especially in a thick wall, the window may consist of three parts: the outer, or glazed window arch, the inner or scoinson arch, and the space between, or rere vault. In the best examples, as, for instance, in the presbytery at Lincoln, in the east transept at Durham, and in the triforium at S. Ouen, Rouen, the rear arch has tracery of an entirely different pattern from that of the window. This development of double

After Bond.

Double tracery, Durham, east transept.

tracery in the eleventh and twelfth centuries is to some extent a reflection of poor wall construction, in which the outer and inner faces were of dressed stone, the middle being filled with coarse rubble. The wall was necessarily thick to contain within it the lines of the forces of the vaulting. In order to obtain the maximum amount of light, the early windows simply had a broad internal splay, so that the inner arch was considerably wider than the outer. Partly for the sake of strength, but more certainly for the sake of internal beauty and continuity of surface, there arose the fashion of constructing an inner system of tracery which was unglazed. Occasionally, but rarely, as for instance in the presbytery at York, this arrangement is reversed, so that the outer tracery is open and the inner glazed, giving a continuous but rather flat surface from within.

After Viollet-le-Duc.
Rose window, Notre-Dame, Paris.

Circular and Rose Windows. The wheel windows of Romanesque times are the forerunners of the large rose windows which form such effective features of the cathedrals of France. In England, except perhaps in the ruined west front of Byland and the original east front of Old S. Paul's, there was nothing to compare with the wonderful round windows of Chartres, Rouen and Sens cathedrals. The design of these and other continental windows varies according to the date, and the whole evolution of French tracery can be studied from circular windows alone: from the plate tracery examples in the west fronts of Laon and Chartres, through the geometric windows of Paris and Reims, down to those with flowing lines, of which the finest is probably that in the south transept of S. Ouen, Rouen. Even when a window had vertical lights, the French often filled the head with an enormous traceried circle, as, for instance, in the great window in the south transept of Beauvais Cathedral. At this point the virtuosity of Gothic architecture had reached its limits, and the decoration seems no longer subordinate but has acquired a significance of its own, independent of mere structural necessity.

CHAPTER IV

DECORATION

THE interiors of many medieval churches, as seen today, are so clean and colourless that it is often difficult to imagine what they were like originally. From descriptions, and such fragmentary evidence as survives, they seem to have presented a blaze of colour from floor to roof. The windows were filled with stained glass, just enough relatively clear glass being left to admit light and to frame the dazzling figures of saints, apostles and martyrs. The walls were painted, and the mouldings of arches picked out with colour and gilding; the floors were covered with encaustic tiles in yellow, red and brown, and further enriched with polished brasses and incised memorial slabs. There were sculptured figures set in niches, all gay and painted, as was the woodwork in roofs and choir stalls, and the ironwork in screens was commonly gilded. Now, in place of the coloured walls we too often have only scraped stone, clean new plaster or—worse still—rubble walling with the joints picked out in black mortar. The brilliant glass has in many cases remained, but often it has disappeared, to make our churches, especially those of the later phases when the areas of window were large, appear more like great conservatories than places of worship.[1] The difference between our churches then and now is as great as between painting and an engraving: the composition remains the same, but the colour is absent. On the Continent, the treatment which the churches received in the last two centuries was even more drastic than in this country, and often without the excuse of Puritanism. Cleanliness may be next to godliness, but too often it has tended to destroy both art and history. What is wanted in

[1] Having had the advantage over Simpson of being able to see the remarkable effect of the removal of stained glass, either through war damage or as a precaution against it, I am not absolutely in sympathy with the derogatory implications of this sentence. A wonderful sense of space is obtained when one can see, through tracery, the sky and the trees in a churchyard outside. This might have attracted the medieval builders if they had been able to manufacture an absolutely clear glass in reasonably large pieces. It is certain that the Cistercians would have preferred this to the closed, jewel-box effect of, for instance, La Ste. Chapelle, Paris. (*Ed.*)

old churches is the cleanliness of the painter, not that of the charwoman.

Colour can be introduced into a church in three ways. It may take the form of coloured light through windows; it may be applied decoration, such as marble veneer, paint or tapestry; or it may be achieved by the employment of different coloured materials used structurally. In Italy, brick and marble or brick and stone are interchanged with the happiest results, although at Siena, where black and white are used in equal bands, the effect is too startling to be pleasant. In France and Germany, materials of different colours are rarely used, but in England, especially in the thirteenth century, the use of polished Purbeck marble in conjunction with the local stone is common. In the nave of Salisbury and throughout the whole of Westminster Abbey, the columns, surrounding shafts, capitals and bases are all marble. At Worcester only the shafts, the abacus of each capital and the top members of each base are of marble, the remainder being stone. The shafts in jambs of triforiums, clerestory and aisle windows, doorways and porches, are also commonly emphasized by contrasting materials. The contrasts now are in many cases too marked, especially at Salisbury, where the jump from the dark Purbeck of the piers to the white stone of the arches is too abrupt, so that the effect is disagreeably sharp and cold. It may not always have been so, or at least such a contrast may not have been the original intention of the builders. The white stone of the arches and walls was probably painted, often in rich reds and occasionally yellow, so that the effect would have been totally different.

Mural Painting. Before oil became the general medium for mural decorations early in the fourteenth century, work not executed in fresco was done in tempera, fixed sometimes by a final coat of oil. Tempera differs mainly from fresco in being applied to a dry surface and not to fresh, damp plaster. Sometimes the work was done direct on stone, but more often a thin coat of stucco was first laid to give a smooth surface and to prevent absorption. The process is exceedingly old, extending back to the civilizations of Egypt, Greece and Rome, and it seems to have been practised all through the Middle Ages in all countries. Until the end of the thirteenth century the palette in the West was limited to reds, browns and yellows. Although many fragments painted in this way have survived, all are more or less damaged. Many have been covered by later paintings, or by plaster, to form a key for which an earlier

painted surface has been hacked. Others have been hidden
by whitewash, applied either by Puritans or, it has been
suggested, during periods of great sickness. After the plague
visitations, the disinfection of churches was as necessary as
the disinfection of homes, and much of the whitewashing attributed to the Reformation may have been done earlier to prevent
the spread of disease. Whatever the reason, the damage was
irreparable.

With the introduction of oil as a medium in the fourteenth
century, greens and blues were added to the palette and predominated in the colour schemes. Figure paintings were not so
general as they had been in the thirteenth century, and the artists
concentrated on furniture and fittings. The walls were merely
covered with diaper patterns enlivened by sprigs of flowers and
leaves, and sometimes with more elaborate conventional designs
reminiscent of Florentine woven fabrics. The mouldings of arches,
especially, were painted, and the fillets gilded. There are many
examples of this abroad, though little survives in England;
instead, we still retain many fine painted screens, pulpits, choir
stalls, tombs and timber roofs, especially in the eastern counties.
The medieval artist had no respect for the natural colour or grain
of oak; that feeling for material is entirely modern. Oak and stone
were painted so that in many cases not a square inch of the natural
material showed. In St. Albans Cathedral, the shrine of the saint,
although of Purbeck marble, is painted blue and green with
gilded tracery and mullions. The paintings on the mouldings of
many Norfolk screens give one a fair indication of what the
painting on stone moulding was like, and enough fragments
remain on stone in different churches at home and abroad to
prove that both wood and stone were treated alike. In stone vaults
the carvings of the bosses were brilliantly painted and often
gilded. The ribs, too, sometimes for only a short distance from the
bosses, and the infilling where plastered, were often enriched
with colour.

The colour schemes of the medieval painters were a succession
of contrasts. A broad effect was obtained, not by the use of one
single colour but by the juxtaposition of many colours, no one
being allowed to prevail over the others. One moulding might be
green, the next red or blue, or white with small sprigs of flowers
painted on it (this last was reserved for hollows), and the dividing
fillets were either gilded or painted a strong yellow. A complete

accord must have existed between mason and painter; otherwise, such schemes would have been impossible, since colour completely changes the appearance of mouldings. By its aid some can be emphasized, others almost obliterated.

Considerable controversy has arisen at times over the quality of the colours used. It has been held that they were crude in the extreme, and the present fine tones are attributed to time alone. As proof, examples are cited in which whitewash or plaster has recently been removed. In thirteenth-century work the colours possibly were crude, although the linseed oil that was often the final coat must have toned them down. It has been suggested that when whitewash has been removed from old work, the glazing coat has unfortunately been removed also, and that the colour remaining is very different in tone from what it was when the painters left the work.

Fragments alone remain to enable one to judge the extent to which colour was employed externally on churches, but these are enough to show that in most cases both colour and gilding were applied to the figures, canopy work and walling behind, in porches and doorways. Colour has to be sought for in those churches which luckily escaped entire renovation through lack of funds. The less renowned the church, the greater the likelihood of finding remains of decoration. The north and south porches of Chartres Cathedral are famous throughout the civilized world, and it is useless to search for colour in them; yet there can be no doubt whatsoever that they were painted and gilded originally. Both paint and gold, however, have been cleaned off with a thoroughness worthy of a better cause. It is only in the crevices that anything can be discovered at all, and even in these the patches are so minute that their nature is not clear. Over the west door of Angers Cathedral a considerable amount of red, blue and green remains, and the bands, etc., on the garments of the figures, the wings of the angels, and the animals, of which there are several, are gilded. In the triple west porch of Sées, Normandy, the same three colours were used extensively, mainly on the mouldings and on the walling behind the figures. The great west front of Wells (Pl. 9), with its 176 full-length statues, was brilliantly coloured. The niches were dark red, and the figures and drapery painted a yellow ochre, with the eyes and hair picked out in black and the lips in red. In the central group of the Virgin and Child, the Virgin's robe was black with a green lining, while the Child's robe was crimson, the composition being set on a background of red and green diaper. There is evidence, from plug-holes, that the statues were further enriched with gilded metal ornament. Above, the row of angels was painted rosy red. Altogether the effect must have been startlingly different from its present sandy monochrome, and according to one authority, 'there can be little doubt that to modern taste the front, in its original condition, would have appeared exceedingly vulgar'.[1] It was, however, a healthy and vigorous vulgarity, which enjoyed the grotesque as well as the sublime, which could make waterspouts into fearsome gargoyles, could carve the hidden misericords with riotous domestic scenes portraying such common everyday incidents as toothache and wrestling and witch-ducking, and which, while obviously delighting in the depiction of the terrors of Hell, at the same time reached sublime grandeur in representing the features of an adored Apostle, saint or king.

That the quality of the painting on the sculptures may not have been as crude or as gaudy as the above descriptions suggest is evident from the records of high payment to painters. Nearly as much was spent on painting as on carving, and this love of colour seems to have permeated all Gothic art. It may well have been as delicate and skilful as the carving. It may have been as brilliant as the painting on glass or in the illuminated manuscripts of the time.

Figure Sculpture. Apart from the intrinsic beauty of medieval sculpture, two reasons account for its special effectiveness. The first is that it was executed by men thoroughly in harmony with the work surrounding it, and in close touch with those who carried out that work; and secondly, that the sculpture in most cases is framed in. The sculpture is complementary to the architecture, and the sculptor was simply one of the members of the masons' yard, who might be required to construct a vault or dress a stone as well as carve a capital or an angel. Although it is obvious that some sculptors developed particular skill in figure work, there is no evidence that because of this they were esteemed more highly, or were better paid, than their fellow-craftsmen.

As a general rule, medieval figures stand in niches with canopies or arches over them, or else are carved on the tympanum of an entrance, in which position they are still framed by an arch. In Paris, Chartres, Amiens and other great French cathedrals, they

[1] Laurence Stone: *Sculpture in Britain in the Middle Ages*, 1955, p. 108.

occur in bands of arcading along the west fronts. In jambs of doorways they often partially take the place of shafts and, in the orders of the arches over, they, with their canopies, form concentric bands of great richness. In the fronts and sides of the buttresses on the west front of Wells Cathedral they are in profusion, standing in niches or seated or crouching inside quatrefoils or trefoils. Inside, they rarely touch the structure. They are reserved mainly for reredoses, as in Winchester Cathedral and Christchurch, Hampshire, for screens round choirs, as at Chartres, and for tombs, pulpits, fonts and other fittings. There are exceptions. On the inside face of the west wall of Reims Cathedral is some fine sculpture and still finer carving in panels. The angels in the spandrels over the triforium arches of the eastern arm of Lincoln Cathedral have earned it its title of the Angel Choir (Pl. 9). Even finer than these, though much smaller, are the figures over the seats of the Lady Chapel of Ely Cathedral, which in pose and in the treatment of the drapery have an almost Classical character.

The outstanding exception to the rule by which sculpture was enclosed or set in a niche or frame was to be found in the figures which stood above the rood screens in every church. In England, by the order of 1547, the crucified Christ and the attendant figures of Mary and John were everywhere destroyed. The loss to our artistic heritage was inestimable, for these compositions must have been not only the dominant religious focus in every church, but also, presumably, of the highest craftsmanship. Today, where the screen survives, it often ends in a discordant horizontal line and is finished with cresting, often of a later date. In France, in the eighteenth century, the removal of the barrier between clergy and people which the screens provided led to similar destruction, so that out of the two hundred and fifty major churches only one, Albi, has its western choir screen *in situ*.

By the end of the twelfth century much of the archaic feeling noticeable in Romanesque sculpture had disappeared, and the faces and forms had become more realistic and the lines of drapery more flowing. The sculpture on the north and south porches of Chartres is representative of the work that followed. That on the south is earlier and finer than that on the north, and its restraint and architectural suitability are greater. Both porches are mines of wealth; but while giving them due praise, it is possible to have a sneaking preference for the earlier and more conventional rendering found in the figures of the west doorway of the same cathedral. The work of the pioneers of a movement is often more fascinating than that of those who have carried the medium to what one is pleased to call perfection. It is more individualistic. It may have more faults, be more open to criticism; but being less correct, it is often less cold.

Of greater significance than the sculptured figures, so far as architectural history is concerned, are the detailed carvings which are integral with the structure and which enrich the mouldings of the arches, the capitals and bases of the columns, the ribs and bosses of the vaults, the pinnacles and the buttresses—in fact, wherever the eye can see and, surprisingly enough, often at points which one can scarcely see at all.

Structural Enrichment. From 1150, the concave or 'bell-shaped' capital was characteristic everywhere, except in Italy and Spain, which never thoroughly assimilated Gothic architecture nor entirely discarded Classical influences. In France the proportions and forms already determined in Romanesque times were largely retained until the fifteenth century. Only the abacus was occasionally octagonal on plan, and the mouldings varied a little. The carving was Corinthianesque throughout the period. In England, on the other hand, there were continuous experiment and change. About the middle of the thirteenth century, the top member was usually octagonal and the lower members and bell shape circular. A hundred years later, all parts, even the bell itself, were made octagonal. Capitals became smaller in proportion until, in the fifteenth century, they seem to have lost all importance and indeed were sometimes omitted altogether.

The carving in the Early English capital was a foliated version of a volute, springing from the necking mould in crisp, compact bunches and usually called the 'stiff leaf' capital. The foliage was strictly conventional, and grew from a firm stalk. This stiffness disappeared about the middle of the thirteenth century, when the aim seems to have been to give as exact a rendering of nature as possible. In some cases this realism was carried too far, so that the capital lost all feeling of strength and had instead a curious crumpled character. The best carvings in England of this period are at Southwell, Exeter and Beverley. Southwell chapter house is the richest of all. Here the skill of the craftsmen in reproducing nature is exceptional. Even the backs of the leaves are finished smooth, and in one instance, perceptible only by looking up from below, there is a small animal carved behind the leaves. No two capitals are the same, but while there is remarkable fidelity in the accurate representation of different botanical species, it is noticeable that there is not the same regard for uniformity of scale. Thus, as Professor Pevsner has pointed out in his *Leaves of Southwell*, 'Hawthorn leaves are no smaller than maple leaves.'

After the Black Death, considerable deterioration is evident. The carving is cramped and knotty; foliage is reduced to a collection of bossy, undulating leaves with sinuous edges. It is all in harmony, however, with the architecture, which at that time was dominated by the flowing S-line. It accords with the curvilinear tracery and the ogee arch, but sculpturally the carvings lack the vigour and pleasant convention of the thirteenth century, or the realistic beauty of the first half of the fourteenth.

A similar change occurs in the conventional ornaments which enrich the mouldings. Between 1150 and 1250 the most characteristic ornament is called the 'dog-tooth'. It is common throughout England and in Normandy even as far south as Le Mans, where it occurs in the window over the doorway of the south tower of the cathedral, and it is met with occasionally in other French cathedrals, notably Laon. The usual statement is that this feature is derived from the 'nail-head' of Romanesque times, elongated and elaborated; but it is much more likely to be a modified version of the chevron, no longer continuous but split up into separate ornaments. At this period it is almost the only ornament. It occurs between shafts, half buried in hollows, sometimes standing out boldly from surrounding mouldings. It is used in arches, piers, labels, string courses, jambs of windows and doorways, the ribs of vaulting; in fact, everywhere.

At the end of the thirteenth century the dog-tooth disappeared and was replaced by the so-called 'ball-flower', which consists of a small sphere enclosed by three or four slightly open leaves. Absolute monotony is avoided by varying the 'hang' of the flowers, but at best the ornament is hard and unsympathetic, even after due allowances are made for the nature of the material in which it is carved. It is more satisfactory when it alternates with a square, four-leafed open flower, especially when, as often happens, the two are connected by a stalk so that a running pattern is formed. In the aisle windows of Gloucester Cathedral and Leominster Church, the jambs, heads, mullions and tracery are all peppered thickly with ball-flowers, the number of which the curious have counted

CAPITAL, SOUTHWELL MINSTER (*c.* 1300)

CROCKETS & CAPITAL
LINCOLN CATHEDRAL
(*c.* 1200)

DOG-TOOTH
(*c.* 1180)

CHEVRON
(*c.* 1080)

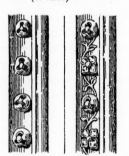

CROCKET,
ELY LADY CHAPEL
(*c.* 1350)

BALL-FLOWERS

DIAPER,
LINCOLN CATHEDRAL

BOSS
S. MARY,
BURY
S. EDMUNDS

A TUDOR
ROSE

and recorded.[1] In the great circular west window of Chartres the ornament carved round its openings (and in the labels over it and the side windows of the front) is a species of ball-flower earlier in date and more beautiful than the English variety. The leaves are folded back, not brought forward, and the whole of each flower, not merely the centre, resembles a ball. In the church of S. Pierre de la Couture, Le Mans (*c.* 1150), in the labels over the arches of the windows, are flowers which are also earlier than those in England. In some of these the flower is quite open, in others only half-open, and the effect produced by the variations is exceedingly good.

A similar change is to be noticed in the treatment of crockets, which in the thirteenth century were small, compact curls, whereas afterwards they were designed to appear as an almost continuous upward ripple along the edges of every pinnacle. In a way, these and other sculptures represent a triumph for the decorator over the architect.

Towards the end of the fourteenth century there was an extraordinary reaction, and the demand for architectural sculptures, other than mere mouldings and mechanical panelling, almost disappeared. The outstanding works are the carvings of screens and misericords in wood, and monumental tombs in alabaster. It is noticeable, especially in the treatment of the misericords, how the religious spirit seems to have departed. At times, indeed, there is a crudity which one cannot imagine being permissible in any church work today. A favourite subject is that of the virago belabouring her husband. At New College, Oxford, where there are some sixty-two misericords, not one is of a religious subject and many are savage caricatures.

Stained Glass. Stained glass is the one art which we associate almost exclusively with the church, and largely with the Gothic period. It is also the one art which has best survived the attacks of time and Puritanism. Until glass was made in large pieces, the only way the medieval glazier could fill a window opening was by joining small pieces together with strips of lead, usually of an H-section and soldered at each joint. Lead, because of its softness, made it possible to join together complicated shapes, and the window as a whole had considerable flexibility. This was an

[1] Edmund Sharpe, the eminent Late Victorian authority on Gothic architecture, says that each window of Leominster Church has 820 ball-flowers of different sizes.

advantage when it came to springing the window into prepared channels in the stonework, but it was a disadvantage in the face of wind pressure on large surfaces. To remedy this, the window had to be braced by a system of iron T-bars, which were at first arranged vertically and horizontally. This introduced a governing factor in design, since the glazier's job was to provide a series of separate leaded panels which could be simply fitted into the iron grid.

Generally, it may be said, the colour effects of medieval windows are not the result of painting, but arise from the use of pieces of coloured glass in which a separate piece has to be used for each change of colour. There are two important exceptions. The first involves the use of silver stain (a discovery of the fourteenth century), which can be applied to a portion of white glass to give areas and gradations of colour from the palest yellow to deep orange. The second is by means of flashed glass, in which a thin film of colour (in the Middle Ages, limited to reds and blues) is fused on to a white backing. The colour may be ground away in places to give the effect of white and colour on a single piece of glass. Today the same effect is achieved by the use of acid. Apart from these two exceptions, the basic design of a stained-glass window depends upon the arrangement of flat patches of colour, worked on in parts by monochromatic shading and drawing. This shading consists in brushing on to the glass an enamel made of oxide of iron mixed with oil or gummed water, which is then fired until the enamel is fused on to the glass.

Hugh Arnold[1] has divided the study of medieval stained glass into three periods, which in England coincide chronologically with Early English, Decorated, and Perpendicular. The first period lasts until the end of the thirteenth century, and is almost entirely limited to that century, for few remains of earlier glass exist. At Le Mans Cathedral we learn of windows filled between 1081 and 1097 with glass '*sumptuosa artis varietate*', and at Chartres the windows over the west front, together with the great figure of the Virgin in the south choir aisle, and some fragments in the choir of the abbey of S. Denis, near Paris, are of the second half of the twelfth century, but most of the early glass has been lost, partly because it was not an integral part of the fabric, but was usually fitted into removable wooden frames. What little there is shows that the designs, with the

[1] *Stained Glass of the Middle Ages in England and France*, 1913.

exceptions mentioned above, were similar to the designs for stone carving, and that scrollwork founded on the classical acanthus was the prevailing motif. It is at York, Canterbury and Chartres that we find the best examples of the first period.

In the first period there are two distinct styles: the dark and richly coloured windows of the school of Chartres, and the light windows, of glass called *grisaille*, of which the 'Five Sisters' at York is the supreme example. In both the ironwork provides a controlling factor of the design. In the coloured windows the figures are usually small, so that each panel constitutes a composition in itself. In both types there is a mosaic-like quality, and brushwork is strictly limited. In grisaille, the bulk is white, and the windows depend for their effect upon an irregular studding of jewels of colour and perhaps a border. These windows seem to have been introduced where an additional amount of light was considered desirable. No attempt was made, apparently, to get uniformity throughout. In the coloured windows the figures are often of different sizes and do not necessarily start at the same level. It is also difficult to find any iconographical scheme behind the sequence of the windows. The choice of subject seems to have been left to the donors, who would naturally choose their patron saints. At Chartres the various town guilds contributed, and their windows illustrate members at work—hatters, butchers, tanners, furriers, etc. In the latter part of the thirteenth century the ironwork was bent into geometric patterns to provide medallions, or inset squares, and these were often filled with individual compositions with inscriptions, which were scratched out of the darker enamelled ground. In later periods the letters were painted on the surface, and were therefore darker than the background.

In the second period, that is, in the fourteenth century, the coloured figure work was often combined with grisaille, thus simplifying the problem of lighting. Ironwork was reduced by the introduction of tracery; naturalistic plant forms, diaper patterns and architectural canopies were often drawn above the principal figures. In place of the relatively wide lancets of six to nine feet, the windows were now subdivided by mullions at three- to four-foot intervals and crowned by tracery, so that all that was necessary to provide wind bracing was a series of horizontal bars, which were much slighter than in the previous century and did not dominate the composition. Silver stain was used as early as 1300 at York, and was commonly limited to haloes, gold crowns, hair and canopies. The sculptured canopy, depicted by means of yellow stain and line drawing on clear glass, was a convenient way of filling tall and narrow lights which could not satisfactorily be occupied by the short and broad figure of a single saint. Curiously, these canopies never have a base, but the supporting shafts simply end at the line of one of the frame bars. Nor is there any attempt at perspective. The drawing of the figures, too, is different. In place of the stiff Byzantine poses of the previous century, the figures and the drapery have adopted a sinuous S-bend like the tracery above, which gives a willowy gracefulness that can be exactly paralleled in the illuminated manuscripts of the time. Single figures, one to each light, are the rule. They are about life size, richly coloured, in a setting of almost clear glass of lozenge-shaped panes, painted with a diaper pattern. Round the outside there is occasionally a border of delicate leaf patterns echoing the colour in the central figure, and separated from the mullions by an inch, sometimes less, of absolutely clear glass. This edging is of great value in forming a bright frame.

Towards the end of the fourteenth century and throughout the fifteenth, English glass was in advance of anything abroad. The general character in this, the third period, was dominated by an increased area of white glass, by larger pieces of glass and the use of leads to emphasize and assist in the drawing. The transition occurred at Gloucester in the great east window. Here are depicted the coats of arms of those nobles who died at Crécy in 1346. It is, in effect, a war memorial, with figures and canopies in white relieved by touches of yellow stain and with columns of light in ruby and blue, so that a vertical striped effect is achieved. The grisaille and mosaic-like quality of the earlier centuries are abandoned in favour of regular, straight-sided, diamond-shaped 'quarries'. Canopies, in the fifteenth century, were extraordinarily elaborate and dominated the designs as never before. It seems as though the stained-glass designers, like the metal-workers who contrived the monumental brasses and the woodworkers who erected canopies over choir stalls, were all dominated by the designs of masons. One might have expected less dependence on the part of the stained-glass artists, who were able to produce highly original figures of great delicacy and skill. Sometimes, it is true, they were able to fill a window with many figures, grouped in such a manner that although separated from one another by mullions, they yet formed a single picture; but as a rule the arrangement was to set each individual figure on a pedestal within a niche looking like stonework and culminating in a flourish of crockets, finials, buttresses and pinnacles.

The most beautiful examples of fifteenth-century glass are at York Minster and at Fairford parish church. The great east window at York, depicting the Creation, is 78 feet high and filled with 117 panels, each illustrating a subject from the Bible. The artist was John Thornton of Coventry, and he was commissioned in 1405. In colour and in drawing it has been reckoned the finest window in Europe. Here the canopy work is limited to the head of each light, the shape of which would have been awkward to fill with the subjects alone, and much of the detailed quality is achieved by delicate shading and stippling. At the same time there is a grand scale about the design which is different from anything at Chartres, where the individual windows are jewelled mosaics which must be examined in detail to get the maximum enjoyment; at York each panel forms a part of one great colourful scheme, to be enjoyed as a whole.

At Fairford the style is quite different. It marks the beginning of what might have been an entirely new development, and one more in line with contemporary oil-painting in the Netherlands. The backgrounds are landscapes, and sometimes, in place of imitative stone canopies, there is a sky with white clouds and circling birds. By the use of yellow stain on blue glass a green for grass and trees is produced. The mullions are often ignored and the composition spreads across whole traceried windows. The figures are drawn with such skill that they have been, without the slightest evidence, attributed to Dürer. In this church, more than in any other, there seems to be an iconographical scheme, so that the church illustrates in an orderly sequence the Gospel story, leading up to the Passion at the east end and ending with the Last Judgment at the exit.

Monumental Brasses. A peculiar and specially decorative feature on church floors of the Middle Ages is the monumental brass memorial. This was an economical substitute for the more elaborate carved tomb or effigy. It had also the advantage that it did not in any way obstruct the space required for service. Usually these memorials consisted of plates of brass laid on pitch, inset into the stone pavement and secured with brass pins so that they finished flush. In England it has been estimated that there are some 10,000 such memorials, whereas on the Continent only about six or seven hundred have survived. While it is considered likely that the idea of brass memorials originated on the Continent and spread to England, there is a marked difference in character between the two. As a rule the English examples have the figures cut to the outline and inserted into the stone slab which serves as a background. In Flemish and other continental examples, the figures are engraved in the centre of the rectangular brass plate, and the background is filled with diaper and scroll decoration.

(*Victoria and Albert Museum. Crown Copyright Reserved.*)

Monumental brass, Westley Waterless, Cambridgeshire, showing Sir John de Creke and Lady, *c.* 1325.

The figures usually lie on their backs, with pillowed heads and their hands joined in prayer; the feet of women are draped so that only the toecaps show, and those of men rest on an animal, either hound or lion. There is no evidence to support the popular belief that a lion symbolized death in battle and a dog death at home. No attempt seems to have been made, in early examples, at portraiture. The men are invariably shown in the prime of life and the women stylized, with smooth unlined faces.

The earliest surviving brass in England is that of Sir John D'Abernon, *d.* 1277, of Stoke D'Abernon in Surrey, and the earliest abroad is dated 1231 at Verden, near Hanover. The best are in England up till 1450, after which there was a decline in quality; the brass was thinner, and the features and drapery were cross-hatched to give shading and suggest a three-dimensional character. Though a few easily identifiable brasses were imported from the Continent, the majority were manufactured in England—in London, York and Norwich.

Examples are to be found in every county, but the greatest concentration occurs in those areas, such as Essex and Norfolk, where good carving stone was scarce.

The medieval brasses have been considered important chiefly for the information which they give on costume, armour and heraldry, but they are also of value as works of art and in the architectural details which many display. Harmony between the monument and the current architectural style is the rule. Many of the memorials have engraved brass architectural frames. These, in their decorations, their crocketed canopies and finials, cusping and buttressing, echo faithfully the prevailing fashion. It is interesting to note that here, as in so much medieval work, the aim does not seem to be to provide a memorial that is necessarily in harmony with the style of the surrounding architecture, but rather one that is in harmony with current practice. The fact that the architecture was, say, round-arched Romanesque would not suggest to a craftsman of the fourteenth century the adoption of that old-fashioned style.

CHAPTER V

NORTHERN FRANCE

THE revival of church building in northern France began about 1140, at the time when the great Norman achievements in England were nearly complete. The country immediately surrounding Paris and to the north and east—the only part of France which then directly admitted the French king's rule—was at that time slowly emerging from a period of great depression, which was not finally dissipated until the accession of Louis le Jeune in 1137. This king's reign marks a new era in France—political, social, and architectural. With the help of the famous Abbot Suger, his chief adviser, the power of the throne rapidly increased; the strength of the semi-independent rulers of Flanders, Aquitaine, Anjou, and the rest slowly but sensibly diminished. The land became peaceful, and peace brought prosperity. The countrymen could till their fields without a constant fear, almost a certainty, that bands of marauders would render their labour vain. The trade of the town-dwellers increased, and the merchants soon became strong enough to assert their rights and to claim and receive privileges of charter which they had not previously enjoyed.

The people, both in town and country, began to interest themselves in matters of religion to a far greater extent, and in a more thoughtful manner, than they had before. The authority of the bishop, the people's representative, became more widely acknowledged; in fact the bishops regained to a great extent, if not entirely, the power they had exercised in the days before Charlemagne and before the ascendancy of the monasteries. The monastic Orders were still strong, indeed were multiplying in number; but the fact that the Benedictine Order was no longer sole and supreme was an indication of weakness. It is not too much to say that the revolt of S. Bernard and the establishment of the Cistercian Order at the end of the eleventh century marked the beginning of the decline of monastic domination. The cause of that decline, however, was largely the growing intelligence of the people. Previously the attitude of most laymen towards the Church had been either one of absolute dependence upon monkish guidance, or else of fervent opposition to that guidance. By the middle of the twelfth century both feelings had undergone considerable modification. On the one hand, religion was becoming better understood; and on the other, the monks in their wisdom realized that the best way to disarm opposition was to work in harmony with others for the advancement and good of the Church. Thus, in the building of the choir of the abbey church of S. Denis, near Paris, in 1140-4, the people banded themselves together to raise the money required, acting in concert with the Abbot Suger, the man who, amongst his contemporaries, did more than any other to advance church architecture in France in the twelfth century.

No doubt there were Romanesque churches in this northern area of France, but they were few and insignificant compared with those of Normandy, Burgundy, and Provence. Even in Paris the church of S. Germain-des-Prés was quite small before the addition of the Gothic chevet, and S. Geneviève was even smaller. No records exist to tell of any cathedral. Elsewhere, in the provincial capitals, the cathedrals seem to have been so unsuited to twelfth- and thirteenth-century tastes that they were pulled down and rebuilt.

S. Denis, near Paris. The west front of the abbey of S. Denis was completed in the year 1140, and the rest of the church built '*stupenda celerite*' within the next four years. The west front is round-arched Romanesque, the east end pointed Gothic (Pl. 1). Between the two, unfortunately, a later nave has been interposed, so that the artistic effect of Suger's church is to some extent destroyed. Indeed, how much of Suger's work has survived is uncertain. Much may have been altered when the nave was rebuilt in the thirteenth century, and when Viollet-le-Duc restored the church in the nineteenth. From Suger's own comments it is clear that he did not regard himself as the innovator of a new style; on the contrary, he declared that he had searched everywhere for whatever was of the best, combining in one structure—the choir—a chevet, as at Avranches or Fécamp, a triforium gallery and clerestory as at the Abbaye-aux-Dames in Normandy, a pointed arch as at Autun, and flying buttresses as at S. Germain-des-Prés.

The fervour with which all men threw themselves into the task of building the great cathedrals of northern France is a proof both of the prosperity of the country and of the better understanding which existed between all classes of the community. A large percentage of the diocesan revenue was devoted to the work; the canons helped with their share; the nobles and rich burgesses gave large sums; the people contributed what they could, sometimes their chattels, sometimes their money, or else their time and strength to transport the materials required. For the extent and character of the undertakings, the ambition for great things that inspired them, the boldness (as at Beauvais) with which the most audacious feats of construction were attempted, and the stupendous conception of design, we can find no other explanation than the spirit of the age. A contagious impulse to build, unparalleled in history, seems to have affected all classes. Here is an extract from a contemporary record:

> In this year [1144], at Chartres, there were seen for the first time the faithful harnessing themselves to the wagons that were laden with stones, wood, provisions, and whatever else was needed for the works at the cathedral. As by the might of magic, its towers rose heavenward. It was not only here, but wellnigh everywhere in France and Normandy and in other lands. Everywhere men were humbling themselves, everywhere doing penance and offering forgiveness to their enemies. Men and women were to be seen dragging heavy loads through swampy places, and in holy songs praising the wonderful works of God that He was doing before their eyes.

Large sums were realized by the display of relics, which were carried about the country to stimulate the generosity of the faithful. The requests for funds were, in some cases, by no means confined solely to the diocese in which the cathedral was being built. Anthyme Saint-Paul[1] recounts how, in the rebuilding of Laon Cathedral in the twelfth century, begging expeditions were made one year throughout the whole of northern France and penetrated the next year as far as England.

Designers and Builders. One fact in particular illustrates the altered conditions under which the great French cathedrals were built: the workmen were in nearly every case laymen. Previously much had been the work of the monks themselves, who had supervised the erection and found the money. The monasteries had been the centres of intellectual and artistic life. Now, in the middle of the twelfth century, the teaching of apprentices in technical matters passed to the lay master masons. It is natural, therefore, that when the bishops, Chapters and people took the building of cathedrals into their hands, they should prefer laymen as their head

[1] *Histoire Monumentale de la France*, Paris, 1884.

S. Denis, Paris; choir

Le Mans Cathedral; nave

Plate 1

Chartres Cathedral; aerial view

Plate 2

Chartres Cathedral; Royal porch, west front

workers. Many of these were as cultured as the majority of clerics or nobles, and they probably took good care that the general education of their apprentices was as sound as their own. By the middle of the twelfth century the corporation of Freemasons was fully established; about 1200, the University of Paris was founded, and in 1253 the Sorbonne.

The organization of masons differed in one important respect from that of other trades, for their work forced them to move to different localities where building work was in progress, while shoemakers, tailors, bakers and others lived among their customers. The mason's work did not come to him, nor could it be carried out in his own home. When any great church or building was to be erected, masons were sent for from all the neighbouring towns or districts. At a time when writing was extremely rare, it was essential that some means should be devised by which a mason could obtain the assistance and hospitality of other masons on the road, and by which his skill or rank could be recognized. To this end a set of secret signs was invented to enable each mason to recognize another as such, and to make known his status to those of equal rank. The master masons were skilled craftsmen who had served their apprenticeship and mastered the technicalities of their trade. They dictated the plans and general ordinance, drawing them on parchment sufficiently well to make their meaning clear to the subordinate workmen. The full-size details and mouldings were drawn on the spot, probably on boards. Whether the men who did work of this description should be termed architects, or masons, or masters of the work, is an academic question which hardly requires discussion, except that the term 'mason' is confusing, inasmuch as it conveys a totally wrong idea of the position these men occupied. The laymen who, in France towards the end of the twelfth century, took the place of the builders and monks of the previous century, were men of substance, held in high repute by their patrons and townsfolk.[1] Their interests, as the sketchbook of Villard de Honnecourt shows, were not limited to the masonry structure, but embraced all the accessories as well. The post of master mason to a cathedral was a high and responsible one and descended in some

[1] C. Enlart gives, in his *Manuel d'Archéologie Française* (Paris, 1902), a list of Gothic churches in France, with the names of many of the men who in turn superintended the work. Some are commemorated in the names of streets. Thus at Amiens, facing the south transept of the cathedral, is the Rue Robert de Luzarches, and at Reims on the north side of the cathedral, the Rue Robert de Coucy.

cases from father to son, as at Amiens Cathedral where, after Robert de Luzarches, Thomas de Cormont was succeeded by his son Renaut; or as at Strassburg, where Erwin von Steinbach's two sons continued the work he had begun. The spirit of the age was such that there was no fear of lack of continuity or harmony between the workers in different crafts. There was absolute sympathy between all branches, and to this sympathy the beauty and completeness of the French medieval cathedrals is largely due.

There can be no doubt that by the end of the twelfth century French architecture was far in advance of that of the rest of Europe. Many of the cathedrals in England and Normandy had been already completed, and the need for new cathedrals no longer existed. The fact that so little had been produced in northern France in the eleventh century was no drawback in the twelfth. From the surrounding districts, Burgundy, Normandy and the south, the builders could select those features which seemed to them the best. The result was a progress unhampered by the past and unparalleled in the rapidity of its development. In 1140 there was no cathedral of the first rank in northern France. By 1223, at the death of Philip Augustus, twenty cathedrals had been erected, or were in course of construction, in and around the Royal demesne.

It is in the choir of the abbey of S. Denis (Pl. 1) that we find the Gothic system of construction perfected, although it still retains the semi-circular arch over its lower windows and traces of Romanesque feeling in its carvings. Viollet-le-Duc suggests that Suger, conscious of the decline of monasticism, was eager to create an abbey as fine as other works then being built. We cannot, unfortunately, be certain that the present structure is Suger's work. Pierre Lavedan, in his *l'Architecture Française* (Paris, 1944), is prepared to accept only the crypt and the plan of the ambulatory as belonging to the twelfth century. Were it not for Suger's writings, other churches not similarly recorded might claim a prior place. Certainly the church, once the cathedral, of Notre-Dame at Senlis cannot differ much in date from S. Denis. The nave of Lisieux Cathedral (Normandy) is pure Early Gothic, and is described by Enlart as having been begun in 1141; Sens Cathedral, which was designed by the same William who later became master mason of Canterbury, was begun about 1140–43. In attempting to trace the growth of the Gothic style, many authorities give different dates. It is enough for our purpose to accept the fact that from 1140 onwards many major works were being undertaken, and although they all have their own distinctive characteristics, all exemplify a striving towards the spaciousness, height and precise articulation of structure that typify the Gothic style.

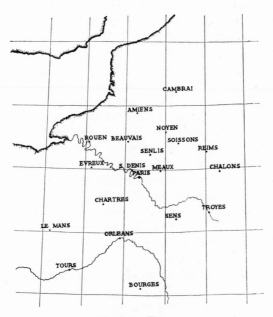

Northern France.

Early Examples. The nave of Le Mans Cathedral (*c.* 1153) is a striking example of the conversion of a Romanesque unvaulted nave of ten bays, with arcades of semi-circular arches supported by columns, into a Gothic nave, vaulted throughout with ribbed vaulting, without the removal of the nave arches (Pl. 1). These arches were originally of two orders, unmoulded, the outer order having a projection of only a few inches.[1] The lower order of each bay was removed, and underneath the upper one was built a pointed arch which, being narrower than the other, allowed room for the great clustered piers, the outer members of which were carried up to the vaulting to support the massive transverse arches and the diagonal and wall ribs of the vault above. As an example of

[1] The easternmost bay on both sides remains unaltered as far as the arches are concerned, so that the original design is easily seen.

adaptation it is a monument to the ingenuity of the medieval builders.

The alternation of large and small piers which is seen in the nave of Le Mans is a characteristic of Romanesque architecture which occurs also at Noyon and Senlis. Noyon is distinctly transitional. There are pointed windows in the apse, and round openings in the adjoining wider bays. Viollet-le-Duc thought it was probably built by workmen released from S. Denis. It is a large building with a vaulted triforium and, between this and the clerestory, a second triforium passage, defined by a blank arcade of round-headed arches. Romanesque taste persists also in much of the carving and in the plan which, with its apsidal transepts, is reminiscent of the Romanesque Cathedral of Tournai in Belgium. Alternate clustered and small piers are seldom found in French architecture after 1160. They belong to that Norman tradition exemplified at Jumièges in Normandy, and Durham in England. Between 1160 and 1200 plain cylindrical columns—sturdy but never heavy, as at, say, Gloucester or Tewkesbury—were general, and these were often employed to support as many as five independent vaulting shafts in addition to the arches of the arcade, as at Laon, Lisieux and Notre-Dame, Paris. Afterwards, these gave way to columns with attached shafts, as at Chartres and Reims.

Of all the early examples the cathedral of Laon deserves special mention. It is one of the very few cathedrals that have no chevet. It terminates in a square east end, and has a long choir and transepts of considerable projection. There are a chapter house and a cloister on the south side and, close at hand, an old episcopal palace. This description might almost apply to an English cathedral; but there are many important differences. At the east end, instead of an immense wall of glass and tracery there is only a circular window; instead of a dominating central tower there is only a short lantern, covered with a pyramidal roof, but, by way of compensation, there are other towers to mark the western end and the termination of the transepts. Villard de Honnecourt sketched them in the thirteenth century and wrote: 'The most beautiful I have seen.' Everywhere the arches are pointed, and all the vaults are sexpartite except that over the crossing, which is quadripartite. The original cathedral had been burned by the citizens in 1112, when they had been refused a promised charter. About 1160 the present building was begun, and in 1205 it was completed. Then the apse was demolished and the eastern arm prolonged until it nearly equalled the nave. In spite of the pointed arches—and some of these are almost semi-circular—there is much that is Norman: there are the cross galleries at the ends of the transepts, like those of Cerisy-le-Forêt and Winchester, the central lantern, as at the Abbaye - aux - Hommes, and the two-storeyed apsidal chapels which resemble those at Christchurch Priory. Even the sexpartite vault originated in Normandy, and the dog-tooth enrichment which occurs again and again is Romanesque rather than Gothic. Laon contributed at least one notable innovation: the west front, with its great triple-bayed cavernous porch, lined with sculpture, its central rose window, and its twin towers connected by an arcaded gallery to form a square top, set a fashion that was to prevail throughout the thirteenth century in the design of the cathedrals of northern France (Pl. 3).

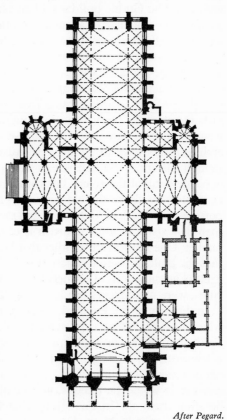

After Pegard.

Laon Cathedral.
Scale 100 *ft.* to 1 *in.*

Sites of Cathedrals. Nearly all the cathedrals of northern France are surrounded by streets and hemmed in by houses. There is none of the greensward and quiet dignity of an English cathedral close. The cathedral belonged to the people and was sited in the midst of the city, accessible without encroaching on private precincts. And so, and especially at Amiens and Chartres, the cathedral dominates all the surrounding dwellings, and from a distance stands out, a great black mass and a landmark in the country around (Pl. 2). Because of such close surroundings it is difficult, as a rule, to obtain a good view of any cathedral except from a distance. Most of the east ends are enclosed, and visible only from private gardens—often those of the bishop or archbishop—while the approaches to the west fronts, or to the fine transept entrances, are often poor in the extreme. The Gothic builder seldom planned his cathedral as the termination of a vista or avenue. In some of the Romanesque and later monastic churches there was, no doubt, originally something of the nature of an atrium or forecourt to the west. At Chartres, Sens, Notre-Dame, Paris and the Abbaye-aux-Hommes, Caen, there are such open spaces opposite the main entrances. The east end of Le Mans Cathedral stands free, and at Bourges a magnificent view of the cathedral, with its long unbroken roof line, can be had from the formal garden to the south-east; this is one of the finest architectural views in France. At Auxerre one can get a good, though distant, view of the east end of the cathedral from the opposite bank of the river. The cathedral, raised above its double crypt, towers above the old bishop's palace, and only the lower portions are hidden. But these are rare exceptions. Even when there is a space or a forecourt, it is often occupied by a crowded market. One must assume either that land was too valuable or else that the builders were indifferent to everything except the church itself. The cathedrals of France, built in the congested hearts of the cities, were monuments to the skill of the citizens.

In France, as in England, there is no one great cathedral to which one can refer as the standard of perfection, no Karnak or Parthenon or Sancta Sophia, which may be cited as the supreme achievement of the age. Reims, Bourges, Soissons, Rouen and many others are enthralling. There is, indeed, an *embarras de richesse*. It would be tedious, and involve tiresome repetition, to describe them all. In this study, therefore, only four cathedrals will be described—Notre-Dame, Chartres, Amiens and Beauvais; but so that the characteristics and style may be appreciated, a more detailed analysis of the principal features of northern French Gothic architecture, inside and out, will follow.

Notre-Dame, Paris. The cathedral of Notre-Dame was the first great work in which the Romanesque tradition was absolutely put aside. It is Gothic in conception throughout. Work was begun about 1162, and twenty years later the High Altar was consecrated. At the time of the death of Philip Augustus in 1223, the whole design was completed except for the west front, the towers of which had been prepared for spires that were never built. This vast building, with its double side aisles sweeping round the semi-circular end of the choir, is possibly the first of the double-aisled cathedrals. It was very large and simple, with transepts of slight projection. There were no chapels; these were introduced later not only around the eastern end but also between the great buttresses on the north and south sides. The rows of cylindrical columns which line the nave are very impressive. Above the inner aisle is a high vaulted triforium, and over this a clerestory, with sexpartite vaults retained by flying buttresses which in one span embrace the two side aisles. These buttresses, especially seen from the apsidal end, provide some measure of the advance which had taken place in design only twenty years after the building of S. Denis.

No sooner was work completed than alterations were begun. The high triforium had originally been surmounted by circular openings, which were removed in order to provide taller clerestory windows filled with simple tracery.[1] The chapels were introduced and the transepts lengthened by one bay. All these alterations were not completed until 1315. Finally, when Viollet-le-Duc restored the cathedral in 1846–79, the central flèche, 148 feet high, was erected at the crossing.

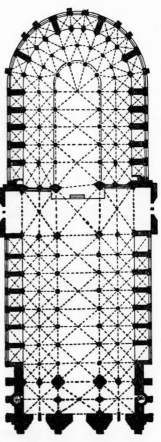

Notre-Dame, Paris.
Scale 100 *ft.* to 1 *in.*

The vaulting around the choir apse presented difficulties. There were five openings around the inner semi-circle, ten between the aisles, and fifteen between the outer aisle and the chapels. This resulted in an irregular system of bays and a curious vaulting problem, which was solved in the most ingenious way, indicated on the plan.

[1] The original arrangement can be seen in Viollet-le-Duc's restoration at the crossing.

Chartres (Pl. 2). The architecture of Chartres marks a further step in the development of the Gothic style. The vaults are quadripartite, there is no vaulted triforium gallery, and the nave is constructed

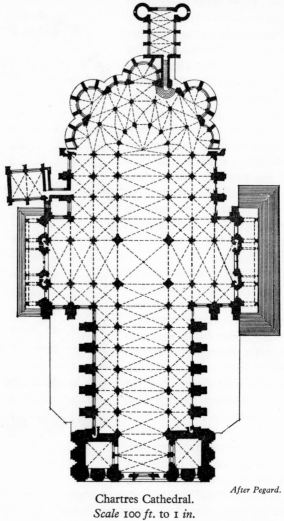

After Pegard.

Chartres Cathedral.
Scale 100 *ft.* to 1 *in.*

of clustered piers. The later cathedrals did no more than perfect these innovations. The introduction at Chartres of quadripartite vaults over oblong bays was a vast improvement on the sexpartite arrangement at Notre-Dame and Laon. The clustered pier provided that vertical emphasis which was lacking in the cylindrical columns of the earlier cathedrals. The abandonment of the triforium gallery and the substitution of a small arcade made it possible to give greater height to the clerestory and the aisles. With all these improvements Chartres would be important enough, but to them one must add the finest twelfth-century sculpture in France and the most wonderful stained glass in the world.

The cathedral of Chartres was founded in the eleventh century, but the bulk of the present structure dates from the rebuilding after a fire in 1194. Only the west front, with its two towers and royal portals between, is anterior to that date. The plan, with its double ambulatory around the apse and its radiating chapels, was largely dictated by the crypt of the older church. The rebuilding after the fire was carried through with great speed and virtually completed by 1212. The whole conception was magnificent. In addition to the two western towers there were to be two at the end of each transept, two at the springing of the apse, and a central tower over the crossing; nine towers in all. The central tower was never built, and the other six were never finished, but the two spires over the towers at the west end, of different ages, are unsurpassed in France. Even the southern, and older, of the two, which was probably finished in the twelfth century, has all the elegance which was so fully developed in Germany and England in later centuries.

The royal portals at the base of the western front, and the open porches at the ends of the transepts, are the special glory of Chartres. The arches are all pointed and filled with carving. The jambs are flanked by a majestic procession of colossal statues, exaggerated in height and designed with such skill that they form an integral part of the architectural composition. The long, straight folds of the drapery assist the main upward lines of the doorways. The heads are full of nobility and grace, especially those that are softened by the addition of hair, in long waves and curls to give linear relief to the general stiffness of the figures. Here are sculptures that can only be paralleled in the finest Byzantine mural painting. They have a quality of almost unworldly dignity and rigid formalism which has never been surpassed in the western world.

Amiens (Pls. 3, 4). The cathedral of Amiens was begun in 1220, that is, nearly thirty years after Chartres, and was completed, with the exception of the side chapels, in 1269. It is the largest of the French cathedrals and the most perfect. Here the Gothic system of thrust and counter-thrust, contrived upon isolated points of support, with walls in between reduced to mere curtains of glass, is carried to its logical conclusion. The whole construction is visibly expressed. Every problem has been solved, and the result is an enormous shell, lavishly decorated with glass and with sculpture, a monument not only to structural skill but also to medieval philosophy and Scholasticism. 'The Bible of Amiens', John Ruskin called it. It is almost wholly designed to provide instruction by means of decoration. The central portal carries *le beau Dieu d'Amiens*, and on the ordered jambs are the figures of the Apostles; above these, in two galleries, are the kings of Judah. There is a host of subsidiary figures—over five thousand in all—illustrating the history of the world from the first chapter of Genesis. Interspersed is a guide to moral philosophy, typified by figures symbolic of the vices and virtues. There are the heavenly hosts—saints, angels and archangels—and the denizens of the nether world, thrust in perpetuity into damnation. All this is contrived in such exquisite harmony with the architecture that one hesitates whether to assess the cathedral as architecture or as sculpture. Certainly, in an illiterate age it must have provided instruction in a most forceful way. To all this must

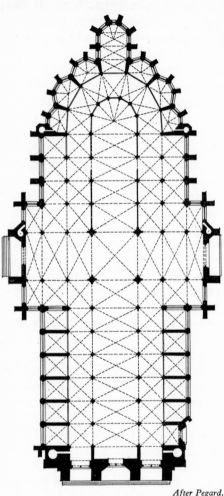

After Pegard.

Amiens Cathedral.

Scale 100 *ft. to* 1 *in.*

be added the ceremonial of the Church, the robes and the costumes, and the relics which, to believers, endowed the whole with a special air of sanctity. The cathedral of Amiens was not only an aesthetic achievement; it was a symbol in physical form of spiritual dedication in medieval France.

Beauvais. At Beauvais the limits of Gothic achievement were reached. Building began in 1247, after the nave of Amiens was complete and the choir well advanced. The inhabitants of Beauvais were determined to surpass the work of the neighbouring city, not only in dimensions but also in constructional skill. The nave of Amiens was 141 feet high; Beauvais was to be 157 feet. The construction of Amiens was light and graceful; Beauvais was to be still lighter and more audacious. Height and slenderness were in fact pushed beyond the limits of safety. In 1284 a part of the great vault fell. Intermediate piers had to be added, two lancet arches being built under the original arcade, and the great oblong quadripartite vaults were transformed into sexpartite, while the vaults to the aisles were strengthened by an additional skeleton rib with pierced spandrels. These repairs were not finished until 1324. The transepts were finished in 1548, and the nave was never built. Beauvais is, therefore, only a fragment, but in many ways the most perfect and

After Bourges.

Beauvais Cathedral. Section.
Scale 50 ft. to 1 in.

beautiful fragment, of medieval art. The chevet has a grace and dignity which is quite lovely, and in extent of window area has no equal. Beauvais is much more than a pretentious *tour de force*; it is the epitome of structural endeavour in the Middle Ages.

INTERIORS

The Chevet. The important characteristic of most of the greater Gothic cathedrals of northern France is the eastern, or altar, end, which has advanced, to suit the medieval arrangements, far from the simple Early Christian apse. This has involved an enrichment of the ground plan by which the choir aisles are carried around the back of the apse in a processional path, off which the chapels radiate, like a great corona at the head of the church. Although few would deny that externally the chevet far surpasses in effect the result obtained by the square east end, as at Laon and so many English cathedrals, it is doubtful if the gain outside is compensation enough for the cramping effect often produced inside. In order that all supports in the chevet shall radiate from one centre, the bays round the end of the choir are too numerous (especially in those churches in which double aisles surround the apses) and too narrow, the piers, as a rule, too slender and the arches, in many cases, disagreeably attenuated in order that they shall be of the same height as the other arches of the choir. In most churches with only a single aisle behind the choir apse, such as Reims and Rouen cathedrals, there are only five bays. At Amiens it is difficult to say whether the apse should be termed one of five or of seven bays, since its springing is on a line with the middle of a bay and not with a pier. This modification of the usual plan is followed at Chartres and Le Mans. In the cathedrals of Bourges and Notre-Dame, Paris, there are, again, only five bays to the apse of each, although both churches have double eastern ambulatories. At Bourges the spaces between the columns separating the ambulatories are unusually wide. At Paris a more ingenious plan is followed: the columns between the aisles are doubled in number. The vaulting of the aisles is naturally affected by this duplication of supports, and the serveries are all triangular in plan, instead of quadrangular.

The success of the choirs of Chartres and Notre-Dame, Paris, is largely due to the fact that in these two churches the faults in apse planning, apparent in others, have been avoided. Chartres, it is true, has more bays at the east end than some churches, but its choir is the widest in northern France, and so the bays are of fair width. Moreover, all the arches of the main arcades throughout the church are stilted, and the little extra stilting of the apse arches is hardly noticeable. At Notre-Dame, the bays of the apse are only a trifle narrower than those at the sides, and all the piers surrounding the choir are of the same size. These facts, coupled with the fine perspective effects east of the apse, due to the number and spacing of the columns between the ambulatories, help largely in making the choir of Notre-Dame the finest in France.

The Triforium. Laon, Notre-Dame, Paris and Noyon have fine open triforiums, vaulted like the aisles, a feature common in the earlier Romanesque work of England, Normandy and Italy. At Laon and Noyon there is an additional triforium passage above the open gallery, with the result that an extra amount of plain wall space is obtained. Originally Notre-Dame also had an upper triforium passageway, and an impression of this can be obtained from Viollet-le-Duc's restoration of the transepts and the eastern-most bay of the nave, where the area between the gallery and the clerestory is pierced by circular openings. This was the original design of the church before it was altered at the beginning of the thirteenth century.

The large gallery triforium is not the rule. In most of the large French churches the triforium is closed by a wall behind the arcade, leaving only a narrow passageway, and this was the usual arrange-ment until the desire for more light and delicacy of structure resulted in the glazing of that wall. The reason for the wall was that the builders, faced with a demand for higher and yet higher vaults, feared for the stability of their churches. To pierce and glaze the wall behind the arcading of what had hitherto been a blind storey did not, however, involve much weakening of the structure, since the ashlar mullions on the outside face were, as a rule, strong and fairly numerous. In the choirs of the cathedrals of Amiens and Beauvais and in the churches of S. Ouen, Rouen and S. Pierre, Chartres, the triple division of arcade, triforium and clerestory is retained, but glass reaches from the top of the main arcades to the summit of the vaults.

Before the triforiums could be glazed it was necessary to get rid of the lean-to roofs which normally covered the aisles and blocked all light from the area between the top of the nave arcade and the clerestory. Lead flats were sometimes introduced, or else high-pitched roofs of double slope, with a gutter on each side at the same level as the base of the triforium. Occasionally each bay of the aisle had its separate high-pitched roof, hipped on all sides as at S. Ouen, Rouen. These numerous roofs add a certain picturesqueness to many a late French church, but detract from simplicity of design.

Proportions. In all medieval work, and not merely in France, the tendency, as development proceeded, was steadily in the direction of increasing the height of the main arcade and of the clerestory, and of diminishing that of the space between them. In the choir of

Le Mans the triforium was omitted entirely, and the clerestory windows started from the top of the arcade. The following table illustrates the development, and at the same time emphasizes the loftiness, at all periods, of the ground storey of French cathedrals.

Name of cathedral	Height from floor to string course under triforium	Height between string courses above and below triforium	Height from string course under windows to apex of vault	Total height
	Feet	*Feet*	*Feet*	*Feet*
Notre-Dame, Paris	37	33	40	110
Chartres	50	16	48	114
Amiens	70	22	48	140
Beauvais	74	20	60	154

A table of dimensions is not enough to convey the atmosphere of a French cathedral. Each has its own distinguishing aura: Notre-Dame, with its robust round columns; Beauvais, with its soaring height and its delicate attenuated clustered piers; Laon, with its simple lancet windows; the complex tracery of Amiens and the glorious harmony of the glass at Chartres. All induce different responses when the first overpowering impression has passed. The sublimity of the French cathedral interior is not easy to describe. There is a sense of ordered spaciousness, of fine logic, which results from the regular rhythm of the arcade and the grace with which the high vaults are supported. There is at first a sense of wonder that such a delicate framework can be sustained, a sense which, after a time, is followed by admiration of the complex mechanics which made the structure possible. 'The arch never sleeps', says the Arab proverb; and throughout a French cathedral one has always the sense of movement; the feeling that stone is always grinding against stone, that the whole, although a triumph of beautifully balanced counteracting forces, cannot possess that stability which a lasting monument should have. It is, of course, but fancy. The French cathedrals have lasted as long as ours and are just as well, if not better, preserved. Beauvais, the most wondrous delicacy of all, was undisturbed by the high explosives that laid waste the proximate housing in the last war. The French cathedrals were the wonders of the Middle Ages; they remain a wonder in this twentieth century.

Bourges. Bourges Cathedral requires a special description

because it is so remarkably different from other cathedrals that have been mentioned. The church has double aisles which run round the apse and down the sides of the nave. There are no transepts, so that the view along the nave is uninterrupted and the whole forms an architectural unity. Great originality is imparted

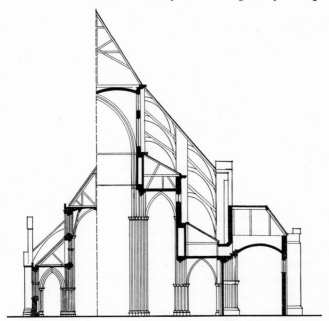

After Britton and Penrose.

(Left) half section, Lichfield Cathedral; (right) half section, Bourges Cathedral.

Scale 50 ft to 1 in.

to the design by the introduction above the intermediate arcade of a triforium and clerestory. The inner aisle is nearly 70 feet high, surpassing the naves of some of our English cathedrals, as, for instance, Lichfield, which is only 57 feet, and Ripon, 59 feet. The nave rises majestically beyond this with its own triforium and clerestory to a height of 125 feet. This design has no parallel in France nor in any other country, and although it may not equal in beauty the sturdier work of Chartres nor the elegance of Beauvais, it produces an effect of great height and spaciousness that is wonderfully impressive. The omission of transepts is a distinct advantage, for the church is less than 400 feet long and the roof runs unbroken from east to west. A parallel in this respect may be drawn with some of the churches in southern France, and as Bourges is about a hundred and fifty miles south of Paris it is probable that southern influence may have suggested such an omission.

The interior characteristics already described are generally unmistakable on the outside. The great height of the majority of French cathedrals rendered a central tower, in most cases, an impossibility. Its accomplishment would have been a *tour de force* from which even the builders of the Île de France shrank, greatly though they delighted in overcoming structural difficulties. There is a short tower at Laon, but the dimensions of the cathedral in both width and height are more modest than in most other examples. The normal substitute was a flèche of wood and lead at the intersection of the roofs—a poor feature compared with the square tower, or tower and spire, so common in England. At Amiens the top of the flèche is 422 feet from the ground, some 20 feet higher than the top of the stone spire which rises above the well-proportioned and comparatively high central tower of Salisbury. Another result of the height of French churches is that the western towers are often dwarfed by the roof. At Amiens the ridge rises even higher than the parapets of the towers.

That there was no objection to towers is shown by the fact that seven were begun at Laon Cathedral: a central tower, two at the west end and two to each transept. At Chartres eight towers were intended, as at Laon but with one on each side over the outer aisles of the choir, just before the beginning of the chevet, instead of a central tower. Only the two western towers, however, were completed, and they were of different periods and of dissimilar design. Rouen, like Laon, was designed to have seven. Reims has six, two at the west end and two flanking each transept. Transept towers, on a big scale, occurred first in the Romanesque part of Tournai Cathedral, Belgium (*c.* 1120), where their lower portions were hidden by the aisles of the semi-circular transept apses which stood in front. In France the whole tower, as a rule, shows. The reason for these towers in French cathedrals may have been an objection to the display in elevation of the sectional outline of a church with a high central part and lower sides. The transepts in France, though of slight projection, have an importance almost equal to the west front itself. At Chartres the porches in front of

aon Cathedral; west front

Amiens Cathedral;
west front

Plate 3

Amiens Cathedral; choir,
looking west

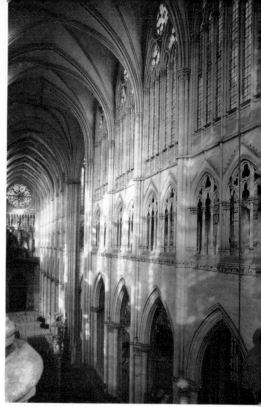

S. Maclou, Rouen; west from

Plate 4

Ste.-Chapelle, Paris; interior

Plate 5

Albi Cathedral; east e[nd]

Albi Cathedral; interior

Plate 6

the transepts, with their wealth of glorious sculpture, are almost as fine as the royal portals. Almost everywhere the north and south doorways, with their large circular windows above, are among the richest portions of the design. The towers of the transepts of Reims and Rouen cathedrals are alike in design. All are unfinished, being carried no higher than the springing of the gable. Transeptal towers do not occur at Notre-Dame or Amiens, and in many cases even the western towers were never finished.

West Fronts. The earliest west front to which the term Gothic can be applied is that of Laon (Pl. 3). Here is found the ordinance which, with only minor modifications, appertains to all French cathedral façades. Two western towers may be said to be the universal rule; portals are generally three in number, Bourges Cathedral being an exception with five; over the central doorway there is a huge rose window—immediately above, as at Reims, or with windows in between, as at Chartres;[1] a characteristic of all churches of the thirteenth and fourteenth centuries in France is a crowning horizontal line to both western façades and transepts. Above the rose window at Chartres a straight band of arcading, filled with figures, forms a parapet. Behind this, set back some feet, rises the gable terminating the nave. Not until the fifteenth century was the gable clearly expressed in the façade. A portion of it appears behind the parapet at Chartres; at Laon it is entirely hidden; at Notre-Dame, Paris, the nave roof is set back on a line with the eastern face of the towers and appears between the open arcading. It should be noted that horizontal lines are far more marked in western and transeptal façades than in any other part. The vertical aspiring tendency, so notable in the interior and elsewhere on the outside, is avoided here.

Doorways. The great portals of France far exceed in magnificence the doorways of English cathedrals. The detail varies, and the later examples are richer than the earlier, but in the main there are few differences. The doorways themselves are generally double, and are always spanned by lintels. Over the lintel is a tympanum framed by an arch of many orders, which forms the head of the portal. The jambs of the portal, the support between the doorways, and each order of the arch, are filled with figures under canopies

[1] At Notre-Dame, Paris, the rose window is separated from the doorway below by a band of figures which is continued across the towers to adorn the whole width of the front. At Amiens, which also has an arcade with figures below the rose window, the separation is widened by a row of windows above the portals.

which form a stupendous array of sculpture. The tympanum also has figure sculpture, generally arranged in bands.[1] In the sculptured tympanums and carved concentric orders of the porches, the Gothic builders were only developing the idea introduced in Romanesque times. There is no difference in principle between early and late designs in this respect. By their multiplication of the arch orders, however, and by their greater skill as sculptors, the French craftsmen of the thirteenth century advanced far beyond their predecessors. No other country can boast such Gothic doorways as France, although Spain and Germany can show some late doorways of the fifteenth and sixteenth centuries which, in richness at least, compare with those of thirteenth-century France.

THE GEOMETRICAL STYLE

With the building of La Sainte-Chapelle, Paris (1240–8) (Pl. 5), French Gothic architecture entered on its second stage, but there was no radical change, except in the tracery of the window-heads. The apex of structural skill was reached at Beauvais, and French Gothic thereafter declined in originality, growing somewhat wiry and hard. The builders, however, fortified by experience, were becoming technically bolder. Plain wall surfaces, both inside and out, disappeared. At Sainte-Chapelle, where there are no aisles, the vaults are simply carried by buttresses which are, in effect, walls set at right angles to the interior to withstand the thrust. There are no other walls from the sill to the vault, so that the whole structure is simply a lantern of coloured glass, contrived to enshrine the inestimable relic of the Crown of Thorns. Such slenderness was not practicable, however, without the extensive use of iron ties. At Sainte-Chapelle a chain was embedded right round the building, and the windows were subdivided by strong gratings of iron bars. Sainte-Chapelle is the first example in which we find the windows occupying the whole space between each buttress and the arch heads completely filled with cusped tracery.

The most striking church of the middle period of French art is S. Ouen, Rouen, begun in 1318 by the Abbot Marc d'Argent.

[1] At Reims the sculpture of the three tympanums was removed, probably in the fifteenth century, and windows were inserted. From the inside the effect is not so bad; outside it is deplorable. About the same time, the simplicity of the gables over the three porches was destroyed by the addition of groups of figures, standing on clouds, and surmounted, in the central gable, by gimcrack tabernacle work.

By the time of his death in 1339 the choir and transepts were finished, but the nave was not begun until 1490 and the central lantern was not completed until the beginning of the sixteenth century. The internal height is much the same as that of Westminster Abbey, although the nave is not so wide. In total width the Rouen church is, however, greater, since its aisles are very broad. The effect of the interior of S. Ouen is quite different from that of the cathedrals we have already described. Not only are the main piers clustered, but the mouldings correspond exactly to the archivolts of the arcades and the vault ribs, and, except for the central shaft carrying the transverse rib, which has a small capital, their lines are carried in a continuous unbroken sweep to the crowns of the arches. The triforium and clerestory are fused into one unifying design by the elimination of wall surfaces so that the entire space above the main arcade appears as a continuous grid of tracery. The detail and execution of Marc d'Argent's portion of the church is very pure. Indeed, the choir is almost the only perfect structure of its age. The later nave is florid, but more restrained than one would expect in a building of its date.

English Influence. England had learned a great deal from France towards the end of the twelfth century. A hundred and fifty years later, when France was in danger of disintegration, her kings weak and her lands devastated, England was able to teach in her turn. Her influence did not extend throughout the whole of the country. East and north of Paris there is little trace of it; the churches there are unmistakably descended from the great French cathedrals of the thirteenth century: but in the southern and western districts, which at that time were under the direct rule of the English kings, having close communication with England, many fourteenth-century churches show traces of English influence. At Figeac, for instance, the clerestory windows in the church of S. Sauveur are strangely like contemporary examples in this country. A likeness is to be seen in the Brittany churches, at Guingamp, Quimper, Treguier, etc. The size and shape of the windows, the lines of their tracery and the sections of the mouldings are all more in accordance with English dimensions, proportions and forms than with those of French examples. A large number of the buildings had in fact been built by the English, and although Viollet-le-Duc maintained that the resultant architecture was essentially French, there can be no denying the influence of

England. However, much of the architecture of fourteenth-century France was dull and mechanical, hard and sinewy; then suddenly, without any transitional period, France developed the brilliant style which we call 'flamboyant' and which continued until the middle of the sixteenth century.

THE FLAMBOYANT STYLE

French archaeologists use the term 'Flamboyant' for the last phase of their Gothic architecture, and the word expresses it well, not merely because the tracery of the windows shows flowing, flame-like lines, but also because throughout all the buildings of the period there is a light-heartedness which no other term could describe so well. Contemporary work in England is equally well expressed by the term 'Perpendicular', not only because the heads of windows are filled with vertical bars, and the wall surfaces panelled with upright panels, but also because the architecture, in its main lines, is stiff and angular. The work in France expresses the *joie de vivre*, inherent in the nation, which found expression after the triumph of the French in freeing the country from the English; and English work shows evidence of the gloom which settled over the country after the Black Death and Wars of the Roses and which was not dissipated until the Tudors came to the throne.

The first sign of Flamboyant feeling, according to Enlart, is seen in one of the chapels of Amiens Cathedral, built in 1373, but it was not until some fifty or sixty years later that it appeared in full force. S. Maclou, Rouen (1437–50) (Pl. 4), is the most delightful surviving example, though it was seriously damaged on the 4 June 1944 and was still, in 1954, unfit for public worship. The west front expresses in overwhelming fashion the *joie de vivre* already referred to. It provides a burst of gaiety which the purist might deplore, but which is none the less a tangible and vivid expression of the feeling of relief and delight in the delivery of the country from war and anarchy. The west end of the cathedral at Alençon has a similar porch, but it lacks the abandon which is so marked in S. Maclou. Throughout Normandy there are many other fine churches of the fifteenth century, such as S. Wolfram, Abbeville (unfinished but nevertheless most impressive) and the churches at Caudebec, Dieppe and elsewhere. The two churches which display the richness of this period more extravagantly, perhaps, than any others are Notre-Dame de l'Epine, near Châlons-sur-

Marne, and the abbey church of Vendôme, near the Loire. The west fronts of both are striking, that of the former especially so, with its two towers crowned by spires which are reminiscent of the north-west spire of Chartres.

Although much of the Flamboyant architecture has a national character, it is curious that its outstanding feature, the window tracery, is often borrowed from the English of a century before. The tracery of S. Germain at Amiens (early fifteenth century), for instance, is almost identical with that at Selby (fourteenth century). The difference is that the French carry the decoration further, introducing the wildest extravagance and fantastic forms which often seem unsuitable to masonry construction. The tendency throughout is towards ingenuity and cleverness, often at the expense of lucidity.

A considerable amount of church building was done in the sixteenth century—far more than in England, where Protestant ideas took root earlier—and much of this is a mixture of Gothic and Renaissance detail which is often pleasing. In the doorways of many churches, Beauvais Cathedral and Abbeville, for instance, rich fifteenth-century Gothic masonry surrounds Renaissance woodwork, which is by no means out of keeping. In travelling through France one is often astonished at the dates given to churches in which Gothic feeling is still paramount, although the detail shows that its reign was nearly over. S. Pierre, Auxerre, is a striking Gothic church, and yet it is stated to have been rebuilt entirely in the seventeenth century. S. Nicholas, Coutances, the nave of which belongs to the sixteenth century and the choir and transepts to the seventeenth, is a quite remarkable example of imitation thirteenth-century work. The traditional methods of medieval building are followed religiously, and the church is ribbed-vaulted, while under the tower the corbelling has been copied from that over the crossing in the cathedral. S. Jacques, Lisieux (*c.*1500), has those simple quadripartite vaults which the French clung to until the end, but here enriched with most effective painting dated 1552. These late churches, and many others, show how strong was the Gothic tradition and how, long after the Renaissance movement had reached France, the Gothic style persisted in ecclesiastical architecture.

CHAPTER VI

SOUTHERN FRANCE

THE medieval architecture of southern France, that is, of Languedoc and Provence, was based upon a long tradition of great architecture. First there was the Roman legacy, with its love for large, simple structures, having as few supports as possible, and its preference for open, unencumbered floor spaces; and second, there was the Romanesque achievement, which grew out of this and produced the aisleless plan and the extraordinary series of domed churches in the district around Perigueux.[1] The development of this domical style was abruptly broken by the Albigensian wars (religious conflicts between the north and south of France) and the subsequent division of Languedoc in 1229, when its eastern portion was acquired by the French Crown. Thereafter the buildings borrowed some Gothic forms from the north, but retained certain outstanding southern peculiarities: these were the wide naves, the internal buttresses and the complete absence of flying buttresses. No cathedral in northern France has a span equal to that of Albi Cathedral (60 feet). Not even in the sexpartite-vaulted churches of the north did any double bays equal in size the single quadripartite-vaulted bays of, say, the church of the Cordeliers at Toulouse. In detail the southern churches may not differ much from the northern; in plan and general ordinance, however, they belong to a totally different school. Sculpture is rare, in spite of the fact that in Romanesque times the south had produced at Moissac, Vézelay and S. Gilles some of the most magnificent and unusual carved decoration in the world. The reason for the change lay partly in the impoverishment of the country after the Albigensian wars, and partly in the austerity advocated by the new mendicant Orders of Francis and Dominic. Further, the building material available in certain areas did not encourage ornamentation. In Auvergne there was the lava rock, in Limousin, granite, and in Toulouse, brick. At Albi and Toulouse alone in France can one study the almost exclusive use of brick on a large and important scale.

[1] See Vol. II, pp. 93–8.

Most southern churches can be grouped under two heads:
(1) Churches without aisles, but with chapels at the sides between internal buttresses of considerable projection, as at Albi Cathedral.
(2) Churches with aisles, the aisles being nearly as high as the central nave, as at Poitiers Cathedral.

Albi (Pl. 6). The cathedral at Albi (begun 1282) and the numerous churches in Toulouse form a group in which can be studied the essential differences between northern and southern ideals. Almost all are built in red brick. Even the jambs of the windows and the buttress offsets are generally of brick, although the mullions and tracery are in stone. Nearly all are aisleless, but the naves and choirs of most are surrounded by chapels, built between the strong internal buttresses which carry the thrust of the vaults. Albi is not only a church; it is also a fortress, linked with the fortifications of the archbishop's palace and the ramparts which crown the escarpments rising from the River Tarn. At the west end a square, donjon-like tower, with great circular buttresses at the angles, takes up a central position. There is no western doorway: this fact alone marks a difference between northern and southern work; nor are there any transepts, and the narrowness and height of the bays are most impressive. The entrance is on the south side, and consists of a magnificent flamboyant stone porch,

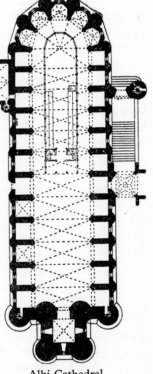

Albi Cathedral.
Scale 100 *ft. to* 1 *in.*

called the 'baldaquin', which by its ornateness is in striking contrast to the severity of the main structure of the cathedral. Albi is certainly the most imposing church in the south of France. The buttresses outside are segmental and of very slight projection. They are built, like the walls, with long, thin, brown bricks and wide mortar joints, no attempt being made to add decorative trimmings.

The appearance inside is, at first sight, a little disappointing after the towering height of the outside and the unusually lofty proportions of the windows. A hundred feet is a good height for a vault, but when the vault has a span of about sixty feet and the springing line is no higher from the floor than the width of the nave, the proportion is not happy. There is no structural division between nave and choir; the chapels continue along the nave and round the apse in an unbroken sequence. To achieve this the choir is isolated in the eastern half of the nave by means of a stone screen, which allows a free passage to the chapels. Over the chapels which thus surround the church are galleries, the vaults of which are as high as the main vault. The galleries, like the aisles below, are divided into distinct bays by the huge buttress walls. Altogether the effect is most imposing. The structure is stupendous; the ribs of the vaulting, two and a half feet thick, are an indication of the massive construction. The great vaults are supported entirely by the buttresses, each of which is five feet thick and twenty feet deep. One misses, it is true, the perspective effects which are obtained with open aisles and triforiums, but the plan for congregational purposes is superior in many ways to the triple division which is almost universal in the large churches of the north.

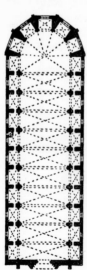

The cathedral at Perpignan, begun about the same time as Albi, has a similar plan and like dimensions, although its height is a trifle less. It differs from Albi mainly in that it has no galleries over the chapels (which are much higher than at Albi) and that over the arched openings to these chapels are uncusped, circular windows, one to each bay. Clerestory windows of this kind are common in Italy and Spain, and probably found their way to Perpignan over the Pyrenees.

The Church of the Cordeliers, Toulouse. The church of the Cordeliers (Franciscan Grey Friars) at Toulouse, now destroyed, was like the cathedral at Albi, but in this case the buttresses were pierced to form an ambulatory. In many ways this must have been the finest church in Toulouse. Its plan, except for the apsidal end, and its dimensions resembled those of King's College Chapel at Cambridge. The nave was nearly as wide as that of Albi, and there were low chapels opening out on either side, but no

Church of the
Cordeliers,
Toulouse.
Scale 100 *ft.*
to 1 *in.*

galleries. Outside, the buttresses appeared above the lean-to roofs of the side chapels, and were connected by arches above the windows. This type of design was a favourite in Toulouse, and still exists in the three surviving bays of the church of the Augustines and at Toulouse Cathedral. It occurs also at Bordeaux, where the western portion consists of a vast nave without aisles, 60 feet wide and nearly 200 feet long.

La Chaise Dieu. A connecting link between the plans of Albi and Poitiers (the two major types referred to above) is found in the church of La Chaise Dieu, in Auvergne (*c.* 1344), although chronologically it is later than either. It is one of the best examples of a monastic church in France. The nave consists of only three bays, whereas the choir has seven. The stalls, one hundred and forty-six in number, return at the west end and separate the monks' part from the smaller portion allotted to the people. The nave and choir are about 50 feet wide. At the sides are aisles, which continue round the church but stop at the east end against the five radiating chapels which open directly out of the choir. These chapels are unapproachable from either the nave or aisles; they belong exclusively to the choir. The church is like Poitiers Cathedral in having neither a triforium nor a clerestory; it differs from it mainly in the narrowness of the aisles, which, although lofty, are little more than ambulatories.

Poitiers. Poitiers Cathedral (1160) is the best example of a church having aisles almost equal in height to the nave, and it is possibly the earliest of the Gothic examples. The aisles are not only about the same height, but are almost equal in width to the nave. The lighting is entirely from the aisles and from the west and east ends. Because of the great height of the aisles and the absence of side windows in the nave walls, the aisle windows are considerably larger and of greater importance than in the northern type of church. Poitiers Cathedral has no chevet; its east end is square, although in the thickness of the wall are apses, as in Early Christian architecture. The transepts are mere chapels and of little importance. The most extraordinary feature of the church is the deliberate introduction of false perspective by the convergence of the sides towards the east end. The vault, too, diminishes in height towards the east end. The result is to give an appearance of much greater length than the church really possesses. In the church at Pontaubert, Burgundy, the chancel arch and vault are dropped towards the east in a similar way, and the springing line of the vault of the apse at the end of the chancel is even lower. In the church of Montréal, also in Burgundy, the gradation in height is obtained in a still more subtle fashion: the transverse arches of the nave are stilted; those of the chancel are not, the result being that the vault of the latter is a few feet lower than the nave vault. In all three churches the differences in height are not obvious. Only above the chancel arch are they at all apparent, for at that point a small portion of wall shows above the nave vault. These subtleties and refinements give some indication of an amount of care and thought normally only associated with Classical architecture. They are devices that are not only legitimate, but are also worthy of special praise.

Church of the Jacobins, Toulouse. Toulouse is the most important centre for the study of the architecture of southern France. In addition to the examples already mentioned, there is one church—the church of the Jacobins (*c.* 1300)—which has a most unusual plan. It has two naves of equal height, divided from each other by tall cylindrical columns which reach from the floor to the springing of the vault and make the church appear far more lofty than, say, the single-span cathedral of Albi, although in fact it is ten feet lower. Nothing else like it exists in France. The central shaft in the choir made possible a most ingenious solution to the vaulting problem around the apsidal end. The side chapels are low, without galleries, and the buttresses, which appear outside, are treated in the same way as at the church of the Cordeliers and the church of the Augustinians.

Church of the Jacobins, Toulouse.

Scale 100 *ft. to* 1 *in.*

Altogether there are few towns in France which can compare with Toulouse in the variety of its churches. They are proof that the Gothic of the north, with its nave and aisles, its flying buttresses and its inside divisions of nave walls, is not the only Gothic worthy of study. The fame of Chartres, Reims, Paris and Amiens has eclipsed the southern work; but in the bold use of great unrelieved masses of brickwork and in simplicity of plan and section there is an architectural logic in southern Gothic which is notable and important.

CHAPTER VII

ENGLAND. THE GREATER CHURCHES

THE accession of Henry Plantagenet (Henry II) in 1154 marks the end of the Norman dynasty and the beginning of a new era in English architecture. To Henry, England was not merely the largest of the provinces which made up a kingdom extending from the borders of Scotland to the borders of Spain; it was also the most important, because it was independent. As Duke of Normandy, Henry had to do homage to the King of France, but in England there was a growing independent nationalism which, during his reign, led to the development of an art freed from the continental tradition and entirely different from that in Anjou, Maine and Aquitaine, all of which lay within Henry's domain. Nearly a century had passed since England had come under Norman rule, and during that time great changes had naturally taken place between the two races, between the conquerors and the conquered. The old conditions, under which a hard-and-fast line was drawn between Normans and English, were still maintained so far as the highest posts in Church and State were concerned; but, in the growing towns especially, the barriers were broken down, and by intermarriage many of the leaders, even Henry himself, were half of English blood. A more powerful reason for fusion was the identity of interests between all burghers, no matter what their descent. Union between the two races was necessary in order to obtain civic freedom and security, and to repel more easily the predatory aggression of the barons and the extortions of the king.

It is evident in many ways, and especially in architecture, that the accession of Henry brought unity to the country. The king was as much a foreigner to the Normans as to the English, and just as much a fellow-countryman of both. At the same time, it was long before there were any changes in the court and in the Church. The barons and the prelates remained Norman, with the addition of a few Angevins. No bishop or abbot was English, and no Englishman was appointed to a see until the thirteenth century. But a break had been made in the Norman succession, and the break brought about a change. It came gradually, for the Benedictine monks still controlled all the great monastic churches of England and still looked to Normandy, or to Burgundy, the cradle of their Order, for guidance in architectural matters. Until the end of the twelfth century, as conservative here as their brethren were abroad, they continued to build on the old lines, as at Ely and Peterborough. It might have been thought that the union of England, Anjou, Aquitaine, etc., under one ruler would have led to the importation of southern methods of building into this country, but such was not the case. Although the inhabitants of the above countries were, in a sense, fellow-countrymen, Angevin characteristics—the aisleless plan for large churches, domical vaults and heavy transverse arches—found no echo in English work.

It was the growing activity of the Cistercians which occasioned, in part at least, the break with the Norman tradition. Their centre was at Cîteaux, and their first settlement in England was at Waverley, near Farnham. In the first half of the twelfth century the Cistercians flocked to England, and as a rule established their abbeys in remote and often waste places. They led the country in estate management, and were largely responsible for the development of the wool trade with Flanders. Although the Cistercians were not the originators of the square east end which is so characteristic of English Gothic, there can be no doubt that they made it popular. They were also among the first to use the pointed arch in England. At Buildwas, Rievaulx and Fountains, all largely built before 1150, pointed arches occur in the arcades, although at Buildwas the general design is frankly Romanesque, the substitution of the pointed arch for the semi-circular being the only modification. The complete Gothic structure was not developed until nearly the end of the century, that is, fifty years after the building of the choir at S. Denis.

The Transitional Style. What is commonly called Transitional, that is, transitional from Romanesque to Gothic, occurs in England during the latter half of the twelfth century. In this style there is an increasing lightness of all parts, a mingling of pointed and semi-circular arches—the former being used for main arcades and for vaulting, the latter for heads of windows and other small openings —and a change in mouldings and ornamentation. The work is transitional in a double sense; it not only marks the transition to a new style but it also expresses a change that was taking place in social and economic life and which culminated in the Magna

Carta, 1215. The period was by no means one of stagnation, but the advance was only partial. In France, on the other hand, contemporary art was advancing towards perfection, while English art seemed by comparison timid—to be slowly and carefully feeling its way. For this the quarrels of Henry II with the Church and barons, the restless ambition of Richard I which emptied the exchequer, and the double dealing of John with the Pope and his own people were mainly responsible.

Although French Gothic of the latter half of the twelfth century was considerably in advance of contemporary work in England, and although relations with France were close though not always friendly, there are very few examples in this country which can be classed as direct evidence of French influence. Indirectly there may be many, for the English builders cannot have been ignorant of the great achievements then being accomplished across the Channel. The first great work in which we can trace the germs of English Gothic is the choir arm of the metropolitan cathedral of Canterbury (Pl. 7), and it was the work of a Frenchman, William of Sens. It was begun after a disastrous fire in 1174, which had destroyed all to the east of the central tower but the crypt, the lower parts of the aisle walls, the eastern transepts and two of the original chevet chapels. Certainly there are features which are entirely French. The mouldings of the arches, the carving of capitals, the shape of the abaci, the starting of the vaulting shafts from above the capitals, and the sexpartite vaults can be attributed to France. The coupled columns of the eastern apse are similar to those of Sens and some churches in Normandy. But there were two innovations which must be associated with England. These are the use of Purbeck marble shafting and the treatment of the clerestory, with its thick wall and pierced gallery. In Anglo-Norman Romanesque it had been customary to build the walls with an outer and inner skin of ashlar, filled between with rubble and mortar. At Canterbury, the outer and inner walls are divided by a passageway. This separation of the inside and outside walls had remarkable consequences. The inner wall could be treated differently from the outer and become, as at Lincoln, an open arcade. Later, towards the end of the thirteenth century, it was to result in those fantastic double-traceried windows which are peculiarly English.

The Early English Style. The connecting links between the transitional work of the second half of the twelfth century and the fully-developed Gothic of the thirteenth are best to be seen in the cathedrals of Wells and Lincoln. The S. Hugh's choir of Lincoln (Pl. 7) and the nave of Wells were both begun about 1190. The designer at Lincoln was Geoffrey de Noiers, but whether he was an Englishman or someone brought by S. Hugh from Burgundy is a matter of dispute. The intro-duction of eastern transepts suggests the great church at Cluny, and the double apses to the eastern end may also be regarded as foreign, but are quite as likely to have been decided upon by the bishop as by the architect. The great transepts and the aisles of the smaller tran-septs, which were built later, have sexpartite vaulting, and the vaulting shafts of the former start, French-fashion, from the tops of the capitals of the piers. Otherwise, all is funda-mentally English. The clerestory has its inner arcade, independent of the windows, and the feature has been carried yet further in the double arcading which runs under the win-dows around the aisle walls. Trefoil arches supported on shafts stand in front of pointed arches against the wall, crossing one another. The idea may have been taken from the intersecting semi-circular arcades which are so common in Romanesque work, but only in England was it developed in this manner.

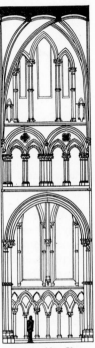

Bay of choir, Lin-coln.
Scale 25 ft. to 1 in.

The most extraordinary feature of the Lincoln choir is the vaulting, which shows an irregularity in the plan of the ribs that is unique. There is, for the first time, a constructional ridge rib, but instead of being crossed at the centre by diagonal arches, the ridge is divided into three parts by three intermediate ribs on each side (see p. 112). Simpson saw this as an early attempt to reduce the size of the vaulting compartments, a desire which animated all English builders throughout the following centuries and led to de-velopments in vaulting peculiar to England; but Geoffrey Webb provides a more attractive but equally English theory. He considers that it was a device to emphasize the east–west axis and to avoid the right-angled junction which inevitably follows in a quadripartite intersecting vault. 'If this be accepted, it is a striking example

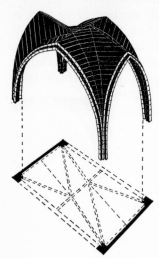

Arrangement of Lincoln choir vault.

of the preoccupation with the effect of linear pattern made by the vault ribs. . . . This preoccupation with linear pattern is evident throughout the work at Lincoln to a far greater degree than at Canterbury.'[1]

It may be said that at Lincoln English Gothic had arrived. With the one exception in Westminster Abbey, and that only as regards its plan and proportions, there is no church built subsequently which can truthfully be said to owe its plan, its ordinance, or its detail to French influence. At Lincoln, at the close of the thirteenth century, English designers had established a national style. Viollet-le-Duc said:

After a most careful examination I could not find in any part of the cathedral of Lincoln, neither in the general design, nor in any part of the system of architecture adopted, nor in the details of ornament, any trace of the French school of the twelfth century. The vaults have not at all the same construction as the French vaults at the end of the twelfth century. The construction is English; the profiles of the mouldings are English; the ornaments are English; the execution of the work belongs to the English school.

At Wells, too, the break from foreign influence is most noticeable in the change in treatment of the triforium which took place when the building of the nave followed the completion of the transepts. In the transepts, the vaulting shafts had sprung from the string course immediately above the main arcade, but in the nave this vertical element was curtailed so that the shafts sprang from corbels in the spandrels of the triforium arches; and those arches, which had been set in pairs in the transepts, now ran continuously along the whole length of the nave, giving that feeling for linear horizontality

After Britton.
Bay of nave, Wells.
Scale 25 ft. to 1 in.

[1] Geoffrey Webb: *Architecture in Britain: The Middle Ages*, 1956, p. 77.

Canterbury Cathedral; choir

Plate 7

Lincoln Cathedral;
choir vault

Salisbury Cathedral

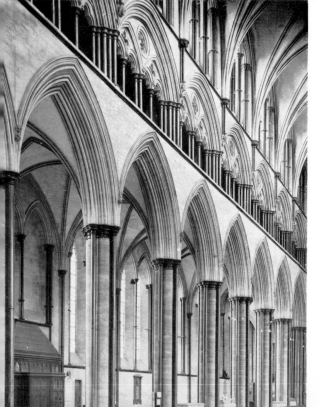

Salisbury Cathedral; na

Plate 8

which is so characteristically English and in such contrast with the French will towards vertical expression.

After the completion of the choir of Lincoln, and while the reconstruction of the nave and transepts was in progress, work was begun on an entirely new cathedral at Salisbury. Salisbury is the only medieval cathedral in England which remains exactly as it was planned. All the others were subject to remodelling, alterations and extensions. With the exception of the cloisters and the superimposition of the tower and spire, the whole cathedral was completed within fifty years. It is, therefore, the most uniform and consistent of all our cathedrals, and is the perfect exemplar of the Early English style (Pl. 8). The foundations were laid on 28 April 1220; it was consecrated on 20 September 1258, and 'it was completed on the 25th March in the year 1266, the whole expense of the fabric up to that time having been 42,000 marks', a sum which G. H. Cook gives as equivalent to a million pounds of our money.[1]

The decision to establish the new cathedral was made by Bishop Richard Poore, who had been Dean of Old Sarum from 1197 to 1214. Here, within the enceinte of a fortress, stood the Norman cathedral, and around it there was scarcely room for the canons' dwellings and for the soldiery. The site was high and windswept and there was a great scarcity of water. Accordingly, with the blessing of the Pope, it was decided to transfer the see to a new site on the plain below, and at the same time to plan a new town. The cathedral and the town are distinguished by their rectangularity; the streets were laid out in a grid pattern with an effective system of canal drainage, which was only covered up a century and a half ago. The cathedral also follows a systematic grid plan, terminating in a strictly rectangular Lady Chapel. It has the long nave and the twin pairs of transepts which may have stemmed from Lincoln and Canterbury, and the west end is finished with a broad screen wall, as at Lincoln, which does not match the section of the church but which terminates at the north and south with small, square turrets. The main entrance is not at the west, but by a porch on the north side similar to that which had already been built at Wells.

Two features of the interior of Salisbury deserve special mention. They are the abundant use of slender, Purbeck marble shafts to support the main arcade, and the unusually squat proportions of

[1] *Portrait of Salisbury Cathedral*, 1949, p. 23.

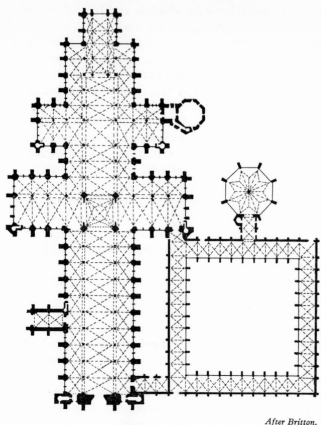

After Britton.

Salisbury Cathedral.
Scale 100 *ft. to* 1 *in.*

the triforium, with its broad low, enclosing arches which Geoffrey
Webb considers may be a personal idiosyncrasy of the designer.[1]

In the fourteenth century the steeple was added, and this certainly provided the most necessary dominant to the whole composition. That such a feature was not intended in the original
scheme is obvious from the slender proportions of the supporting
piers. Some additional support was provided by the introduction
of flying buttresses, but this was not enough, for in the fifteenth
century additional girder arches, like those at Wells, were inserted
between the north and south arches. In the seventeenth century

[1] *Architecture in Britain: The Middle Ages*, 1956, p. 98.

Sir Christopher Wren tried to strengthen the tower with iron ties, but as recently as 1945 the cathedral architect reported that its condition was far from reliable.

Comparison has been so frequently made between Salisbury and Amiens that the present choice of these two cathedrals for this purpose may suggest a lack of imagination, but no others can so well and forcibly bring home the fact that the English and French methods of design were proceeding on totally different lines when these two churches were building. Amiens was begun in the same year and, although finished earlier, had to be partially rebuilt, owing to a fire. In the rebuilding, alterations were made in the original design, especially in the clerestory windows, and it is not, therefore, so complete an example of consecutive building as the English church.

Bay of nave, Salisbury.
Scale 25 ft. to 1 in.

The most noteworthy points about the plan of Salisbury are its absolute symmetry and its rectangularity. So much is said about the irregularity of Gothic work that it is as well to emphasize the fact that, when not tied down and restricted by existing surroundings, the medieval builders adopted plans as symmetrical as any to be found in ancient Rome. The only features which have not their counterparts are the north porch, and the cloisters and

Salisbury and Amiens. Comparative sections.
Scale 100 ft. to 1 in.

chapter house to the south. Salisbury has a nave of ten bays west of the crossing, and a choir and presbytery of seven bays to the east of it, beyond which is a Lady Chapel of four bays, all ending square. The great transepts project three bays beyond the aisles, the smaller transepts two bays. On the east side of both pairs of transepts is an aisle divided into chapels. There are single aisles to nave and choir, and no side chapels. Amiens has a nave of seven bays and a choir of four, or five including the apse. Beyond is the semi-circular chevet, with its radiating chapels. The eastern arm has double aisles, the nave single aisles, with chapels along their outer sides, and the transepts have an aisle on both sides. The transepts project only one bay beyond the outer choir aisles, and that bay on each side is much narrower than any other in the church. There are no eastern transepts. The internal width of Salisbury is 78 feet, exactly half of which is the width of the nave from centre to centre of the piers, the aisles dividing the remaining half. The western arm of Amiens is 103 feet wide, exclusive of chapels, and is divided in the same way. The eastern arm is about 155 feet wide, nearly double that of Salisbury. The differences in proportion become still more marked when the heights are considered. Amiens, the second highest church in France, is 140 feet high from the floor to apex of vault; Salisbury, the third highest in England, is only 84 feet.

The above is enough to show that whereas breadth and height seem to have been the aims of the French builders, the English, modest in these respects, relied more on length. The latter could, in consequence, afford to give their main transepts considerable projection and to add eastern transepts. They could carry a stone tower and spire above the crossing, a far more effective feature than the wood and lead flèche of Amiens, although this does rise some twenty feet higher than the spire of Salisbury. A tower and spire at Amiens would have detracted from, rather than added to, the dignity of the cathedral. No one studying the plan, appearance and main ordinance of these two churches can doubt for a minute that the ideals advanced on one side of the Channel were not those striven for on the other. At Amiens the cathedral rears its whole body above the houses which hem it in on all sides; the tower and spire alone of Salisbury Cathedral form a landmark. But each building tells the same story, although in a different way: the story of the majesty of the Church, of which it is the visual monument.

In English cathedrals the west fronts are the weakest parts of the ensembles, and Salisbury (Pl. 8) is no exception to the general rule; in fact, it is probably the least satisfactory of all. There are no western towers, and a horizontal parapet connects the gable with angle turrets which are poor substitutes. At Lincoln, the base of which is Norman, horizontality is still more marked, since on each side of the central gable is a screen extending far beyond the western towers, which rise behind it, and finishing with turrets similar to those at Salisbury. The two most famous thirteenth-century fronts are Peterborough, with its triple porches—the central one, curiously enough, narrower than those at the sides; and Wells (*c.* 1220), about which more has probably been written than about any part of any other building, mainly because of the beauty of its sculpture, which extends round the towers at the angles as well as along the entire front. The west front (Pl. 9) is unusually wide for an English cathedral, because the towers stand beyond the aisle walls, and do not terminate the aisles as was the usual custom both in England and abroad. Nothing can be finer in the design than the lower part, notwithstanding the insignificance of the doorways, When it was completed and every statue was painted and gilded, it must have presented a stupendously colourful façade. For the smallness of the doorways leading to the aisles there is every excuse; in fact, they are better small, because they give scale. The difference in relative size and importance between French and English entrances is an interesting point of comparison in the work of the two countries. Climate can hardly account for it, and Wells is a proof that it was not lack of skill on the part of English sculptors which led them to dispense with the many figures in the jambs and the multitude of canopied figures in the arched heads which are so characteristic of French work. Other countries copied the doorways of France. England did not.

The eastern ends of English cathedrals, too, are remarkably different from those of France. There the chevet, with its radiating series of flying buttresses leading down from a steeply pitched roof, provides a logical and dynamic conclusion. The east end of Salisbury and other cathedrals spreads itself over much ground, with buildings much lower than the bulk of the cathedral behind. At Ely the result is more satisfactory, for there the choir and presbytery (*c.* 1235) are continued their full height to the east wall; but the large window in the gable only lights the roof space above the vaulting and does not show inside at all. The most important Early English eastern terminations are those at Durham Cathedral and Fountains Abbey. At Durham it takes the form of a Chapel of Nine Altars (1242–80) and at Fountains of a similar chapel, but for seven altars. In effect, they form transepts at the extreme eastern ends, stretching beyond the choir aisles on either side. In both cases the resemblance on plan to the bemas of the greater Roman basilicas is marked, except that there are no apsidal projections. The Durham chapel forms a magnificent vaulted hall, about 35 feet wide, 127 feet long and 80 feet high. Its floor is dropped some six feet below the choir floor, which accounts for the fact that its height is greater than that of the rest of the church. At Fountains the addition is even larger: about 36 feet wide by 132 feet long; but its length was broken by two piers, continuous with those of the choir, which rose to a great height and supported arches immediately under the vault.

The years between 1175 and 1250 define the period called Early English. It is the Doric of our Gothic architecture. At no other period do the designs show such strength, freshness, simplicity and refinement. There is a stateliness and quiet dignity about everything built between these years which had not been reached before and was never equalled afterwards. The work may not have the vivacity and intricacy of the immediately following period, but it possesses other and sounder qualities. The steps by which it was evolved are so unmistakable, and can be traced so easily, that any student of architecture who knows it, and knows also the preceding work in England and contemporary work in France, can see from local examples that its growth was a natural one and that it owed little to outside influence. There are no breaks or sudden changes, such as would have been perceptible if it had been an importation from outside. It is unreservedly English. The dominating features are: first, the emphatic verticality of the windows, as, for instance, in the famous 'Five Sisters' at York— a feature which has led many authorities to call the style 'lancet'; secondly, the introduction of contrasting materials, especially smooth dark marble shafts against white stone walling, as appeared first at Canterbury and later at Chichester, Winchester, and Salisbury; thirdly, the advances in constructive skill, which are especially evident in the use of the *tas-de-charge* at the springing of the vaults and the boss at the apex, and the development of the buttress which, in this period, is carefully located to withstand the structural forces and is in fact greater in projection than it is in width; and finally, there is the wholesale abandonment of the semi-circular arch in favour of the pointed form. All these features belong to the Early English style, but some also occur abroad. The outstanding peculiarity is what Dr. Pevsner calls the 'additive' character of English design. It lacks the spatial unity of French cathedrals. In England there are the duplication of transepts, as at Canterbury, Lincoln, Wells, and Salisbury; the constant extension of the choir by additional bays and Lady Chapels; and the emphasis which is laid upon a three-storeyed scheme—arcade, triforium and clerestory, each strongly defined by powerful string courses, so that even the main shafts which carry the vaults do not come down to the floor but are commonly stopped on corbels at triforium level. Perhaps the most striking of all is the fact that although certain standards seem to have been adopted, there was no slavish copying and no rigid adherence to a single discipline or code of proportions. Every Early English work seems to have its own individuality and character.

The Decorated Style. In 1245 Henry III began work on the rebuilding of Westminster Abbey, and this date and event mark the beginning of a change in style. Henry appears to have taken a keen interest in architecture, but he was so much under the influence of foreigners that his church at Westminster possesses many features that are typical of France. The chevet plan of the eastern arm and the high proportions of the church point to the employment of a French architect in the design. The size of the windows, the number of flying buttresses (Westminster is the only church in England which has double tiers), and the relative width of wall to column are evidence of continental influence. The king's mason at that time was called Henry of Reyns, and it is almost certain that he came from Reims rather than Rayne, or Raynes, in Essex. That the English coronation church was chiefly inspired by its counterpart at Reims is undoubted, but other nearly contemporary buildings, notably Amiens and Ste. Chapelle, provided some features. There are also some details which are English: the use of Purbeck marble, with attached shafts round the columns, and moulded bands; the rounded abacus and the details of capitals, bases, arches, etc. The design of the triforium gallery and wall arcading, the absence of any stilting of the window-heads, the method of infilling adopted in the vaults, and especially the introduction of the ridge rib, all suggest the influence of English

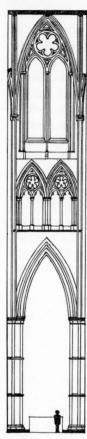

Bay of nave, Westminster Abbey.

Scale 25 ft. to 1 in.

rather than continental masons. What is certain is that by the middle of the thirteenth century the English masons had established a tradition, and although willing to adopt features from France which they felt would be improvements, they were by no means willing to sacrifice others which were to their liking.

The new work exemplified at Westminster marks the first stage in what is commonly called the Decorated style. Foliage and figure sculptures are introduced into the spandrels between the arches, as, for instance, at the entrance to the chapter house (*c.* 1253), which was completed before work began on the main church. These motifs are naturalistic, though stiff, and usually circumscribed by diapers and trefoils. The windows, both in the aisles and the clerestory, consist of two foliated lights of lancet proportions, surmounted by a circular foliated figure. This is set out geometrically by compasses, and differs from the earlier 'plate' tracery (see p. 54), where apertures were pierced in the stone walling. For now the whole arched opening is filled with a skeleton system of slender mullions and arches, which we call 'bar tracery' and which appeared at Reims as early as 1212. Lastly, there is the use of the *tas-de-charge* at the springing of the vaults. This device (see p. 41), apart from its practical and structural value, facilitated the introduction of additional and often largely decorative tierceron ribs.

The anglicization of the style of Westminster is most noticeable in the building of the Angel Choir or presbytery of Lincoln (1257) (Pl. 9). The proportions of the bays in each church are quite different. At Westminster they are only 17 feet 6 inches wide from centre to centre of the columns, and the height from the floor to the apex of the arch is about 42 feet; at Lincoln, the corresponding dimensions are 23 feet 2 inches and 33 feet 6 inches. The triforium in both examples consists of four openings grouped in pairs, but the greater width of the bays in Lincoln makes them appear totally dissimilar. The Westminster triforium is lighted

Wells Cathedral; west front

Plate 9

Lincoln Cathedral; angel choir

Lichfield Cathedral; nave

Exeter Cathedral; nave

Plate 10

Ely Cathedral; the octagon

y Cathedral; Lady Chapel

Wells Cathedral; scissor
arches at crossing

Plate 11

Lincoln Cathedral;
chapter house

Westminster Abbey;
chapter house

Plate 12

by windows on the outside wall, but the Lincoln triforium is dark behind. At Westminster the clerestory windows are each of two lights, uncusped, with a foliated circle above; at Lincoln they are each of four lights, with three circles above, and made doubly rich by the repetition of the design on the inside face of the wall. The vaulting starts rather low at Lincoln, some feet below the clerestory string course, whereas at Westminster it starts in the French fashion, many feet above. And finally, the presbytery at Lincoln, continuing the level of S. Hugh's choir, is only 73 feet high, whereas Westminster measures 100 feet from the floor to the crown of the vault. Certainly there are many differences, but the elements are the same. In both there is a new richness of design, a multiplication of decorative forms and an extensive use of sculpture. The language is the same, but at Westminster the accent is French.

Two other important works should be mentioned on this first stage of the development of the Decorated style. They are the nave of Lichfield (1265–93) and the presbytery and Lady Chapel of Exeter (begun 1280). At Lichfield the arches are sharper than at Lincoln, and the triforium taller in proportion. The clerestory is the most remarkable feature, for it consists of tracery alone within spherical triangles, that is, figures formed by three equilateral arcs (Pl. 9). The tracery consists of trefoil cusped circles, and is linked with the triforium below so that the whole seems like a two- rather than a three-storeyed structure. At Exeter the theme of surface texture is carried even further than at Westminster and Lincoln. The mouldings are finer and more undulating, and the ribs of the vault more numerous (they are in sheafs of eleven from each bay division), so that the infilling becomes no more than the background to an intricately moulded surface.

After Sharpe.
Bay of nave,
Lichfield.
Scale 25 ft.
to 1 in.

About 1290 we enter the second stage in the development of the Decorated style, and pass from what is sometimes called the geometric, to the curvilinear. This work is characterized by the use of the ogee curve, in which the arcs are joined in reverse lines to form flowing patterns. Foliage sculpture becomes more lush and loses much of its crispness in favour of decorative exuberance. Much of the work was richly painted, gilded and incredibly intricate. This is the period of our grander and most ornamental towers and spires, of the great octagon of Ely and of many of our finest cloisters and chapter houses. The end is marked by the opening of the Hundred Years War (1338–1453), by which time nearly all our cathedrals had been built.

Exeter is probably the most complete example of a 'Decorated' cathedral (Pl. 10). Work seems to have been continuous from east

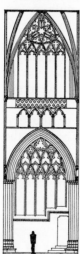

After Britton.

Bay of nave, Exeter.

Scale 25 ft. to 1 in.

to west from about 1280 until the middle of the fourteenth century, with only insignificant variations in stylistic treatment. The triforium is reduced to the merest incidental arcade below the clerestory. The heads of the windows are filled with intricate flowing tracery patterns. The vaults spring from delicately rich corbels and reach, along the ridge line, some of the finest sculptured bosses in the country. The west front is prefaced by an entirely new feature: a projecting triple porch, two storeys high, which stands in advance of the main gable, but this, the culmination, belongs to the third quarter of the fourteenth century and therefore to the succeeding style.

Contemporary with the nave of Exeter was the nave of York. This is remarkable chiefly for two features: first, the incorporation of the triforium within the clerestory arch, so that the arcade is a continuation of the window mullions; and secondly, for the great span of the nave (it exceeds those of Reims and Amiens and all the English Gothic cathedrals). This necessitated a timber construction based upon king post trusses. These are remarkable not only for their extent but also for their ingenuity.

The span of the nave at York was 58 feet, and was far surpassed by the great octagon at Ely, planned to replace the Norman central tower which had fallen in 1322. The decision to form an octagon at the crossing might be an echo of the contemporary fashion for octagonal chapter houses, or, more probably, an expression of the new feeling towards space and against the rigid discipline of right angles. The ogee arch was the first step in this movement; the second, which we see in the niches of the Lady Chapel at Ely (Pl. 11) and in the chapter house at York, was to project forwards the apex of the arches so that they became three-dimensional canopies, or 'nodding ogees'. The final step was taken at Bristol, in the Berkeley Chapel vestibule, where the main vault ribs were detached from the vault surface and appeared as a series of slender stone arches defining, but not enclosing, space.

The octagon at Ely has a span of nearly 70 feet, and was probably the work of Master William de Hurle, the king's carpenter (Pl. 11). The wooden timber vaulting consists of a series of hammer beam trusses, the hammer posts forming the great uprights of the inner lantern. This is also of wood, covered with lead, and although stated by some to be a temporary makeshift it seems difficult to believe that any more solid superstructure can ever have been intended. The Ely octagon is unique, and its construction a most wonderful carpentry achievement which had far-reaching effects on the design of roof trusses in the following century. It is said that the length and breadth of England was searched for suitable timbers. The main supporting beams are, in fact, 63 feet long by approximately 3 feet square, and the problems of transportation and erection must have been stupendous.

While the fourteenth century was notable for its various alterations and reconstructions affecting interior design, the period was remarkable also for additions to the cathedral complex of towers and spires, chapter houses and cloisters. All, of course, had precedents in earlier centuries, but the most significant developments took place in the fourteenth. The great towers of Lichfield, Lincoln, Wells, Hereford, Salisbury and Peterborough were constructed early in the century. They set the standards which were to be followed, often with improved quality, in the hundreds of parish churches throughout the land. The cathedral towers are among the most obvious extravagances of a design system which has so often and so erroneously been regarded as strictly functional. A single tower to carry bells may be justifiable on practical grounds, but when there are three, or even more, they are introduced solely for external effect. The octagon at Ely did at least provide by its lantern an additional source of light at the crossing, and the same may be said of the central towers of Canterbury, Durham, Lincoln and York; but at Salisbury, Gloucester and Wells this potential lantern space is sealed off with a vault so that the tower becomes a purely external feature. At Wells and at Salisbury the construction of the central towers nearly resulted in disaster, and involved the immediate introduction of remarkable scissor, or cross, arches to assist in stabilizing the main supporting piers. The arches at Wells (Pl. 11), and possibly those at Salisbury, are attributed to the same school of masons as was responsible for the open vaulting at Bristol, and are among the most sensational features of all English Gothic architecture, even although, and perhaps because, they are dramatic structural expedients.

The polygonal chapter house is a peculiarly British structure. The earliest example was at Worcester (1120), but that was circular inside. On the Continent, and in most monastic establishments, the usual plan is rectangular, with perhaps an apsidal end. Only in England, in Gothic times, and usually attached to cathedrals served by secular canons, was the octagonal or decagonal form developed. Of these there are twenty-five, and the majority were constructed between 1220 and 1360. The earliest was built at Lincoln and is a decagon, about 58 feet across and vaulted to a central column (Pl. 12). Westminster (Pl. 12), then Salisbury, followed, both about the same size as Lincoln, but octagonal, and also with central columns. The octagon had the advantage in that it provided a

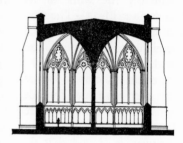

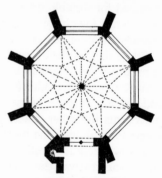

Chapter House, Salisbury.
Scale 50 ft. to 1 in.

greater space for the broader, multi-light window then being developed, and nearly all the later chapter houses seem to have followed the lead of Westminster. At York (1285) and at Southwell (*c.* 1290) the bold step was taken of dispensing with the central supporting column. The span at York was equal to Westminster's, and the builders had to contrive an elaborate imitation of vaulting in timber; but at Southwell the span was less (only about 30 feet across), and stone vaulting was possible without a prop in the middle. The result is a completely unbroken space, which is saved from dullness because it possesses, on the capitals of the columns which separate the peripheral seats, on the tympanums of the canopies, in the crockets and the finials, on the vaulting shafts themselves and the bosses above, the most wonderful collection of naturalistic leaf carving in England.[1] The chapter houses of Southwell, York, Wells and Westminster are remarkable, too, in their approaches by vestibule, passage, or staircase, which seem to have been designed as a prelude to the great assembly hall. The approach at Wells (Pl. 13) is perhaps the most dramatic and ingenious of all, though part of that belongs to the fifteenth, and not the fourteenth, century. It consists of a staircase which leads from an angle of the north transept and sweeps round to the main doorway, lit by traceried windows which follow the stairway, while at the same time a branch stairway is cunningly mitred on the curve to lead towards the north and over the chain bridge.

Cloisters, in a monastic establishment, form the circulatory core of the plan, and the earliest designs in England seem to have followed French precedents by consisting of no more than open passageways with a lean-to timber roof carried by pairs of columns set on a low stone wall. By the thirteenth century, however, cloisters were windows, traceried and sometimes glazed, and covered with a stone vaulted ceiling. The first was at Salisbury (Pl. 13), a secular cathedral, where a new standard of magnificence was set. This was completed by 1284 and consisted of ten bays to each side, enclosing a green garth 130 feet square. From this beginning may be traced, via the quadrangles of the Oxford and Cambridge colleges, most of the story of that most characteristic contribution of English town planning, the eighteenth-century square, such as still survives in Bloomsbury, with its garden in the middle. After Salisbury came Lincoln, much smaller, and Norwich (monastic) with its superb carved bosses. In the fourteenth century, Exeter, Old S. Paul's, Gloucester, Worcester, Durham, Canterbury, Peterborough, Wells, Oxford, Hereford, Chester, Ely and Bristol all began to build or rebuild their cloisters in the latest mode, and Gloucester, in 1370, set an entirely new fashion, that of the fan vault.

The Late Decorated period, that is, the first forty years of the fourteenth century, was notable for an increasing preoccupation with vault design, partly due, no doubt, to the greater amount of light filtering through the new large windows. On the one hand there was the multiplication of tierceron ribs, which we noted at Exeter 1328–42) (Pl. 10); on the other, there was the growing interest in the possibilities of pure pattern-making on the vault surface by

[1] *See* N. Pevsner: *The Leaves of Southwell*, 1945.

means of lierne ribs. The choirs of Bristol (1311) and of Wells (1329) are among the earliest examples of this new approach. At Wells the aim seems to have been to disguise as far as possible the basic constructional form and to introduce instead an intricate linear pattern of foiled figures which disrupt the main lines of the vaults (Pl. 13). The effect is that of a barrel vault, interrupted by similar but smaller vaults over the windows. At Ely, in 1335—concurrently, that is, with the building of the octagon—the choir was vaulted in a more conventional way, but with the introduction of lierne ribs to form a series of six-pointed stars. This was the progenitor of stellar vaulting, and found its most complete expression at the east end of Tewkesbury, where the purpose was apparently to focus interest on the apex of the vaults. The next, and logical, step was to combine the complexities of tierceron and lierne vaults, and this was done at Gloucester (Pl. 14) at the same time as at Tewkesbury, but it belongs to the Perpendicular and not the Decorated style.

The Perpendicular Style. The fact that the opening of the Hundred Years War coincided with the start of the reconstruction of the choir of Gloucester provides a sufficient excuse for the adoption of that date to mark the begining of a new epoch. Certainly after 1337 nothing was quite the same. The war provided a far more convenient outlet for nationalist militarism than had been possible with the Crusades, and the fact that the English claims on France were dubious and largely a matter of genealogy does not concern us here. What matters is that the war stimulated a strong national self-consciousness, which in terms of architecture was expressed in a distinctly national style. The changes and events of the century were immense. For the soldiers, the most important change was the substitution of the cannon for the bow and arrow; in the Church, the preaching of Wyclif, and the consequent agitation of the Lollards, caused dissension and weakness; for the masses, it was a period of change from servile to hired labour. There were years of famine, followed by the Black Death in 1349, which reduced the population of the land from four millions to about two and a half millions. This affected all classes. The farmers were unable to till the land and gather the crops for want of labour; prices rose considerably because of the amount of land thrown out of cultivation, and all workers, while having to pay a far higher price for the necessities of life, were forbidden by law to demand a higher wage than that which had been customary before the pestilence came. In many cases it meant that the shepherd replaced the ploughman. The effects of the Black Death would not have been so disastrous, and the recovery would have been more rapid, but for the continuous wars abroad, and the constant demands on the people's purse which their prosecution entailed. The unrest throughout the land was exemplified by the Peasants' Revolt of 1381. Early in the fifteenth century the victory of Henry V at Agincourt brought glory to the king, but little profit to the people. In 1453 the war ended with the expulsion of the English, and two years later the Wars of the Roses began. This had not the paralysing effect on commerce and trade that civil war generally entails, since it was a barren struggle in which the people took little part; but when, in 1485 at Bosworth Field, Henry Tudor replaced the Plantagenets, England had changed beyond recognition. No century, almost no decade, in the Middle Ages, passed without insurrections or wars, and those of the fourteenth and fifteenth centuries probably damaged architecture far less than the awful calamity of the Black Death. The drop in population meant that the extent of cathedral and abbey church building was less than in any previous century. There is no complete cathedral of the Perpendicular period. In any case, most of the greater churches had been finished, so that we have at most a miscellaneous number of alteration jobs and a few completions of work already begun. But there was by no means stagnation. The energy merely took another form: it was devoted to the building of parish churches. The clergy were poor, and the monastic Orders seem to have been indifferent, but another race of donors was springing up. Increase in trade had brought great wealth to the merchants, and many were willing to spend it royally. The Perpendicular period is therefore the period *par excellence* of the parish church, which will be considered later. The stylistic inspiration, nevertheless, came from the greater churches, from the minor improvements and alterations which were undertaken at the instigation of the court, and which was of a character so distinct that it has often been entitled the court style.

The first evidence of a new development away from the florid and often over-decorated style of the first quarter of the fourteenth century appears to have been shown in the vicinity of London, and it is unfortunate, to say the least, that these most important works no longer survive. They were the Royal Chapel of S. Stephen's in Westminster Palace, which was almost totally destroyed by fire in 1834 so that only the undercroft, now much restored, remains;

and the Chapter House of S. Paul's Cathedral, which perished in the Great Fire of 1666 and of which there are some fragments in the triforium of Wren's cathedral and only the scantiest remains of foundations in the churchyard to the west of the present south transept. Only by reference to drawings and prints are we able to see the novelties of this new development. S. Stephen's lower chapel was begun in 1292, and the upper was started in 1331; and S. Paul's chapter house was under construction in 1332, under the direction of William de Ramsey, who had previously been engaged on S. Stephen's. Both, therefore, precede the reconstruction of the choir of Gloucester. It is possible that some, at least, of the innovations owe their origin to France, and certainly many of the motifs can be traced in earlier French works at Clermont Ferrand, Limoges and Narbonne, but the exploitation of the style to remarkable limits was due not to France but to the English designers of the second half of the fourteenth and of the fifteenth centuries.

The outstanding feature of the style, as its name suggests, is the emphasis on verticality. There is also a new feeling towards space, in which piers and supports generally are reduced to the absolute minimum, while windows are proportionately increased in width. Vaulting, which at first seemed to tend towards increasing intricacy in the meanderings and interlacings of tierceron and lierne ribs, later changed entirely with the introduction of pendants and conoids of masonry (see p. 46). It became fashionable to frame windows and other openings with a rectangular hood mould and to panel the spandrels. It was common to continue the lines of the window mullions below the sills to form blind tracery, so that eventually every surface was enriched and enlivened by rising mullions which met, and cut at right angles, horizontal members, to result in a system of rectilinear masonry panelling. Lastly, there was a change in the form of the arch. At the beginning, the ogee form continued, at least as a decorative feature, but as early as the building of the cloisters of S. Paul's—that is, at the same time as the building of the chapter house—a new, flatter, four-centred arch was used, and this, which is commonly the distinguishing feature of Tudor architecture, became usual by the end of the fifteenth century.

The importance of Gloucester as the first surviving monument to illustrate the new style cannot be exaggerated; for Gloucester, ever since it had received the murdered body of Edward II, was a centre of pilgrimage and architectural activity. Miracles happened,

Salisbury Cathedral; cloisters

Plate 13

Wells Cathedral; stairs to chapter house

Wells Cathedral; choir vaulting

Gloucester Cathedral; cho[

Gloucester Cathedral;
cloisters

Plate 14

and considerable wealth was amassed from devotionary offerings; so much, according to one chronicle, that the monks might have rebuilt their entire church. They contented themselves with remodelling the choir (Pl. 14) which enshrined the tomb. They did not demolish the old Norman structure, but only removed the

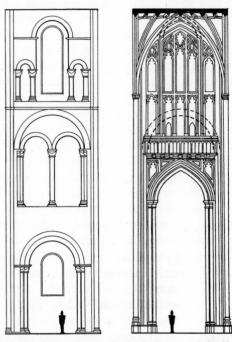

(Left) Winchester Cathedral as originally designed; (right) as altered by William of Wykeham.
Scale 25 ft. to 1 in.

clerestory wall, which they replaced by piers with glazing between. By about 1350 the vaults were completed, the windows glazed, and the new style was revealed. The fashion of remodelling rather than rebuilding was noted, observed and followed throughout the land. Similar face-lifting was undertaken at Malmesbury, Malvern, Norwich, Winchester, Tewkesbury, Sherborne and Oxford. Everywhere large new windows were inserted in the new rectilinear mode, and the walls were refaced with masonry panelling. Every surface was brought into harmony—buttresses, battlements and towers. The pilgrims who had found their way to Gloucester returned to their homes to spread and reproduce the wonders of the new mode. The most astounding feature of Gloucester was the great east window. This filled the area between the side walls with one wall of glass and, to give additional structural stability, was planned as a shallow three-sided bow. It measures 38 feet across by 72 feet high, an area about equal to that of a tennis court (36 feet by 78 feet), and exceeding that of any other window in England.

The technique of Gloucester was followed at Winchester with improvements to internal proportions, by William Wynford when he began to remodel the nave in 1394. In the old Norman church the three divisions of arcade, triforium and clerestory were approximately equal in height. William raised the piers to the level of the floor of the triforium, abolished the triforium itself while maintaining a passage gallery higher up, and panelled the wall at the sides of, and below, the clerestory windows. The arches of the main arcade he made four-centred, but they are not so flat as they were later, and consequently do not look weak. Over the arches ran a boldly carved and moulded string course, which formed a strong division between the upper and lower storeys.

The fifteenth century saw the beginning of the end of Gothic art in England. It was a glorious end. English Gothic did not flicker and linger and drag out an inglorious life. Still full of strength and vigour, it laid itself down with majesty and pomp, with all the trappings of carvings, sculpture and colour, and surrounded by a richness and wealth of ornament such as had never been known before and has never been equalled since. Between 1430 and 1520 some of the most remarkable English ecclesiastical work was undertaken. Little was done to cathedrals, except to finish a tower, as at Canterbury, or to add chantry chapels—outside, as at Lincoln Cathedral, or inside, between the columns, as at Winchester. Bath Abbey Church (c. 1500–39) is the only large monastic church begun after the middle of the fifteenth century, but extensive alterations were made to Malvern Priory Church (1450–86) and to the Abbey Church of Sherborne (1436–1504),

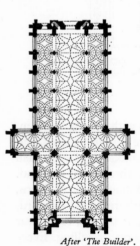

After 'The Builder'.

Bath Abbey.
Scale 100 *ft. to* 1 *in.*

where the nave piers are richly panelled and the vault is a fan vault.

The fan vault is probably the last remarkable development of English Gothic architecture, and the earliest major example is to be found in the cloisters of Gloucester (Pl. 14), of which the south-eastern bays were completed between 1370 and 1377, though it is possible that the idea may have originated in a small way in some of the tomb canopies, as, for instance, that of Sir Hugh Despenser, who died in 1349 at Tewkesbury, and in the chapter house of Hereford, which was built 1360–70, but of which only drawings and a description survive.

While the new vaulting technique was adopted in a number of additions and alterations to cathedrals and abbeys, as, for instance, in the nave of Bath, the aisle and retrochoir of Peterborough and the crypt of Canterbury, the most important examples are to be found in a number of chapels, royal and collegiate, which, if inferior in size, surpass the greater churches in richness. The most famous are King's College Chapel, Cambridge (begun in 1446, the fan vault not being finished until early in the sixteenth century) (Pl. 15); S. George's, Windsor (1475–1528); Eton College Chapel (contemporary with King's, Cambridge); and Henry VII's Chapel, Westminster (Pl. 15), finished a few years after his death by his successor.

The Henry VII Chapel, with its side chapels, is almost a church in itself, and the same may be said of the Royal Chapel at Windsor. King's College Chapel is a chapel, pure and simple, since although it has low aisles which form side chapels, these are cut off from the main body. The chapel proper forms a magnificent hall, 45 feet wide, 284 feet long and 81 feet high, vaulted with one of the most successful fan vaults in England, because it is one of the simplest. This building really marks the end of the English Gothic achievement. In place of walls there are windows, and the roof is carried by deeply projecting buttresses. It is all clear-cut and logical, a masterpiece of three men: Richard Ely, Robert Westerley and, for the vaults, John Wastell. The architecture that came after was either an elaboration, as at Henry VII's Chapel, where the art of the mason seems to have been allied with that of the embroidress to produce a wonderful craftsmanship at the expense of structural logic, or was contaminated by an admixture of Renaissance detail. In Henry VII's Chapel the metal screen surrounding the tomb is really fine English medieval craftsmanship, but the tomb itself is not English; it is the work of Torrigiani, the best known of the first batch of Italians who came to our shores to spread a new style. The transition from medieval to Renaissance had already taken place in Italy. Brunelleschi, the first of the Renaissance architects, died in Florence in the year that work began on King's College. When the vaults were nearing completion, Bramante was already building a new S. Peter's.

With the beginning of the sixteenth century there were no further developments in the Gothic style in England. There were only revivals, and they were concerned with lesser buildings, not with greater churches. At Oxford, for example, the conservative tradition is evident at Christ Church and Wadham Colleges, and in the outlying districts in the Midlands and the North people continued to build in much the same way as their forefathers had, and with little difference in detail. In fact the Gothic spirit lingered in England until, by a strange irony of fate, it was destroyed by a movement in favour of a Gothic revival. An insistence on the letter rather than the spirit of the style cut the thread of the tradition which had descended from father to son for generations, and the spirit of revivalism destroyed the last vestiges of vernacular art.

In this chapter it has not been possible to refer to all, or even the majority, of the great works which were undertaken during the Gothic period in England. To remedy this defect without burdening the reader with unnecessary reiterations, I am following the method adopted in the previous volume by giving below a summary of the outstanding features of our cathedrals, abbeys and monasteries:

BATH 'ABBEY'. Monastic cathedral—Benedictine. Built (1501–39) on the foundations of the nave of the original Norman church. It is in all essentials a complete Perpendicular cathedral. The designers were Robert and William Vertue. Aisles are kept to an absolute minimum and separated from the nave by four-centred arches. There is no triforium. The clerestory windows fill the area from the top of the arcade to the roof to give a complete glass-house effect. The culmination is a fan vault which is contrived over rectangular bays. At the east end is an unusual square-headed window of seven lights, built up in five tiers, the uppermost being filled with rectilinear tracery. The central tower is rectangular on plan, its proportion being dictated by the foundations of one of the bays of the Norman nave.

BEVERLEY MINSTER. Secular Canons. No Norman work. The Lady Chapel, choir, double-aisled transepts and east bay of nave are good examples of Early English work (1225–45), with interesting interlacing arches in triforium. The nave, except for east and west bays, is Decorated (*c.* 1320–*c.* 1349) and has fine flamboyant tracery in windows and arcading. The west bay and the great west front are Perpendicular (*c.* 1380–1430). The most noteworthy features are: the west front, which surpasses that of York, because the towers are not absorbed by the central façade but are clearly defined from ground to pinnacle; inside, the Early English arcaded staircase which led to the chapter house; the Percy tomb, which is the most sumptuous piece of Decorated work (1336–40), where even the cusps are ogees and everywhere there is carving and undercutting and intricate flowing foliage; and the choir stalls, which are late (1522–5) and contain superb canopy work.

BRISTOL CATHEDRAL. Originally an Augustinian abbey church; made a cathedral at the Dissolution of the monasteries (1539). Along with Exeter, may be taken as our only nearly complete Decorated cathedral. The rectangular chapter house and a few fragments are all that survive of the Norman church. The tower is Perpendicular, and the nave and western towers, by George Edmund Street, were a Victorian construction echoing the style of the choir. The chief interest is, therefore, in the original choir (1298–1340), which is unique in two important respects: it is the only example in which the aisles are of the same height as the main vault; and the vaults over the aisles are of a novel skeleton construction, consisting of transverse arches which carry beams, with pierced spandrels between, from which, at the centre, spring conoids of masonry to sustain double lateral vaults. The main piers are no more than a series of mouldings, rather than a collection of shafts, and have no capitals, so that the mouldings continue upwards without interruption to form the arches. The great east window (*c.* 1280) is a fine example of curvilinear tracery.

BUILDWAS ABBEY. Cistercian. Ruins. Norman and Transitional (*c.* 1148), as at Fountains. Main arcade with pointed arches, no triforium, and simple round-headed lights above. Early English vaulted chapter house.

CANTERBURY CATHEDRAL (Pl. 7). Benedictine. Nothing remains of Lanfranc's cathedral (1070–77) but the foundations of three apses; nor of Conrad's 'Glorious Choir' (1096–1126). The present choir (1175–80), by William of Sens and William the Englishman, is Transitional, with round and pointed arches. Apart from the lavish use of Purbeck marble shafts, the general character, with its Corinthianesque capitals and sexpartite vaulting, is French (cf. Sens and Noyon). After completion of the choir the next major undertaking was the rebuilding of Lanfranc's nave (1377–1458) by Henry Yevele. Here the emphasis on verticality is most pronounced. The triforium is reduced to a minimum. There are superb lierne vaults with innumerable bosses. This work was completed by the building of the south-west tower (the original north-west tower remained until 1834, when the present Perpendicular tower was substituted).

The supreme achievement was the central—the Bell Harry—tower (1433–97), by Richard Beck, completed by John Wastell. Inside, there is a magnificent fan vault above the crossing. The weight of the tower (235 feet high) necessitated the introduction in the sixteenth century of a series of girder arches.

Of the conventual buildings, the most interesting is the cloister on the north side of the nave, which is Perpendicular and has a remarkable series of heraldic bosses in the vaults. Off this opens the chapter house, with thirteenth-century arcading below and a rich painted timber barrel vault, 90 feet long by 30 feet across, above.

CARLISLE CATHEDRAL. Augustinian. Of the Norman church only two bays of the nave and part of the south transept remain. The choir was built in the thirteenth century and remodelled and completed in the fourteenth century. It is relatively intact, but has been spoiled a little by modern reconstructions. There survives, however, the great east window, which was described by Thomas Rickman as 'by far the most free and brilliant example of Decorated tracery in the kingdom'. It still retains in the tracery the fine original glass, but the nine main lights are modern.

CHESTER CATHEDRAL. Originally a Benedictine abbey church; made a cathedral at the Dissolution. Founded 1093. Of the Norman church only the north transept and lower stages of the north-west tower remain. The choir was built 1200–1350 and the church extended by incorporating a new building, which became the south transept. The nave was built between 1323 and 1492. The choir stalls are outstanding. They are late fourteenth century and incorporate some magnificent tabernacle work.

CHICHESTER CATHEDRAL. Secular Canons. Essentially a Norman church (1088–1148), with considerable Early English additions. The retrochoir, built after fire of 1187, is interesting Transitional work in which there are traces of French influence, especially in the carving of the capitals. The spire was fourteenth century, but rebuilt by Wren and again by Scott. Impressive Decorated windows to south transept. Curiously irregular cloisters on south side with Perpendicular arcade.

DURHAM CATHEDRAL. Benedictine. *A priori* the greatest of our Norman cathedrals and the least altered in Gothic times. Its importance to the student of Gothic architecture largely rests on the fact that it was here that the ribbed vault was first evolved (certainly in England and possibly in Europe), and therefore it may be claimed that here the germs of Gothic may be seen. By 1140 the whole of the cathedral was completed and the choir and nave had been vaulted with ribbed vaults, having pointed, not semi-circular, transverse arches, sustained by flying buttresses which were concealed beneath the triforium roof. In spite of this, the spirit is Norman rather than Gothic. In 1175 work began on the Lady, or Galilee, Chapel (curiously at the west rather than the east end), and this is still Norman in the shape of the arches and their mouldings, though with a lightness and grace suggestive of Gothic; but this was only possible because the arches and columns were required to carry merely a timber roof.

The first major Gothic undertaking was the Chapel of the Nine Altars, by Richard of Farnham, at the east end, which was begun in 1242. Here emphasis is laid on the vertical by using grey polished marble shafts everywhere. The windows, except for the central oriel, are generally lancets, and the Joseph window in the north is a magnificent example of double tracery. The vaulting is a curious combination of quadripartite and sexpartite bays. The last important works were the erection of the Neville screen (1372–80), which was manufactured in London, and the great central tower (Perpendicular), which was erected upon the Norman base storey (1465–1500) and is comparable in style and character to its counterpart in Canterbury.

The cloistral buildings are unremarkable, except for the kitchen designed by John Lewyn, which is astonishing. It is a square room turned into an octagon by four cornerwise fireplaces, with a central louvre carried on ribs to form an eight-cornered star. This technique of vaulting also occurs in Muslim work at Cordova, but has no parallel in England.

Durham, vaulting to kitchen.

ELY CATHEDRAL (Pls. 10, 11). Benedictine. Although Ely is essentially a Norman cathedral, with an exceedingly fine nave and an outstanding Transitional west front, the crowning glory is the octagon at the main crossing, which was built after the collapse of the tower in 1322. This octagon was probably the work of John Ramsey and William de Hurle. It consists of four principal arches rising the full height and width of the nave, choir, and transepts, and four large windows above the level of the arcades filled with curvilinear tracery on the diagonal sides. From the capitals spring eight segments of timber vaulting, the ribs of which are linked by an octagonal collar; this in turn carries a slender upper lantern with a ring of windows. There is nothing finer or structurally more daring in Gothic architecture. The effect of the pool of light in the very centre of the church is stupendous.

Coincident with the building of the octagon, three bays of the choir were reconstructed in characteristic Decorated work. They are very florid and lavishly enriched with cuspings and crockets, and the whole is crowned with a complex lierne vault. The remaining six bays of the choir are Early English (c. 1240) and like, but not so fine as, the Angel Choir at Lincoln. More interesting is the Lady Chapel (1321–49), an almost independent structure on the north-east corner with fine arcading and crocketed ogee arches and canopies. A lierne vault spans the full 40-foot breadth, and the windows are large and curvilinear.

EXETER CATHEDRAL (Pl. 10). Secular Canons. Except for the Norman transeptal towers and the Perpendicular west front, this is a complete Decorated cathedral. Work began at the west end, and the Lady Chapel was completed and vaulted before 1300, the choir was finished by 1310 and the nave by 1350. The plan is completely symmetrical, and the outstanding architectural feature is the vault, which runs uninterrupted (there being no central tower) from end to end. It is a tierceron vault, with eleven ribs spreading from each capital and rising to the ridges, where they are punctuated by a most exquisite and interesting series of carved bosses (*see* C. J. P. Cave: *Medieval Carvings of Exeter Cathedral*). The west front, which was added by William Joy from 1346 to 1375, is unusual. It was built in three planes, and incorporates a great window of complex tracery and a screen of sculptured figures in tiers of kings, saints and angels, all under canopies but much damaged.

FOUNTAINS ABBEY. Cistercian. Ruins. The nave of eleven bays is of twelfth-century Transitional work, having Romanesque piers carrying pointed arches, while above there are round-headed clerestory windows. The new east end (1205–47), which incorporates a transept intended to hold nine altars (cf. similar but later arrangement at Durham), and the tower, which was added in the early sixteenth century on the north side of the main transept, are the most important Gothic parts.

The monastic buildings, also in ruins, are chiefly twelfth century and interesting as examples of Transitional work. There is a fine vaulted kitchen and a refectory with tall, shafted, lancet windows.

GLASTONBURY ABBEY. Benedictine. Ruins. Important largely because of its antiquarian rather than its architectural interest. The most complete fragments of the church are the Lady Chapel (1186–7) at the west end, which is Transitional, and the presbytery, which is thirteenth century. The abbot's kitchen is the only intact building. It dates from about 1440 and consists of a square buttressed block, from which rises an impressive octagonal roof with a central lantern.

GLOUCESTER CATHEDRAL (Pl. 14). Originally a Benedictine abbey church; made a cathedral at the Dissolution. Norman nave of seven bays capped by thirteenth-century quadripartite vault, which springs awkwardly from triforium. The east end and transepts, which are also Norman, were transformed into Perpendicular after 1330 by a most remarkable piece of masonic scenery. The Norman surfaces in the interior were pared off and a thin screen of tracery applied. In the choir the clerestory was added to increase the height by about 20 feet, and a complicated lierne vault was superimposed. The ribs seem like a network of applied decoration. Behind the choir the Norman ambulatory, with its ponderous piers and triforium gallery, was unaltered. At the east end the scheme was finished by an immense Perpendicular window, which was bow-shaped in plan to increase the visible area of glass and at the same time to provide greater rigidity to the structure. This work marks the beginning of Perpendicular architecture, though it may have been inspired by slightly earlier work in the chapter house of Old S. Paul's.

The Lady Chapel, which was built beyond the choir and is reached by a rich vestibule, was constructed nearly 150 years later (1457–83), and echoes the scheme of the choir, but is furnished with two tiny transepts with open minstrel galleries. The central tower (1450–60) necessitated some remarkable internal flying buttresses, which appear across the ends of the arcades, as well as by flying arches across the transepts. The cloisters are the finest in England. They were built (1357–1400) with fan vaults on all four sides, and are probably the earliest examples of this type of construction.

HEREFORD CATHEDRAL. Secular Canons. Chiefly Norman work (1079–1145) and much restored and reconstructed in the last two centuries. The north transept (rebuilt 1245–68) has interesting slender windows and geometrical tracery; the central tower (rebuilt after 1325) is a fine Decorated work with innumerable ball-flower enrichments, and originally carried a timber spire; and the two-storeyed north porch (1520–30) is a fine Late Perpendicular addition.

LICHFIELD CATHEDRAL (Pl. 9). Secular Canons. The great example of Decorated architecture and the only cathedral which retains its three spires, one over the crossing and two over the west front. Nothing of Norman work remains above ground. Building began at the choir at the end of the twelfth century and proceeded down the nave (1250–80); the central tower was built *c.* 1300 and the cathedral finished with the Lady Chapel (1320–36). The nave has pointed arches (sharper than those at Lincoln), a tall triforium, and most unusual clerestory windows formed of three equilateral arcs filled with three trefoil cusped circles. From the floor to the base of the tierceron vaults, triple shafts run up without a break. The Lady Chapel, by William of Ayton, lit by very tall traceried windows consisting each of three lights with trefoils ranged in series above, marks the culmination of Decorated architecture. It is without aisles and terminates in a polygonal apse.

LINCOLN CATHEDRAL (Pls. 7, 9, 12). Secular Canons. Like Salisbury, Lincoln is almost entirely a creation of the thirteenth century. Of the Norman cathedral (1074–92) all that survives is the central portion of the west front. The rest was largely destroyed by fire in 1141 and by earthquake in 1185. Work on the new cathedral began, under the direction of Geoffrey de Noiers, with the building of a choir of five bays with transeptal chapels and terminating in a three-sided apse (1192–1200). The vault is of a most unusual and eccentric form (see p. 111). This work was completed by the building of the main transepts and a central tower. These transepts have sexpartite vaults, and on the north wall there is a remarkable circular window (the 'Dean's Eye'), which is a very advanced example of plate tracery. This should be compared with its opposite number on the south wall (the 'Bishop's Eye'), which was inserted after 1320 and is a notable example of Decorated tracery. In 1237 the central tower collapsed, but work was not stopped and continued down the nave towards the Norman remains of the western end (1235–45). This nave is covered by a very early example of tierceron vault, and the style generally shows a considerable advance on that in the choir. Purbeck marble is used for the shafts throughout, and the foliage on the capitals is exceptionally fine. In 1256 the apse of the choir was taken down and the choir extended by five bays. This section is the famous Angel Choir, so called for its thirty sculptured angels in the triforium. It was not completed until the beginning of the fourteenth century, and is the culminating achievement of the cathedral. The only other works of importance were the completion of the central tower (1307–11) and the belfry stages of the west towers, which were capped in the fifteenth century with timber spires. These spires remained until 1807.

Apart from the cathedral, the outstanding building is the chapter house (1220–35). This is a ten-sided building and one of the earliest polygonal chapter houses in England. It has a diameter of 62 feet and the vault, which is unusually complicated, is dependent on a central pier from which springs a sheaf of ten ribs. The flying buttresses which are a distinctive feature outside were added in the fourteenth century.

NORWICH CATHEDRAL. Benedictine. Founded 1096 and completed in about forty years. The Lady Chapel, which was a rebuilding of about 1250, was removed in the sixteenth century. In 1361 the wooden spire and part of the central tower collapsed, and this necessitated the reconstruction of the choir. Finally (1464–72) the lierne vault was built over the Norman nave. The choir (1362–1499) is the most beautiful part, with its lantern-like clerestory and lierne vaults, sustained outside by a ring of flying buttresses. Unlike the Gloucester choir, the lower stages, that is, the arcade and the triforium, were not touched, so that the effect is of a Late Gothic structure superimposed upon a Norman church. There is a fine doorway (*c.* 1305–10), possibly by John Ramsey, leading from the cloister to the cathedral, with radiating figures on the arch. The cloisters on the south side have tracery of different periods and contain a magnificent series of bosses.

OXFORD CATHEDRAL (Christ Church). Originally an Augustinian abbey church; made a cathedral at the Dissolution. The smallest and most complicated of our cathedrals. It contains fine work of all periods. The Norman church was completed *c.* 1180 and has a remarkable nave and choir design, in which the main arches incorporate the triforium gallery, and subsidiary arches, bracketed from the piers, spring at a lower level to form the arcade. The nave has a panelled timber roof, and the choir a wonderful fan and pendant vault (1478–1503) of a kind that was later to be developed in the Henry VII Chapel at Westminster. In the thirteenth century an Early English Lady Chapel was added to the north side of the choir aisle, and beyond, and parallel to this, is the so-called Latin Chapel (1350–5), with its fine curvilinear tracery. Early in the sixteenth century, the three western bays of the nave were pulled down to make way for 'Tom Quad', and the rest might have followed, if Wolsey had had his way, to make room for a new chapel for Cardinal College.

PETERBOROUGH CATHEDRAL. Originally a Benedictine abbey church; made a cathedral at the Dissolution. Although the main bulk of the cathedral was not finished until 1192, the design is pure Norman, and there is no trace of Transitional feeling. The aisles have quadripartite vaults, and the nave has a thirteenth-century timber ceiling. In 1193–1230 a new west front was added, consisting of three immense portals, of which the central is curiously the narrowest. There are gables above each opening, which preserve their original sculptures and incorporate wheel windows. A small fourteenth-century porch is fitted into the central opening and this, by a passage, leads to the main doors of the Norman nave. At the east end the 'New Building' or retrochoir was erected 1496–1508, ending square and enveloping the lower stages of the Norman apse. It is roofed with one of the finest fan vaults in England.

RIEVAULX ABBEY. Cistercian. Ruins. Of this, the first Cistercian foundation in England, all that remain are the internal arcades and walls of the choir. All is Early English, severe and plain (1145–1203).

RIPON CATHEDRAL. Church served by Secular Canons; promoted to cathedral 1836. Saxon foundation, with original crypt. Church rebuilt *c.* 1180–1230. Chancel completed *c.* 1300. Nave early sixteenth century. All thoroughly restored by Scott in the nineteenth century.

The outstanding feature is the west front, which is Early English and consists of two massive towers (originally capped with spires), with three portals all giving access to the nave. Above this are five lancets, and above them five more, but stepped, and above these again three small lancets filling the apex of the gable. The flanking towers also have lancets, but do not reach much higher than the apex of the gable. The total effect is fine and simple. Inside, the chancel is the most notable part, with beautiful choir stalls. Much of the character is French rather than English. There are tall clerestory windows and a slight triforium passage, and the vaulting shafts run up from the tops of the moulded capitals of the piers to carry a wooden tierceron vault with excellent carved bosses.

ROCHESTER CATHEDRAL. Benedictine. Important for its fine Norman work rather than for its Gothic additions. The nave clerestory and the timber ceiling are Perpendicular (*c.* 1490) and the presbytery and transepts are Early English. The Lady Chapel, situated to the west of the south transept (1500–12), was intended to be finished with fan vaults but these were never built.

St. Albans, junction of Norman and Early English work.

ST. ALBANS CATHEDRAL. Originally a Benedictine abbey church; promoted to cathedral 1877. Although basically a Norman structure, the church embodies features of all periods. The Norman cathedral was virtually finished in 1088, and largely constructed of Roman bricks from Verulamium. Of this the central tower, the transepts and nine bays of the north arcade and three of the south arcade in the nave, remain. In 1195 alterations were begun at the west end by increasing the nave by three bays and adding a new west front. The designer was Hugh de Godelif. Unfortunately the front was drastically altered in the fifteenth century and almost entirely obliterated in the nineteenth century by Lord Grimthorpe. The junction between the Norman work and the Early English on the north side, where the main mass of the pier is Norman and the upper courses and capitals are Early English, is extraordinary. From 1257 to 1325 the choir arm was rebuilt, but most of this was so thoroughly restored in the nineteenth century that it is difficult to say how much is genuine. The Lady Chapel (1308–26) all but completed the church, and this, with its curvilinear tracery and ball-flower enrichments, is a fine example of Decorated. In 1323 five of the Norman piers on the south side collapsed, and the work of reparation of this section was carried out in the Decorated style. Thus, in the nave of St. Albans, we have a curious combination of Norman, Early English, and Decorated work. The last important undertaking was the construction of Duke Humphrey's Chapel (1445), which is one of the most splendid and elaborate examples of Perpendicular work, complete with fine, open tracery and niches and crowned with a fan and pendant vault.

ST. DAVID'S CATHEDRAL. Secular Canons. Impressive Late Norman nave (*c*. 1180–1200) with exceptionally rich Early Renaissance coffered ceiling (*c*. 1520). Choir under tower still retains its screens on all four sides. The presbytery (thirteenth century) shows little advance on the style of the nave, except that the arches are pointed. Farther east the Lady Chapel (1290–1328) was detached from the main building, leaving a curious unroofed space between. This space was roofed over (*c*. 1509–23) by a superb fan vault of the Gloucester type, but much lighter. The outside is uninspiring. West front by Scott; tower, originally low, has fourteenth-century Decorated middle storey and an awkward, slightly overhanging, top storey which was added in the sixteenth century.

SALISBURY CATHEDRAL (Pls. 8, 13). Secular Canons. Remarkable for the symmetry of its plan and the uniform style of its architecture. It is the only cathedral which remains almost exactly as it was conceived, a perfect monument to thirteenth-century Gothic. Only the tower and spire are later. The plan is completely English and owes nothing to Normandy nor to the Île de France. It consists of a nave of ten bays with a porch on the north-west; transepts of three bays, a central tower, then a choir of seven bays with transepts of two bays, an ambulatory or retrochoir and a Lady Chapel. Building began at the eastern end (1220) on virgin soil, and the cathedral was completed and consecrated in 1258. In 1330 the low central tower was raised by Richard de Farleigh to a steeple, the loftiest in England. The erection of this afterthought, which is in the Decorated style, necessitated considerable strengthening to the works below. The imposition of 6,000 tons of masonry on to four slender piers immediately caused movement and settlement. Flying buttresses were built outside, and girder arches, like those at Wells, were inserted across the north and south walls of the crossing.

The inside of the cathedral is remarkable for the quantity of Purbeck marble shafting and for its elegance and lightness. In the Lady Chapel the shafts, nearly 30 feet high and only 10 inches in diameter, jointed in two lengths with bronze annulet rings, carry the ribbed vault and the timber roof above that. The whole of the vaulting is simple quadripartite, and the windows generally are grouped lancets. Architecturally, the weakest feature is the triforium. The space between the top of the arcade and the bottom of the clerestory was insufficient to allow an ordinary pointed arch, with the result that the arches spring obliquely from the capitals and give an unfortunate squat effect.

The cloisters and the chapter house were built shortly after the completion of the cathedral (1263–84). The tracery here is geometric. The chapter house seems to follow in size and general design that of Westminster (1253), and is particularly notable for its series of sculptured reliefs. It is a great advance on the Lincoln chapter house (1220–35), where there are only pairs of lancets on each side. Here the whole wall area between the piers is filled with geometric tracery, producing an effect of wonderful delicacy.

SELBY ABBEY. Benedictine. Nave of eight bays, which is interesting as Transitional and experimental work. Transepts Norman, restored. Tower rebuilt 1908. Chancel of seven bays, Decorated (1280–1320) with some fine windows and glass.

SOUTHWARK CATHEDRAL. Originally a priory for Augustinian Canons; promoted to cathedral 1905. Date of original church uncertain. Retrochoir and tower restored nineteenth century. Nave rebuilt 1838 and again 1890–97. The only original portion is the chancel, which is of the thirteenth century, but this too is much restored.

SOUTHWELL MINSTER. Church served by Secular Canons; promoted to cathedral 1884. The nave and transepts, with towers at west end and crossing, are Norman. The chancel and second pair of transepts are a model of Early English work (1234–60). In 1290 the chapter house, polygonal but without a central column, was begun. The scheme includes a portal, a vestibule and a corridor leading from the chancel. The windows here are triple lancets, grouped together at the head with three trefoils. The sculptured capitals are particularly remarkable for their naturalistic carvings of foliage (*see* Pevsner: *The Leaves of Southwell*). The other outstanding feature is the pulpitum, or rood screen (1320–30), which is vaulted with flying ribs, that is, ribs independent of infilling panels. Below, there is much characteristically intricate carved crocketing and blank tracery. In the fifteenth century the large, unusual west window was inserted in the centre of the Norman front.

TEWKESBURY ABBEY. Benedictine; now a parish church. Nave Norman (after 1087) with tremendously high pillars, from the capitals of which spring fourteenth-century lierne vaults, partly obscuring the original clerestory. The Norman choir was also remodelled in the fourteenth century and new chapels were built around, leaving only the main pillars and the ambulatory vaults relatively intact. Large new windows were built above the arcade, involving the removal of the triforium and substitution of a small walkway at the base; a complex lierne vault completes the scheme. In the fifteenth century a vast Perpendicular window, with pointed arch, was inserted in the west front, rather awkwardly, under the remarkable recessed Norman round-arched central feature.

TINTERN ABBEY. Cistercian. Ruins. The church was completed *c.* 1320 with a nave of six bays (curiously, without any triforium), a crossing with aisled transepts and then four bays in the presbytery, which has a square east end. The style is restrained Decorated with simple geometric tracery.

WELLS CATHEDRAL (Pls. 9, 11, 13). Secular Canons. There is no Norman work, and this is the first all-pointed English cathedral. It was begun *c.* 1175, and the choir, transepts, nave, and north porch were all completed by 1230 (cf. Salisbury, 1220–58). The west front was undertaken 1230–60, and the end capping towers were begun 1365 and completed 1435. Finally the cloisters were added (1430–58). Thus Wells illustrates works from all periods of Gothic and, what is more important, the standard of workmanship and carving throughout is exceedingly high. The nave remains as it was built, with a well-designed continuous triforium arcade (superior to that of Salisbury), and simple ribbed vaults without ridge ribs and with 'stiff leaf' carved capitals to the arcade. The upper parts of the choir were reconstructed by William Joy, together with the building of the retrochoir (1329–43). Here the vaulting is Decorated of the most complex lierne type, and the east wall is incipient Perpendicular, not only in the tracery of the window but also in the way the mullions continue below to form vertical panellings.

The Lady Chapel, built in the first quarter of the fourteenth century, was originally intended as a separate octagonal unit, but by a complex arrangement of Purbeck columns with exquisite foliated capitals was linked and vaulted to the retrochoir.

The west front is the finest in England. It is a veritable sculpture gallery, with insignificant doorways (the main entrance is by the northwest porch). The central tower was built 1315–22, with alarming consequences to the structure below, which necessitated the introduction (1354) of great inverted arches across the choir, the nave, and the transepts. These, with their open circles in the spandrels, are the most sensational features of Wells, and indeed of all English Gothic architecture.

The chapter house, reached by a curiously contrived branching staircase, is one of the most beautiful of its kind. The centre pier is a

cluster of Purbeck shafts, from which ribs ascend to bosses at the
ridge and return to the angles of the octagonal wall with scarcely any
interruption of capitals.

WESTMINSTER ABBEY (Pls. 12, 15). Benedictine. Virtually nothing remains of the Norman abbey. The present building was begun in 1245
and the chancel and transepts were completed within ten years, to the
designs of Henry of Reyns (Reims) and John of Gloucester. From
about 1375 Henry Yevele was working on the nave. The Henry VII
Chapel was built 1503–12, probably by Robert and William Vertue,
and the western towers were built to the designs of Hawksmoor after
1734. Much of the present exterior is the product of nineteenth-
century restoration, chiefly by Scott and Pearson. Architecturally,
the outstanding feature of Westminster is that it is almost entirely
French in style and proportion. It is far higher than any other English
church. The nave is 103 feet high and 38 feet wide, and is restrained
outside by tiers of flying buttresses. The chancel, with its ambulatory
and radiating chapels, follows almost exactly the pattern of Reims.
The windows, with their bar tracery, trefoils and quatrefoils, stem
from Amiens and Ste. Chapelle. The only English features are the
extensive use of Purbeck marble shafting, the herringbone infilling of
the vaults, with their ridge ribs to cover the awkward joints, and the
large triforium galleries.

One of the most extraordinary facts about Westminster is that the
nave, built at the end of the fourteenth century, should have been
carried out in the old (that is, thirteenth century) style of the chancel,
and did not incorporate any of the more fashionable features of the
time other than mere variations to the profile of mouldings.

The *tour de force* of Westminster is the Henry VII Chapel. It consists of a nave and aisles, with five radiating chapels, and buttresses
which are octagonal turrets connected by sweeping fliers and capped
with crocketed domes. The windows form a series of bays, with
Perpendicular tracery which continues as panelling around the buttresses and walls to form an all-over grid. The chapels are fan vaulted
with pendants, and the nave has a pendant vault on rectangular bays
of unsurpassed intricacy and workmanship. It is sheer embroidery in
stone, in which the thickness in places is no more than $3\frac{1}{2}$ inches.

The other notable part of the Westminster complex is the chapter
house, which is octagonal, with flying buttresses, and reached by a
stairway and an inner and outer vestibule. The windows are of four
lights, nearly 40 feet high and 30 feet wide. The original decorative
tiled pavement and some traces of wall paintings survive.

WINCHESTER CATHEDRAL. Benedictine. Of the Norman cathedral
only the transepts and the crypt survive intact. The choir and retrochoir were rebuilt after 1202, and are fairly straightforward Early

King's College Chapel, Cambridge; nave

Plate 15

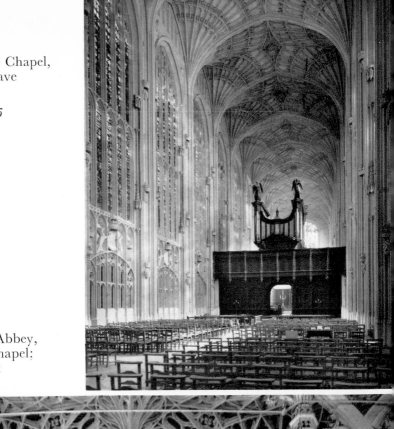

Westminster Abbey, Henry VII Chapel: pendant vault

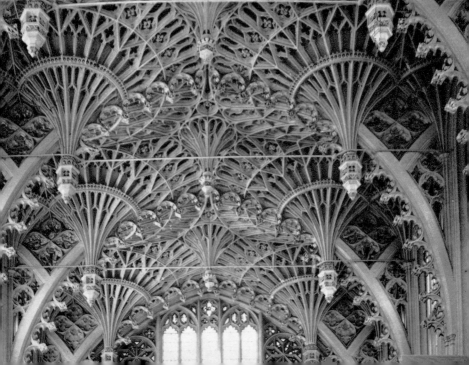

Cologne Cathedral;
from the south-east

Strassburg Cathedral; detail
of west front

Plate 16

English works with later Perpendicular windows and a fine timber vault with carved and painted bosses (*c.* 1505). The west front (*c.* 1360) is uninspiring. The outstanding transformation was the reconstruction of the Norman nave to the designs of William Wynford (1394–*c.* 1450). This is often compared with the Gloucester choir, but at Gloucester only the inner faces were pared and a new skin of masonry applied. At Winchester the nave was completely altered. The old work was cut down and worked into new mouldings, and even the arches were changed, so that only the core of the Norman piers remained intact. These are still sturdy, but are moulded into a new elegance. The Norman triforium is virtually abolished, since the arcade of four-centred arches is carried up to a small pierced parapet, above which rise the stone-panelled bases of the clerestory windows. The whole is covered with a superbly original lierne vault. Also at Winchester there are some good choir stalls (1308–10) and a series of magnificent fifteenth-century tombs and chantries in the retrochoir.

WORCESTER CATHEDRAL. Benedictine. Apart from the crypt (1084–92) nothing remains of the earlier churches on the site. In 1170–80 two western bays of the nave were erected in a remarkably advanced Transitional design. The triforium storey is particularly interesting, with its graded trios of round arches and rosette ornaments under a single pointed arch; this seems to forestall plate tracery, and precedes the Lincoln choir by thirty-five years. This work was followed by the building of the choir and the retrochoir (*c.* 1224–69), and the remaining seven bays of the nave (fourteenth century), which are all characteristic works of their periods but much restored. There is a fine Perpendicular screen to Prince Arthur's Chantry in the south choir aisle, and the cloisters (1404–38) are well preserved Perpendicular work with continuous lierne vaults and good carved bosses.

The really notable features are the north porch and the central tower, which are attributed to John Clyve, who also vaulted the nave (1375–95). The tower is described by John Harvey as 'the finest individual tower design of the whole Gothic period in England'.[1]

YORK MINSTER. Secular Canons. Only the crypt survives of the Norman cathedral. Rebuilding began about 1226 with the erection of the present transepts—the south with a great rose window and the north with the tall lancets of the 'Five Sisters'. The nave was begun in 1291 and completed in 1345. It may be taken as Late Decorated; indeed, the way in which the triforium gallery is linked by the mullions with the clerestory foreshadows Perpendicular. The nave, like the transepts, is exceptionally wide and has timber vaults. Lastly, the eastern arm, the central tower (which acts as an immense lantern at the crossing) and the western towers are Perpendicular.

[1] *The English Cathedrals*, p. 133.

The chief glory of York is in its windows and in the glass which fills them. The grisaille glass of the five lancets in the north transept is succeeded by the rich and colourful fourteenth-century windows in the clerestories and aisles. The west window has complex curvilinear tracery of a pattern which was to be surpassed later at Carlisle, and there is a rectilinear window at the east end, of the fifteenth century, which has double tracery below and presents in 117 panels, each about a yard square, the Bible story from the Creation to the Apocalypse.

The chapter house is also notable. It is octagonal, 58 feet across, without a centre column, and the vaults are in timber imitating stone. Below, there is a delightful arcade with projecting polygonal canopies. Here, too, are grisaille windows, a little later than the 'Five Sisters' and richer and warmer in their colouring.

CHAPTER VIII

ENGLISH PARISH CHURCHES

O F all countries, England is the most remarkable for the number, beauty and variety of its parish churches. They cannot compare in size, as a rule, with those abroad, but they have a distinction of their own. The great number of country examples we possess is due to our insular position, which saved our forefathers from the constant fear of attack from neighbouring States so common on the Continent. The whole of England was dotted with villages, and each had its own church. In some cases the village disappeared and only its church remains, as at Magdalen Laver, Essex. Often the villages touched one another, like Pevensey and Westham, Sussex, where two churches stand within a stone's throw of each other, or Willingale Doe and Willingale Spain, Essex, where two churches share the same churchyard. In France, Germany and other countries, villages were few and far apart. The bulk of the population, for safety, were forced within walled cities. Farmers and agricultural labourers, who lived outside, had in many cases to trudge far to church, as in Brittany at the present day, where in many parts the church serves a large outlying district. Not only are there more country churches in England, but the number in towns is, or at all events was, far greater. Norwich at one time boasted sixty-one churches, and York nearly as many.

The majority of parish churches were small, and their construction and general ordinance differed in many respects from those of the greater churches already described. Almost all had open timber roofs. In France, on the other hand, the majority of town parish churches were vaulted, and there was nothing in their design to distinguish them from cathedrals; in size, even, they were often as great. S. Mary Redcliffe, Bristol, is one of the few in England of which the same may be said. Its plan, with aisled nave and choir, projecting transepts (each with east and west aisles) and Lady Chapel, its elaborate vaults and the internal divisions of its nave and choir walls, belong to a cathedral rather than to a parish church. The number and smallness, as a rule, of English town churches are early evidence of an independence in religious matters which led the burghers to erect a church for their exclusive use. The priest they could regard as *their* priest. And so the churches were crowded together in towns, hemmed in by houses and often hardly visible to the casual passer-by, yet each possessing its own regular congregation.[1]

English parish churches are of various shapes and sizes. Many are the result of piecemeal building and rebuilding over several centuries. Very few retain their original plan. Apart from the addition of towers, porches and vestries, the parish church expanded in length and in width. This lateral extension is one feature which distinguishes the parish church development from that of the cathedral. In length the nave might be extended westwards and the chancel eastwards, but, more significantly, north and south aisles might be added, or increased in width, and commonly chapels were built beyond these, until the final plan had not the remotest resemblance to the original. To attempt to enumerate the many peculiarities in plan resulting from such alterations would be a tedious, lengthy task and also an unprofitable one. The simplest form of church consisted merely of a nave and chancel, with or without a tower at the west end. To this was often added a porch on the south side, and occasionally one on the north as well. In the early centuries of medieval architecture the entrances in parish churches were nearly always lateral; it was not until the fifteenth century that a doorway in the western wall of a tower became customary. With few exceptions, the chancel had a square end and was built without aisles. It was nearly always raised above the nave, and the altar, with very few exceptions, had one or more additional steps surrounding it; in large churches there were often as many as seven, or even nine, steps from the nave to the level on which the altar stood, the number as a rule being odd. In addition to the step or steps at the entrance to a chancel and round an altar, one step west of the altar rail separated the choir from the space reserved for the clergy at the extreme east end. Besides the altar in the chancel there was often one at the east end of each aisle, as is conclusively shown by many existing piscinae in the side walls, although the altars themselves have long ago disappeared.

[1] Occasionally a portion of an abbey church was granted to a parish, as at Chester, where the south transept of the present cathedral was far larger than the north and, with its eastern and western aisles, formed a church in itself.

Vestries were not general until the fifteenth century, and were as a rule placed on the north side of the chancel.

No definite rule can be stated for the proportion of the nave to chancel in parish churches, but roughly speaking, the later the church, the smaller the chancel. The parish church was the people's church, and it was therefore the nave and aisles that were extended, while the cathedrals and abbeys were more the concern of the priests, so that there choir extensions were more usual. In early thirteenth-century work one frequently finds a chancel two-fifths of the total length, as at Cobham, Kent, and sometimes chancel and nave are equal in length, as at Broadwater, Sussex. In churches of the fourteenth and fifteenth centuries a common proportion was three to five, the nave frequently consisting of five bays and the choir, when aisled, of three. In some examples built towards the end of the latter century, the east end was shorter still, thus paving the way for the time when, after the Reformation, the chancel almost disappeared.

The proportion of the width of aisles to nave also varies considerably. In early work the former were generally narrow. In the fourteenth century they frequently approximated to the proportions customary in cathedrals, that is, the width of the nave was double that of each aisle, as at S. Patrick, Patrington, Yorkshire. This church, however, differs from the majority of English parish churches in having transepts of three bays, each with an aisle on both sides, and a lofty tower over the crossing crowned by a spire. In the following century the aisles were sometimes nearly as wide as the nave, as in the fine church of Walpole S. Peter, Norfolk, where the nave is 19 feet 2 inches wide and the aisles 17 feet; and in S. Mary Magdalene, Gedney, also in Norfolk, the nave of which is 21 feet 6 inches wide and the aisles 19 feet 6 inches. In both churches the chancels are without aisles. At Thaxted Church, Essex, the aisles are actually wider than the nave. Occasionally the churches followed the plan of the Dominican Order and had but one central arcade, which divided the church in two longitudinally, as can be seen in the plan of the old church of S. Mary, Truro, one half of which still remains as the outer aisle of the choir of the present cathedral.

The most striking characteristic of fifteenth-century churches is their spaciousness. They were built for congregational worship in the days when the power of the monastic Orders was on the wane, and often at the sole expense of private donors who were laymen. The central idea that governed their plan was the desire to accommodate as many people as possible. With this object in view, both naves and aisles were as wide as could conveniently be spanned by timber roofs; the piers were as far apart as possible and were, moreover, as slender as stability would allow. The western arms of the majority of churches of this period were fitted with fixed seats with ends elaborately carved, and many of these still exist, notably in the western counties.

The internal division of nave, triforium and clerestory, customary in cathedrals, is rare in English parish churches. S. Mary, Redcliffe, Bristol (mostly *c.* 1375–1440) has already been mentioned as the most conspicuous exception (p. 147). This church is vaulted throughout, and although the triforium does not, strictly speaking, exist, there is a considerable space between the arches of the arcade and the windows above, which is treated with elaborate panelling similar in design to that of the choir of Wells, finished a few years previously. Many of the earlier churches have no clerestory windows. In some cases the rafters of the nave roofs are continued down to the aisle walls, so that all three divisions are covered by one roof. In others, the aisle roofs are of considerably flatter pitch, and there is a small portion of walling between the eaves of the nave roof and the top of the lean-to side roofs. This occasionally is pierced with quatrefoils or trefoils. In churches of the first half of the fourteenth century, even such small clerestories are rare. The typical aisled church of that period is lighted entirely from the sides and from the end walls. The aisle roofs are sometimes lean-to, and sometimes double pitched like the nave, so that each end shows three gables. Because of the absence of clerestories, early fourteenth-century churches are invariably low, and this is most noticeable when nave and aisles are approximately equal in width and roofed in the same way. As a result, the churches do not dominate the landscape, but the towers or spires serve as landmarks. The west end of Patrington Church, for instance, is only 46 feet high from the ground to the apex, whereas the spire rises to a height of 170 feet. Such disproportion, if such a term can be applied to what is really a beauty, is never found abroad. The love for length and lowness, so marked in English cathedrals, is still more characteristic of English parish churches.

In the latter half of the fourteenth century, clerestory windows were introduced and became almost universal. In many examples they form a continuous band from the west wall of the nave to the wall over the chancel arch, and when the chancel is aisled they are sometimes continued along that as well. Considering the added light they give, it might have been thought that the aisle windows would have lost their importance and become small. The contrary was the case; they too increased in size. For this the love of stained glass was chiefly responsible. The desire for it was always existent throughout the Middle Ages, and in the fifteenth century it approximated to a disease. Windows reached from buttress to buttress, from plinth to parapet, and walling almost disappeared. The mason became little more than a frame-maker. Notwithstanding the large proportion of glass, the churches were not over-lighted, because the glass was coloured. Neither, from the inside, was there the feeling of insufficiency of wall space which strikes one so strongly now that clear glass has taken the place of the other. Void and solid blended. This was especially the case in eastern counties, where the outside face of the walls of many churches was panelled. But the result outside was not altogether satisfactory, for the elevations often looked flat, because stained glass from the outside has a very opaque appearance, and the difference between the sunk panelling and the pierced is consequently not very noticeable.

It will be obvious from what has already been said that it is impossible to generalize about parish churches as one can about cathedrals. The reasons for the remarkable developments which took place in the building of parish churches in post-Romanesque times can be attributed largely to the establishment of the Orders of preaching friars, which necessitated suitable auditoria, and to the custom of chantry foundations, either by private benefactors or by religious, and later trade, guilds. A chantry is an endowment for Mass to be celebrated at an altar for the well-being of the benefactor during his life and for the repose of his soul after death. The Guild chantries served the same purpose, but on a co-operative or common benefit basis. While the chancel altar itself might serve for a chantry, it was usual to endow separate chapels. The size and magnificence of such chapels is not only an indication of the piety and munificence of the donors, but also a reflection of the relative prosperity of the parish at the time of the building. It is, for instance, in regions such as Norfolk and Somerset, at the time of the development of the wool trade, that the most extravagant and extensive additions were made. Other factors played a part in determining regional characteristics. There was the availability of materials, which encouraged local developments of flint work in East Anglia, granite in Cornwall and brick and timber in Essex; and there was the influence in stylistic terms of the greater churches. At York and Norwich, for example, there were in effect schools of builders, whose influence on neighbouring parish church buildings was considerable. The cathedrals set stylistic standards in details which the parish churches followed, but in one important respect—the development of timber roof design—the parish church designers made a notable contribution.

Open Timber Roofs. The open timber roof, treated decoratively, is almost exclusively an English feature. Most of the basilican churches of Italy have coffered ceilings, and in the few in which the timbers show, as in S. Miniato, Florence, the design is of the simplest character and the only decoration is paint. Even at Verona, where S. Zeno and S. Fermo Maggiore have more elaborate roofs, the inner surface is still panelled. In France, a church of any size is generally vaulted and, as mentioned before, most of the parish churches are large. Some small churches are unvaulted, but the carpentry of their roofs shows little ingenuity in design and not infrequently consists of timbers arranged to form a pointed barrel roof, which is covered on the inside by plain boarding, with or without small ribs reaching from wall plate to ridge. The supremacy of the mason in France, and the square miles of oak forests which England at one time possessed, account to a great extent for the difference between the two countries.

Very few roofs survive in this country from earlier than the thirteenth century, but it is reasonable to assume that the complex systems which were adopted in the fifteenth and sixteenth centuries were the culmination of a series of experiments of which, because of the perishable nature of the material, little evidence survives. It is particularly interesting to notice, however, that in the earliest example—the Bishop's Palace in Hereford—the roof is in fact contrived in imitation of masonry construction. The masons would seem to have determined the fashions which the carpenters followed. Even in the intricate joinery of choir stalls the forms and details of vaulted canopies, complete with buttresses, pinnacles and tracery, all seem to imitate stone construction. At York, Selby and St. Albans the vaults are of timber, but ribbed in imitation of stone.

It is likely that ordinary tie beam construction, with king or queen posts and sometimes ceiled, was the usual method of spanning a large roof. That the pitch was very steep, about 60° or more, can often be proved by an examination of the weather tabling on the east side of the western tower, even although the existing roof may be much later and flatter. Many early roofs were destroyed in the fifteenth century, when the nave walls were raised to form a clerestory. The roofs which took their place were usually of a much shallower pitch, and designed to ensure that the thrust was not too great for the raised walls. Many are nearly flat, and almost invariably all the timbers show from wall plate to ridge. Usually the timbers are large in section and beautifully framed and pinned and, except for the rafters, elaborately moulded. Six inches by four inches is a common size for rafters, and these are generally laid flat so that the width of the underside of each is the greater dimension. All the timbers are oak, and no metal ties or nails were used.

Medieval open timber roofs can be divided into two main classes: (1) trussed rafter roofs, in which there are no principals; and (2) framed roofs, in which the structure is reinforced at intervals by trusses. The second class can be subdivided into tie beam roofs of the king post or queen post type, arched braced roofs, and hammer beam roofs.

In trussed rafter roofs there is no additional supporting framework. The rafters are spaced about eighteen to twenty-four inches apart and usually project beyond the outside wall face to give 'dripping eaves'. They do not, therefore, rest directly on the wall plate, which generally lies along the centre of the wall, but are connected by sole-pieces notched into it and laid across the wall. The rafters are further supported by vertical struts connecting the other, or inner, ends of the sole-pieces. Thus, triangular trusses are formed at the base of every rafter. Each pair of rafters is also united by a collar about one-half to two-thirds above the start of the roof, which may be strutted from the rafters. All the different timbers are halved, pegged or tenoned together. In some examples the struts are curved, like braces, and a wagon or barrel roof is thus formed, which is either pointed or semi-circular. A moulded cornice (the only part of the roof which is not structural) usually conceals the ends of the sole-pieces. The defect of this type of roof was that it did not have an adequate longitudinal tie, there being no connection between the pairs of rafters except at the level of the wall plate and by means of the boarded covering. This weakness was to some extent remedied, in some of those

After Brandon.

Heckington, Lincolnshire, trussed rafter roof, span 10 ft. 9 in.

roofs which had a polygonal or wagon shape, by interior boarding divided into panels with moulded ribs. Considerable care was exercised in the spacing of the timbers, so that all the panels should be approximately square and equal in size. At Wimbotsham Church, Norfolk, there is a good example of a many-sided panelled roof, and in the west of England, in Cornwall especially, there are several panelled wagon roofs, mainly of the fifteenth century.

Roofs with tie beams were used in all the centuries of Gothic art, and were most common in the early work where the high pitch allowed the introduction of king or queen posts, supplemented by curved braces. The function of these posts was to provide struts to carry a longitudinal ridge piece or purlins. The idea of using the king post as a tension member, that is, suspended from the apex of the truss to carry the tie beam, was never considered in the Middle Ages. This meant, however, in the king post truss, that the tie beam was being loaded at the centre, which was its weakest point, and as an alternative a queen post type was often adopted, in which two uprights were introduced, thus distributing more evenly the load on the tie beam. A further expedient was to use a tie beam so shaped that it curved slightly upwards, but more

After Brandon.

Wimbotsham, Norfolk; boarded trussed rafter roof, span 25 ft. 9 in.

After Brandon.

S. Martin's, Leicester; tie beam roof, span 23 ft.

important was the provision of curved braces beneath the tie, which were tenoned into vertical wall pieces resting on corbels.

In the numerous flat-pitched roofs of the fifteenth century, the space between the tie beam and the principal rafters was so reduced that it was often simply filled with pierced or carved panelling. In such cases the tie beams usually rose slightly towards the centre and, in conjunction with curved braces underneath, formed a series of four-centred arches. In all open roofs the ridges were heavy timbers, often elaborately moulded and frequently supported by curved braces which ran longitudinally from principal to principal. In many cases the intermediate purlins were similarly strengthened.

After Brandon.

Starston, Norfolk; arched braced roof, span 21 ft. 10 in.

A type of roof which seems to provide a connecting link between the trussed rafter roof and the framed roof is the arched braced roof. Here the method adopted was to introduce, in place of tie beams, two large curved members rising, as a rule, from the sole-pieces up to the collar and thus forming an arch. Sometimes the collar was dispensed with and the braces were continued from the ridge down the wall face to rest on corbels, some feet below the top of the wall, as, for instance, at Starston, Norfolk.

The most ingenious type of all is called the hammer beam, and this is also the richest. It was the favourite form in England in the fifteenth century, although, like so much of English Gothic, it may have originated in France. Certainly an early example is to be found in Villard de Honnecourt's sketchbook of about 1240; but the hammer beam roof was never so common in France as it became in England, where it was used for both wide and narrow spans. Indeed, at Westminster Hall (1394–1402) over a span of 65 feet we have the earliest and the greatest example of all.

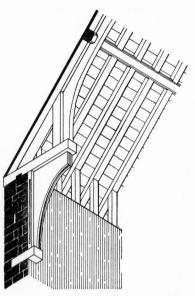

Construction of hammer beam.

The hammer beam truss incorporated features of all the other types discussed. The construction of the foot of each truss is much the same as in a trussed rafter roof, except that the sole-piece projects horizontally into the roof space and is supported by a wall-piece and brace. This extended sole-piece, the hammer beam, then supports a strut and another arched brace. In some roofs there are two or even three hammer beams to each truss, one above the other. At Westminster Hall there is an unusually strong pair of braces, which start from corbels and unite all the timbers (see p. 217). The suitability of the hammer beam roof for wide spans is well illustrated in this building and in the halls of many Inns of Court as well as in parish churches. A hammer beam is preferable to a tie beam whenever the width is greater than a single beam can bridge, since scarfing is avoided and, owing to the science displayed in arranging the timbers so as to transmit all thrusts on to the wall, the interior space is unspoiled by horizontal members.

One feature of Gothic roofs which deserves mention is that the purlins are invariably tenoned into the principal rafters and do not rest upon them as in ordinary modern roofs. This method, though structurally unsound, has aesthetic advantages, since it brings all parts closely together and the mouldings can mitre with one another with excellent results. The trusses generally come over the piers

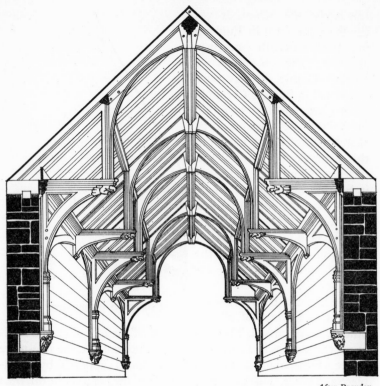

After Brandon.

Trunch, Norfolk; hammer beam roof, span 19 ft.

or solid walling, but occasionally over the windows or arches, in which case they are unrelated to the buttresses outside. At each end, east and west, a half truss is invariably introduced to finish the roof design and frame in the purlins and common rafters.

There are very few open English timber roofs without some carving on them, and all were originally richly painted and gilded. The cornices were crowned by battlements or cresting, and frequently were pierced or carved. The spaces between the timbers of the trusses were filled with similar pierced panels or carvings, and at the ends of the beams in hammer beam roofs were frequently carved angels with outspread wings, while in some cases the actual beams were carved to represent angels with their wings folded. Much of the painted decoration has disappeared, but enough remains in many churches to show how rich and effective it was.

White always entered largely into the colour scheme, and 'barber-poling' in white and green or red and white was a favourite treatment for three-quarter-round mouldings. The boarding between the common rafters was frequently painted white, with sprigs of flowers at intervals, or blue, in which case it was studded with lead stars screwed on and gilded. Similar decoration was applied to the rafters themselves and to the timbers of the trusses, care being taken to counterchange as much as possible, so that although many colours were introduced a broad effect resulted. The richest decoration was generally over the chancel, or in the bay of the chancel immediately over the altar. Either was frequently boarded when the rest of the church was not, and gold was applied in greater profusion there than elsewhere.

In many a small parish church, otherwise of little interest, the roof imparts a distinction which parish churches abroad of similar size rarely possess. Indeed, it might reasonably be said that it was in the design of the roof that the English parish church made its most notable contribution to the sum of Gothic architecture. Certainly it is the roof that provides the most perfect surviving evidence of the skill of the parish church builders, and it was fortunately immune from the destruction that followed the Reformation. Between 1545 and 1547 the chantry endowments were plundered for the privy purse. In 1548 all images were removed, and with them most of the ornaments and treasures of the Church. Wooden tables replaced the stone altars, and many stained-glass windows and paintings were destroyed. Mary Tudor's reign of five years (1553–58) was too brief to restore the splendour of the past. In any case, a change in architectural fashion had already been introduced by the court, at the instigation of Henry VIII and Cardinal Wolsey. The break with the Church of Rome came after the seeds of the Roman Renaissance had been sown in England. It was not a consequence, but it was a coincidence. The Renaissance copybooks became the most valuable tools of the builders, and such Gothic as continued to be built in the provinces was little more than reproduction at second hand of stock details, and lacked the original conviction which had inspired the builders of the Middle Ages.

Towers and Spires. Next to timber roofs, the most interesting contribution made by our parish churches to the sum of Gothic architecture was the design of towers and spires. In England, the striking feature is not their number but their variety. They may be square, oblong, round or polygonal; they may be placed at the crossing, at the end of one aisle, centrally at the west end or even entirely detached from the main building; they may be built of stone, brick, timber, chalk or flint; and they may have been erected over a considerable period of time, so that the base may be Saxon or Norman, the centre mid-Gothic and the top Perpendicular. There are almost as many variations as there are towers. No two are alike, and it is not intended here to do more than cite certain principles which apply to the best.

Usually the tower is built with a slight batter, or inward slope, to the outside face of the walls, to counteract any feeling of top-heaviness. This is achieved by reducing the thickness of the wall by about half an inch for every yard in height. Buttresses may be contrived diagonally on the corners, or at right angles to the walls, and are usually set back a little from the corners. In the best examples these buttresses terminate in crocketed pinnacles. The spiral staircase, or vice, may occur at one corner or be placed on the centre of one side. It usually projects like a turret to give an additional vertical emphasis to the design. The amount of ornamentation by niches, arcading, string courses, traceried windows and belfry lights varies, but as a general rule the topmost storey is richer than the base. Where there is a parapet wall, this may be battlemented and enlivened with gargoyles, pinnacles and blind tracery. The finest culmination of all is the spire. This is the most original and the least essential, in a purely functional sense, of all the features of Gothic architecture. It is, in fact, the most particular contribution of Gothic church builders.

In Romanesque times the towers were usually crowned with steep-pitched, slated roofs, generally square in plan. Nearly all later spires, whether in timber or stone, were octagonal. The usual way in which an octagonal timber spire sits on a square tower is very simple. A trimmer is inserted between each pair of hip

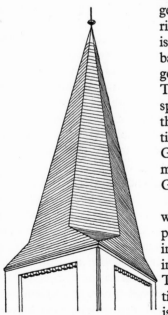

Form of timber spire.

rafters near the base, and from its junctions small trimming rafters are carried to the corner, with ordinary rafters in between. The triangle thus formed covers what would otherwise be an exposed angle. The same form is occasionally worked in stone, but it is most appropriate to wood, where the covering is lead, slates or oak 'shingles', according to the locality. In most stone spires of the thirteenth century in England, each angle is covered by a 'broach', which is an inclined half-pyramid, the top of which dies into one of the canted sides, while the bottom completes the square. The broach and canted sides of the spire are carried on squinches, or corner arches, to form the necessary octagonal base.

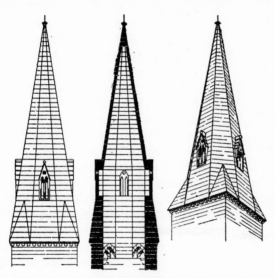

Broach spire.

The chief objection to these spires was that they were extremely inaccessible and difficult to repair, but if a space round the top edge of the tower wall could be kept clear, it could be used for hauling up material from the ground, and if it was protected by a parapet, ladders could be set up against the sides of the spire and would not slip at the foot. This could be done by building an oversailing or projecting parapet, as at Shottesbrook, or by setting the spire back from the tower walls.

In the fourteenth century the latter became the more common method. The tower was finished by a parapet and the spire started behind it. The buttresses at the corners, which had hitherto stopped ·

at the oversailing courses, were now continued above the parapet and crowned by pinnacles, which appeared as miniature editions of the parent spire. A refinement which gave unity to the composition was the linking of the pinnacles with the spire by means of little flying buttresses, thrown from the base of the pinnacles up to the canted sides of the spire. The ultimate audacity, however, was to construct arches springing from each corner pinnacle to form, in the air, a base upon which a spire might be raised. This was done at Newcastle, at S. Giles, Edinburgh, and King's College, Aberdeen.

S. Giles, Edinburgh; detail of spire.

The sides of a stone spire are not more than from six to nine inches thick, according to size. Near the top they are often thinned down to four or five inches. The actual top for a few feet is solid and finished with a finial. All joints are horizontal, a spire being really built up in a series of corbels, and consequently exercising no side thrust, only vertical pressure. Many spires have a slight entasis to prevent the sides from appearing concave, but this is not universal. The arrises, or angles of the spire, often received special attention. Sometimes they might be emphasized by a slender roll moulding, as at S. Mary's, Oxford, and Ledbury. This might be further enriched by ball-flower ornaments, as at Salisbury and the western spires of Lichfield. The most interesting ornamentation was the introduction of crockets. This had a practical purpose, for it provided projections to give ready access to the summit without the expense of scaffolding. These projections are sometimes so obviously spaced that, as Francis Bond states, 'there can be no doubt that they were purposely designed to give foothold to the steeplejack'.[1]

As a general rule, the later the spire, the steeper its slope. The angle of English spires of the thirteenth century is rarely more than 75°, and those constructed of timber are less steep than those of stone. However, the spires of Salisbury, Norwich and Lichfield are about 80°, that of Patrington Church, Yorkshire, a trifle more,

[1] *Gothic Architecture in England*, 1906, p. 626.

and that of Louth Church, Lincolnshire, as much as 85°. Richly ornamented spires are rare in England. The Patrington spire has some arcading round its base, but generally, simple lines are allowed to show from parapet to finial, banded in places, and in the fourteenth century crocketed at the angles. The windows or lucarnes vary in design according to date, but are seldom more than single lights, or pairs of lights, crowned by a gable. On the Continent they may be more elaborate. In France they were often covered with scalloping cut in the stone, and in the fifteenth century the spires were often almost concealed by a network of little buttresses, carved panels, niches and crocketed canopies. In Germany, special attention was paid to spires, and although only a few were built in stone, these were extremely elaborate, while those in timber showed considerable variety.

The question of whether a tower alone or a tower and spire combined is the more effective depends on circumstances. In mountainous districts spires do not look so well unless they stand in a wide valley. At the foot or side of a hill their height is dwarfed by the mass rising above them. In the Lake District in England, most of the towers are without spires, and are broad and stumpy. Spires are most telling on flat or undulating country, and for this reason are especially numerous in the Shires—in Rutlandshire, Northamptonshire, Leicestershire, etc. The Boston 'Stump' is an exception, for it is a landmark for miles around in the Fen District, and is probably more striking than if it had a spire. In towns, towers and steeples are the dominating features, as, for instance, at Oxford, Rouen and almost any other medieval city. S. Bernard, when he forbade towers in Cistercian Houses, missed the opportunity which the Benedictines seized of emphasizing the whereabouts of their churches.

CHAPTER IX

GERMANY

I T makes for a curious confusion that the Goths contributed little to Gothic architecture; that Gothic architecture should more properly be called Frankish architecture. The age of the Goths, the Visigoths and the Austrogoths had long since passed. They had, in the sixth century, supplied a Teutonic infusion to the Roman world and been converted to Christianity. Between 800 and 1200 their contribution to Romanesque art was considerable, but so long as the Hohenstaufen dynasty ruled over Germany the builders clung to the traditions of their forefathers and apparently paid little regard to the changes that were taking place in neighbouring countries. They continued to build churches, for instance at Bamberg, Bacharach and Naumburg, that were practically identical with those of a hundred years before. In the cathedral of Limburg-on-the-Lahn (*c.* 1212–40) the influence of the French cathedrals of Laon and Noyon is seen in the internal proportions, but externally the design is pure Romanesque. When the Hohenstaufen dynasty came to an end in 1254, the crown was made elective, and direct heredity became an obstacle to succession rather than a help. Constant wars followed between rival claimants and their supporters, and the country, for a long period, was split up into what were virtually a number of separate kingdoms, the larger cities also claiming an independence which they had not before possessed. The Hohenstaufen rulers, who spent so much time in their Italian domains, had individually done little to advance architecture in their native country, but under them their dominion was at least united, and one style of architecture was general, even if it was old-fashioned.

The transformation from the heavy Romanesque to the lighter and more graceful Gothic had taken place in France and England in the twelfth century. Original effort on the part of the Germans in the thirteenth century seemed, therefore, unnecessary. In any case, the confusion in government which obtained in Germany made natural progress an impossibility. It is not surprising that the builders of Germany looked to France for inspiration. This may be regretted, for out of the German Romanesque there might have grown a school of pronounced national character. Amiens was taken as the exemplar, and the men of Cologne threw to the winds the old traditions and started German architecture afresh on French lines. Cologne Cathedral was not quite the first church to be built in the French fashion, but owing to its size and importance it exercised an influence on subsequent work which could not have been equalled by any number of smaller buildings. Nevertheless, in spite of French inspiration, the German Gothic architects contributed some important features. To Germany we owe the traceried spire, the popular use of brick and terracotta, and the hall-church. This last was undoubtedly the most important. It involved a nave and aisles of equal, or almost equal, height and produced a feeling of spaciousness which was only paralleled in England in some of our parish churches towards the end of the medieval period. The reason for the hall-church in Germany was probably practical rather than aesthetic, for it would seem that religious developments in Germany were closely connected with the preaching Orders, and this made it desirable to bring the whole congregation in nave and aisles into closer relation with the pulpit.

There was no 'transitional' style in Germany, nor was there an Early Gothic style. At most there was a mixture of German Romanesque and fully-developed French Gothic. At Magdeburg Cathedral the first architect introduced Gothic features, but the second reverted to the Romanesque. The choir, like that of Reims, has polygonal chapels, and was founded in 1212; but the nave, which is later, is Romanesque with widely-spaced piers. At Limburg-on-the-Lahn the plan and general ordinance is truly French, but there is nothing Gothic about the outside; and in the church of S. Gereon at Cologne (begun 1212) there is a remarkable domed nave, carried on semi-circular ribs, over a structure which combines pointed arches, clustered columns and traceried windows, all copied, according to G. Dehio,[1] from the cathedral of Soissons.

Liebefrauenkirche, Trier (Trèves). One of the earliest, and at the same time most perfect, of fully-developed Gothic churches in Germany is the Liebefrauenkirche at Trier (*c.* 1240). Its plan is circular, but by a clever disposition of side chapels it appears cruciform externally. The plan seems at first to be most original and without prototype, but it is in fact merely the result of doubling the east end of the church of S. Yved, Braisne, near Soissons

---

[1] *Die Kirchliche Baukunst des Abendlandes*, Stuttgart, 1884.

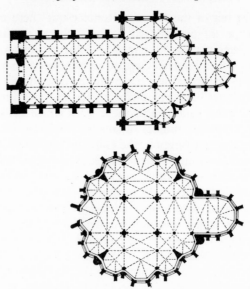

(Above) S. Yved, Braisne, France; (below)
Liebefrauenkirche, Trier.

(consecrated 1216). A similar arrangement occurs at Zanten,
Germany (*c.* 1210). This is not a chevet, for there is no proper
ambulatory, but the chapels radiate and the spatial effects are very
fine. The Liebefrauenkirche has no triforium, and the internal
proportions throughout are excellent. There is a square tower over
the intersection which corresponds to the central dome that
normally occurs in Byzantine work. Indeed, the whole design is
remarkable. The piers are slender and delicate and the vaults are
over 80 feet high, surpassing in many respects the work of the
Île de France. It could be regarded as a logical development of
the Tomb House of Charlemagne, now the old cathedral of Aix-la-
Chapelle,[1] which is about the same diameter, but in place of the
ponderous piers and rounded arches there is all the grace and
refinement of Gothic art at its best.

Cologne Cathedral (Pl. 16). With the building of Cologne Cathedral,
Germany came into line with developments in northern France.
The foundation-stone was laid in 1248, when work was begun on
the eastern arm under the architect Gerard. The design is a clever
combination of the designs for Amiens and Beauvais, and as

[1] Illustrated in Vol. II, p. 133, and Pl. 12.

Beauvais was begun only the year before, and Amiens not yet completed, it is obvious that Gerard must have had access to the drawings.[1] Work progressed slowly and the choir was not completed until 1322. Then the construction of the transepts and nave was begun, but funds failed and when half finished these parts were covered over for service and left. The unfinished portions soon fell into decay, and it was not until the last century that the church was completed. The eastern arm is therefore the only part that belongs properly to the Middle Ages. The original design for the rest existed and was followed with strict archeological accuracy. The result is a complete unity of style and a sad lack of artistic variety. Most of our greater medieval churches were built over the centuries and therefore display an interesting succession of stylistic developments, and it must be admitted that these contribute greatly to their artistic interest.

It must be added that the original design was not without faults, and one can reasonably assume that if the work had progressed at the rate of the building of the choir, there would have been many radical changes. The western arm, although it is the same length as that of Amiens, has double aisles instead of single, and gigantic western towers occupy two of its bays on each side, with buttresses projecting in all directions. These towers are so large and so close together, and they spread out so much, that except when one is immediately facing them they appear to touch. At Amiens the towers were kept comparatively low, and the nave is dominant. At Notre-Dame the western towers also occupy two bays, but the full width of the nave is retained between them, and their buttresses do not spread. Another variation upon the French plan is the large projection of the transepts so that the nave, from most points of view, is swallowed up and only three whole bays stand clear between the transepts and the towers. The eastern arm is the finest part. It is almost an exact replica of the choir of Amiens Cathedral; the dimensions are the same, and the design of the aisle windows of the chevet is practically identical. The plainness of the lower storey acts as a pleasant foil to the later and richer work above. It is all reminiscent of Amiens and Beauvais, and its great width and height, its broken outline and elaborate panelled and crocketed buttresses, produce an extremely imposing effect.

Nevertheless, as a whole Cologne falls far short of its French

[1] *Vide* A. L. Frothingham: *A History of Architecture*, Vol. III, pp. 324–5.

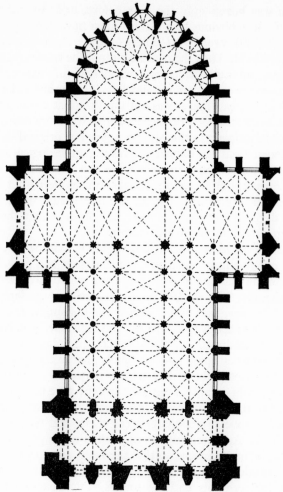

After Sturgess & Frothingham.
Cologne Cathedral.
Scale 100 *ft. to* 1 *in.*

counterpart. Perhaps this is because it is built with such
mathematical accuracy that there is not one inch left for poetry
or for anything irregular or fanciful. The nave, for all its masonic
skill, has a hard, mechanical quality which belongs not to the
period of its design but to the nineteenth century, the period of
its execution. Its almost complete rebuilding after the last war
brings the story of the Gothic Revival up to date.

Strassburg Cathedral (Pl. 16). After Cologne, the most important church designed mainly on French lines was the cathedral of Strassburg. It is much smaller than Cologne, and the eastern part is pure Romanesque. The nave was planned about 1250, and the western front begun, under the direction of Erwin von Steinbach, in 1277. This front is the most noble Gothic work in Germany. Originally the façade was to be square, like that of Notre-Dame in Paris. The two lower storeys were finished in 1298 and the third, which is very elongated, was begun in 1350. On the north side a spire, consisting of corner staircases and a pyramidal series of interpenetrating open octagonal tabernacles, rising to 466 feet from the ground, was erected in 1439. The really magnificent effect of the western front was obtained by the arrangement of free-standing tracery, about 14 inches in front of the main façade, by the open-work gable over the main door and by the marvellously complex and airy filigree work which adorns the tower and spire.

Spires. The Strassburg spire was not the first, nor the last, effort at creating a mason's *tour de force* in open-work tracery. At Friburg, between 1268 and 1288, a single tower was built to mark the termination of the nave, and this was capped by an octagonal spire of exceptional intricacy. At Regensburg (Ratisbon) in 1486 two such spires were built, and at Ulm, about the same time, the greatest of all single steeples was planned, although it was not completed until 1890. It rises over 520 feet from the ground and was probably designed by the architect, Böblinger.

There can be no doubt that the Germans surpassed the French in manual dexterity. They wrought in stone results as wonderful as the Chinese in ivory. The interpenetration of mouldings, if not a German invention, was certainly developed in Germany to a greater extent than elsewhere. The pierced spiral staircases on the outside of the towers of Ulm and Strassburg cathedrals are marvels of technical skill. German canopy work, for mere ornateness, has no equal. The Germans delighted in crockets, finials and fretted parapets, but the pierced spires were their supreme efforts. Openings in spires are occasionally necessary for light, but to produce a termination that is no more than a network of stone, worked out with geometrical science so that it gives the effect of extravagant irresponsibility, is remarkable, particularly when one recalls the severity of the helm roof, which had been the accepted termination for German towers in Romanesque times.

Brick Churches. In the north of Germany, in the cities of the Hanseatic League along the Baltic, and in Poland, there is a series of brick churches of interesting and distinctive character. The walls, the piers, the mullions and tracery bars of the windows, and even the flying buttresses, are of brick. The earliest and most important is the Marienkirche at Lübeck (1270–1310). There is

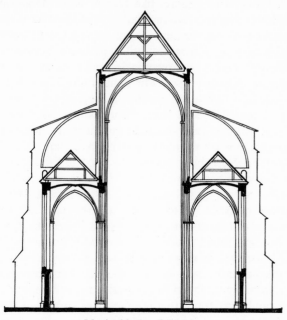

Marienkirche, Lübeck.
Scale 50 ft. to 1 in.

no dependence on French models here, nor is there any apparent connection between the sturdy brick construction and the ornate flights of fancy in masonry to be found in other parts of Germany. The Marienkirche was built by the citizens for themselves, and the plan is as simple as the general ordinance. The nave is 125 feet high, and the side aisles only half as much. There is no triforium, and the arrangement of double-pitched roofs over the aisles has made it possible to carry the clerestory windows right down to the string course above the arcade. This church is worthy to rank in size with the cathedrals of northern France, except that it is short, a fact which, however, makes it more suitable for congregational purposes and which undoubtedly influenced the design of other brick churches erected in the fourteenth century at Luneburg, Wismar, Danzig, Frauenburg in East Prussia, and many other northern towns. In civil and military architecture the independent municipalities within the Hanseatic League developed brick construction in a magnificent and often highly original way. It could be used to produce massive and forbidding effects in the walls and gates of the cities, as at Stendal and the great castle of Marienburg, or it could be used with the most delicate and charming effect, as in the town hall of Braunschweig, where there is an open storeyed portico forming two sides of the city square, and above, a series of dormer gables with open-work tracery to form a first-floor arcade (Pl. 17).

Hall-churches. The most notable contribution made by the Germans to the sum of Gothic architecture was the erection of *hallenkirchen.* These incorporated a nave and aisles of equal height, and were the favourite type of church in North and South

Germany in the fourteenth and fifteenth centuries. It was not an entirely original form, for at Poitiers Cathedral and in southern France churches had already been built on similar lines, but only in Germany was the scheme generally adopted. The earliest example is S. Elizabeth at Marburg (1235–83) (Pl. 17). It is a small and remarkably perfect version of the hall-church. The nave and aisles are exactly equal in height, about 68 feet, and there is, of

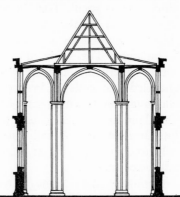

S. Elizabeth, Marburg.
Scale 50 ft. to 1 in.

course, no triforium or clerestory, so that the structure is logically a single storey. In its method of roofing, it differs from most examples which have a single enormous roof spanning over both nave and aisles. At S. Elizabeth the central vault is covered by a high-pitched roof, while each compartment of the aisles has its own little roof of still steeper pitch, hipped in front, which cuts into the main roof at right angles. In some churches, such as S. Severus, Erfurt and S. James, Lübeck, there are double aisles, and yet one roof suffices to cover the whole. Vienna Cathedral, S. Peter, Lübeck, etc., also differ from the Marburg church in that the aisles are a little lower than the nave, the vault of the latter starting about the same level as the apex of the side vaults. All these churches are lit from the aisles and have no triforium galleries.

German architecture is not without faults. The designers were often careless in the way they joined the roofs of the nave and choir. In the Lorenzkirche, Nuremburg, one roof at the east end covers both choir and aisles and rises far higher than that at the west, which is over the nave only. At S. Sebald, in the same town, a similar mistake is made. In Vienna Cathedral the reverse occurs; there the nave roof is higher, and there is a considerable drop to the roof over the choir. That the halves of these two churches were of different dates is no excuse. The want of length no doubt prevented the introduction of transepts or a central tower, which would have concealed the junction.

German churches are usually very short. This is because the choirs are so small. The churches were not monastic; they were built by and for the people, and while the naves are large and spacious the choirs are short, and usually without aisles or ambulatory. The spirit of Protestantism seems to have begun early in Germany, and the long choirs of England or the many-chapeled east ends of France were not wanted. Most German choirs terminate with a semi-octagonal apse. At Erfurt Cathedral the choir has no aisles, and their omission made it possible to introduce enormously tall windows, over 50 feet high, which are enhanced by occurring in a choir which is already raised over a lofty substructure.

Germany stood alone amongst continental countries in the preference for a single tower at the west end, instead of the pair customary in France and England. The great merit of this was that there was a possibility of its being finished. The French in the thirteenth century discovered that a church could have too many towers, and the Germans in the fifteenth century were wise in restricting their ambitions to one. Even then most of the complicated spires which capped these towers were not finished for a century or more, and some have only been completed in modern times.

Towards the end of the medieval period, Gothic architecture in Germany underwent a process of exaggeration exceeding anything in Flamboyant France or Perpendicular England. This took two forms. First, the structural elements were exaggerated and even deformed, and secondly, vegetable and arboreal motifs were introduced in place of tracery, and as wall decoration. In the first one finds the shafts of the columns are twisted spirally up their full height, as in the cathedral of Braunschweig, and tracery weaves across the vaults in an apparently quite inexplicable way. In the second, branches and twigs are carved in intricate confusion over walls and vaults in the manner of Early Victorian rustic furniture. 'There is,' wrote Frothingham, 'more of this sort of architectural debauchery in Germany than in any other country.'[1] Something of the kind, it is true, occurred in Spain and in Portugal. It is the very antithesis of the noble and simple brick architecture of the north, and the great *hallenkirchen* of Lübeck, Marburg, and Ulm.

[1] *History of Architecture*, Vol. III, p. 357.

CHAPTER X

SPAIN

MEDIEVAL architecture in Spain is the product of two civilizations, Christian and Muslim. In the north, Christianity dominates; in the south, Islam. Towards the end of the Romanesque period less than half the country was in Christian hands. The Battle of Tolosa in 1212 marks the beginning of the decline of Muslim influence, but it was not until 1492, with the capture of Granada, that the Moors were finally expelled from the peninsula. Christian Spain was, therefore, regaining its freedom at the time when medieval art was making its greatest advance in other countries, so that the absence of a national school of architecture is not surprising; nor is the fact that the dominating influences in the monuments of Spanish medieval architecture should be French in the north and Moorish in the south.

French Gothic was imposed on Spain just as French Romanesque had been imposed a hundred and fifty years before. But the influence was no longer monastic, for in the thirteenth century it was the secular bishops who were the chief patrons of art. Three great cathedrals were begun: Burgos (*c.* 1221), Toledo (*c.* 1227), and León (*c.* 1250). All were built in that cosmopolitan style which had originated in the Île de France, and all were evidently designed and, doubtless, partly built by French masons. There is no gradual or native evolution of a style, but instead the sudden appearance of a fully-fledged Gothic.

Two features are particularly Spanish: one is the *cimborio*, or dome enclosed by a lantern tower, at the crossing, which was a legacy from Romanesque times; and the other is the *coro*, a choir, which was a completely separate structure and often blocked up the nave, but provided a degree of privacy and dignity during services while still permitting easy circulation around it. The alternative method, used in England, of extending the eastern arm for the choir, was never followed in Spain. The origins of the horseshoe arch in Spain are still uncertain, though it is now generally held that it was not a Muslim introduction. It is to be found in early Visigothic works long before the Wars, and may be traced much earlier in the Near East. It was simply adopted by the Muslims and Christians alike. Of much greater interest is the possible extent to which such essentially Gothic features as the ribbed vault, the pointed arch, cusping and tracery may be linked to Saracenic sources.[1]

Although the cathedrals of Spain were usually secular, that is, served by canons rather than by monks, they are as a rule fully equipped with cloisters, chapter houses and the like for regular community life. In contrast to the French emphasis on height and the English emphasis on length, the Spanish cathedral impresses by its horizontal extent in all directions. In some degree this is due to the multiplication of ironwork screens and the addition of chapels and sanctuaries beyond the normal limits. Spain received its inspiration from many sources, and at the same time produced works of great distinction. Much that was Gothic has since been enveloped in Renaissance and Baroque trimmings; for the prosperous age of Spain came with the discovery and conquest of America. By that time the medieval world had passed.

Burgos (Pl. 18). Burgos Cathedral is almost contemporary with Reims and Amiens and was founded one year after Salisbury. It was commissioned by Bishop Maurice, who is said to have been an Englishman; but he was probably 'English' only in the sense of coming from the English provinces in western France, which were still under the English crown. Certainly the plan and general ordinance of Burgos are French rather than English and have much in common with Rouen and Bourges, though there is none of the French penchant for height and there are other features which give Burgos a specially cosmopolitan air. The open-work spires which crown the western towers are German; they are the work of Hans of Cologne in 1442. The crowning glory is the cimborio over the crossing. This is even later (after 1539) and belongs to that transitional style in which Gothic design was combined with Renaissance detail. At the extreme eastern end is the Constable's Chapel, which was erected about 1487 and is one of the most sumptuous examples of the Late Gothic or 'Plateresque' style. Here is the wonderful open-traceried stellar vault, which was designed by Simon of Cologne, the son of Hans. The vault over the crossing of the cathedral, which was completed

---

[1] For an introduction to this subject, see especially *Cathedrals of Spain*, by John Harvey, 1957.

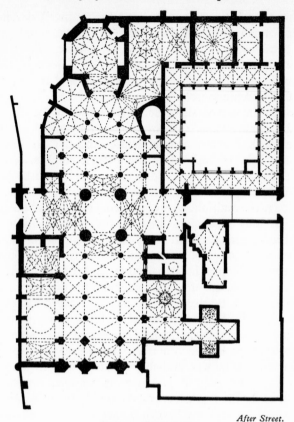

Burgos Cathedral.
Scale 100 *ft. to* 1 *in.*

After Street.

by Juan de Vallejo in 1568, is likewise of open tracery, and follows
the pattern of the Constable's Chapel. It is the last great Gothic
work at Burgos.

Toledo. The cathedral of Toledo, a church with double aisles, is
one of the largest in the world. Only Seville and Milan surpass
it. Its width is 178 feet—equal, in fact, to the widths of Amiens
and Salisbury combined. The plan resembles that of Notre-Dame
(p. 87), for both have transepts which scarcely project at all,
and both have double ambulatories. At Toledo the arrangement
is most peculiar, for instead of having trapezoidal compartments
there is an arrangement of alternating rectangles and triangles.
This type of ambulatory is illustrated in Villard de Honnecourt's

S. Elizabeth, Marburg;
from the north-west

Plate 17

Braunschweig Town
Hall

Burgos Cathedral

Plate 18

Palma, Majorca; south fror

sketchbook, and it is suggested by Camille Enlart[1] that de Honne-court's brother archi-tect, Pierre de Corbi, might be the Petrus Petri, who is buried in the cathedral and who was for a long time Master of Works at Toledo.

Toledo is one of the most impressive cathedrals in Europe, even though it is so hemmed in by other buildings that it is difficult to obtain a

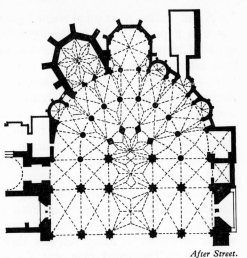

After Street.

Toledo Cathedral, Apse.
Scale 100 ft. to 1 in.

good general view. The north-west tower and spire is Late Gothic (1428–79) and unlike any other in the Gothic world. The south-west tower, unfortunately, was only built up to the first storey and in the seventeenth century was finished with an Italianate dome which is quite out of keeping with the rest. The inside, with its six-light clerestory windows and its carved choir stalls enclosed within a rich masonry screen, is the most gorgeous in Spain.

León. The cathedral of León follows very closely the plan of Reims, but is constructed with an audacity almost equal to that of Beauvais. It is the most truly Gothic cathedral in Spain. Like Beauvais, it is a cathedral without walls, having not only a glazed triforium but also a high clerestory which occupies the whole space between the slender piers up to the arch of the vault. As at Beauvais, it was soon discovered that too small a margin of safety had been allowed, for within a couple of hundred years the building was collapsing and the triforium and clerestory had to be walled up. In 1631 the vault at the crossing collapsed and an incongruous dome was erected over the ruins. In 1865 the south transept had to be completely rebuilt, and from 1880 to 1901 the rest of the cathedral was thoroughly restored and various Renaissance accretions removed. In spite of all these tribulations,

[1] *Manuel d'Archéologie Française*, 1902–4.

León still retains its original stained glass, so that today it looks much as it probably did in the fourteenth century. It is like a splendid lantern, and even France has nothing to compare with it in extent of colour. It has been computed that there are over 2,500 square feet of glass, and nearly all of it dates from the thirteenth and early fourteenth centuries. Architecturally, León does not surpass the cathedrals of northern France, but it does mark the highest level reached in Spain in the style of the Île de France. Subsequently the Spaniards sought their inspiration from nearer home—from the great aisleless churches of Albi and Toulouse.

Catalan Gothic. In the fourteenth century, Catalonia, with Barcelona as its capital, was the centre of the most remarkable architectural activity in Spain. Here were built stone churches which surpassed in many respects their brick counterparts in Languedoc. The usual plan was aisleless, with deep internal buttresses enclosing chapels, with no transepts, and a chevet at the east end. The vaulting, as a rule, was of the simplest quadripartite form, but enriched by large pendant bosses. Over the side chapels there were sometimes galleries, connected by arched openings which pierced the deep buttresses. Windows were tall and narrow and there was little ornamentation.

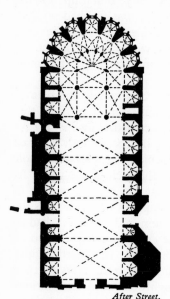

After Street.

Gerona Cathedral.
Scale 100 *ft. to* 1 *in.*

The naves were exceptionally long. At Barcelona the church of S. Maria del Pino (*c.* 1329) has a nave 54 feet wide, about the same as Albi's and greater than that of any English cathedral, with chapels on each side, but no aisles. At Gerona Cathedral the span is 73 feet, excluding the chapels, and the height 117 feet. No vaulted building of such dimensions had been attempted since Constantine built his basilica in Rome. The east end of Gerona was built first (*c.* 1312–66) by the French architects, Henrique, and Jacques Favran of Narbonne, and in itself presents nothing of particular interest, being divided into central and side aisles with radiating chapels round a semi-circular end. Then, in 1417, the great nave of four bays, equal in width to the nave and aisles combined, was begun by Guillermo Bofill. The idea of adding an aisleless nave to a conventional choir was not a new one, for it had been done two or three centuries earlier at La Trinité, Angers, and S. Radegonde, Poitiers, but these are far inferior in size to the Spaniards' masterly *tour de force*. The problem to be solved at Gerona was how to provide space for a large congregation with an uninterrupted view of the High Altar, and in no other example has this been more successfully accomplished. At Barcelona, besides the church of S. Maria del Pino already mentioned, is the still larger S. Maria del Mar (*c.* 1328), designed with the same aim in view, but in a different manner. This church has aisles and consists of a nave of four great bays, each over 40 feet square, with a narrow eastern bay, and an apse beyond surrounded by an ambulatory. There are consequently only four piers to each side, and these naturally offer little obstruction.

While this church, and others in Barcelona, were planned for congregational worship, the cathedral was especially arranged for private devotion. There are as many as twenty-seven chapels inside the cathedral, arranged round the chevet and opening out of the aisles of the nave, and, as though these were not enough, no fewer than twenty-two more are grouped round the sides of the cloister. It is not a particularly large cathedral, but the immense height of the pier arcade makes it appear greater than it is. The section is more interesting than the plan. The columns rise without a break 55 feet above the pavement. The nave vaults (84 feet) and the aisle vaults (55 feet) spring from the same band of capitals, the difference in height being the result of the greater width of the nave. It is the enormous height and slenderness of the piers of Barcelona Cathedral, and other later Spanish churches, which is most striking. In English cathedrals the piers are notoriously

After Bevan.

Barcelona Cathedral. Section.
Scale 50 ft. to 1 in.

short, the height of 30 feet at Westminster being exceptional. In northern France the piers are higher, but not equal to those in Spain. In Amiens Cathedral the piers are 48 feet high, being one-third of the total height of the nave; even Milan Cathedral, with its height of 157 feet, has piers only 55 feet high. Barcelona Cathedral is a masterpiece of Catalan Gothic, and although it was begun in 1288 and not completed until 1420, it is amazingly uniform in its style and treatment. The same system was followed elsewhere, at Manresa (1328), Tortosa (1347) and, on an even grander scale, at Palma (*c.* 1300–1500) on the island of Majorca.

At Palma (Pl. 18) the limits of Gothic structural skill were reached. Like Barcelona, it was built over a period of more than two centuries, and remains a wonderfully unified conception. From the outside, the great nave, which is higher than that of Amiens, is supported by a series of gigantic storeyed buttresses, while the aisles, which are higher than the nave of any English cathedral, are sustained by lesser buttresses, three to each main bay, ranged so closely along the sides that the spaces between scarcely equal the width of the buttresses. The effect is formidable in its sheer massiveness and weight of masonry. Inside, in spite of the narrowness of the windows, the effect is staggering. There is no chevet, no crossing, no transepts and no triforium gallery. It is simply a vast box, a stupendous volume of space 364 feet long, 182 feet across and vaulted to a height of 141 feet, the only interruptions being fourteen slender octagonal piers.

Mudéjar. In those districts which had been reconquered by the Christians and which still retained a large Muslim population, there developed an architecture which is called Mudéjar. It is chiefly limited to the smaller churches, and could be called a vernacular architecture, forming a link between the Christian north and the Muslim south. Muslim taste seems to have survived in the Courts of Spain, and many of the stylistic features of Islamic architecture were kept by the Christian conquerors. Much of the work was, indeed, executed by Muslims who were carpenters, masons, plasterers, etc., and continued their traditional skills whether they had been converted to Christianity or not. The architecture is often of brick and plaster, and the horse-shoe and lobed arches are common. The surfaces of the walls are often decorated with geometric and intersecting arches and with glazed terracotta tiles in a curiously Oriental manner. One of the most remarkable examples of Mudéjar work is the cloister of San Juan

del Duero at Soria, which is of the early thirteenth century. It
is not Gothic, it is not Muslim; it is a mixture of the two. In
Aragon, belfries are the most striking examples of Mudéjar work.
Often they are detached, like Almohade minarets. They are
generally square, without buttresses, and profusely decorated with
surface patterns in brick and terracotta.

Late Gothic. Throughout the fifteenth century and far into the
sixteenth, Gothic architecture persisted in Spain. In 1402 the
largest of all the Spanish cathedrals, Seville, was begun. It consists
of a huge parallelogram, 460 feet long and 295 feet wide, with a
nave 132 feet high. It was completed about 1520, that is, a century
after the Renaissance movement in architecture had begun in
Italy. Architecturally, in spite of its size, its heavy moulded piers
and high arcades, it contributes little to the development of the
Gothic style.

In 1513, at Salamanca, a new cathedral was planned alongside
the old twelfth-century cathedral. Here at a glance may be seen
the limits of national development. The new cathedral covers six

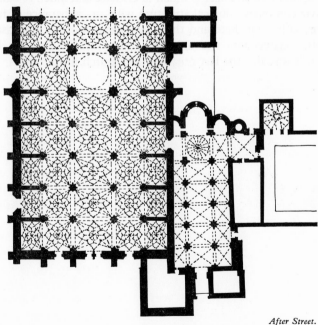

After Street.
Salamanca Cathedral, showing old cathedral bottom right.
Scale 100 *ft. to* 1 *in.*

times the area of the old, and has much in common with Seville. It is a gigantic rectangle, consisting of a nave, aisles, and side chapels set between buttresses. In place of a triforium there is only a small balustraded gallery. The rich mouldings of the piers are carried up and continue, with only the slightest interruption of narrow capitals, up to the most complex lierne vaults. The detail is very mixed; the windows are Renaissance in character, there are Italian pilasters, and the cimborio is plastered and painted with cherubs, flashing rays and gilt scallop shells of monstrous size. Its architect, Juna Gil de Hontañón, designed, a few years later (1522), a cathedral in much the same style at Segovia. This was the last great Gothic undertaking in Spain. Its site on the top of a ridge in the centre of the city is superb. It is a little larger than the new cathedral of Salamanca, and is superior in having a chevet in place of a square east end. But there is little else to distinguish the two cathedrals. Both have the same pinnacles, buttresses and parapets, the same nearly flat roofs and cimborio over the crossing, and the same complex vaults without ridges but with capricious waving lierne ribs. There is much to criticize and much to admire. Segovia combines a logical structure with an exuberance of fancy in the vaults, and here and there incongruous proto-Renaissance details. Segovia was not only the last great Gothic church in Spain; it was also the last great Gothic church in Europe.

CHAPTER XI

ITALY

ITALY is not famous for its Gothic architecture. The reasons are obvious: there are the remains of the marvellous works of the Romans; there are the great Romanesque churches, such as S. Ambrogio, Milan, S. Miniato, Florence, and Pisa Cathedral, which marked important stages in the story of architectural development in Europe; and there are the monuments of that Renaissance movement which had its beginnings in Florence and which forms the basis of the fourth volume of this History. Nevertheless, in spite of its lack of recognition,[1] Gothic art in Italy had many interesting and important features. It was Gothic with a difference: Gothic in coloured marbles; Gothic freely interpreted by artists like Giotto and Nicola Pisano; Gothic in domestic and palace architecture having no parallel in the rest of Europe.

It was inevitable that the architecture of medieval Italy should differ widely from that of other countries in the West. In Rome the basilican plan and ordinance had for so long been accepted as the only possible solution for churches that it naturally affected subsequent progress. At Pisa and in the neighbouring cities a school of building, based partly on basilican and partly on Byzantine models, had been perfected, and this mode persisted in the thirteenth century. In the church of S. Caterina, Pisa (c. 1250) (Pl. 19), for instance, the western façade is like that of the cathedral, even to the irregular spacing of the arcades, although the upper arches are pointed and not semi-circular. The crowning feature of Byzantine architecture, the dome, which was common in so many Romanesque churches, is still a feature of Italian Gothic. At Siena, the dome over the hexagonal crossing was finished about 1265; at Florence a dome was planned in the fourteenth century but not built until the fifteenth; and in S.

[1] In the mid-nineteenth century John Ruskin, in his *Stones of Venice*, and George Edmund Street, in his *Brick and Marble Architecture in North Italy*, to some extent popularized Italian Gothic and encouraged the adoption in England of many of its stylistic peculiarities. Since then, the subject has not had the study it deserves.

Petronio, Bologna (*c.* 1390), a dome equal to that in Florence was contemplated but never built.

Gothic architecture came late to Italy, and the Renaissance began in Florence a hundred years before it obtained a sure footing in France and nearly two hundred years before it swept England. The result is that Gothic art in Italy is virtually limited to two centuries. Nor was the semi-circular arch abandoned. The tower of S. Gothard at Milan, which is purely Romanesque, is of the same date as the choir of Gloucester. In the middle of the fourteenth century the nave of the cathedral of Lucca (S. Martino) was re-built with round arches. There are round arches in the Florentine Loggi del Bigallo (*c.* 1360) and dei Lanzi (*c.* 1375); and so strong is the Classical feeling in these buildings that one hardly knows whether to regard them as evidence of a lingering tradition or as forerunners of the Renaissance.

There were many influences which gave a peculiar characteristic to the arts of Italy. Unlike France and England, Italy was not a nation. It formed a part of the Holy Roman Empire at a time when imperial power was weakening and Papal authority was slight. Indeed, for seventy years (1307–77) the Popes were absent from Rome and were established at Avignon under the control of the kings of France. The result was that the north of Italy resolved itself into congeries of a few powerful city states: Venice, Milan, Florence, and Genoa; in the centre were the so-called Papal States, and in the south lay the Kingdom of Naples. The northern half of the country was thus divided into a number of small, autonomous republics, and this resulted in the development of what is essentially a civic style, a style in which the ducal palace at Venice and the town halls of Florence, Siena, Cremona, and Udine are the material expression. The churches have none of the spiritual mystery of those of France and England, but are light and airy halls with only a little trace of Gothic inspiration. The use of marble had an important effect on their design and led to a much more delicate treatment and a greater regard for sur-face qualities. Finally, there was the special status of the designers in Italy. In many cases they were not only architects, but also painters and sculptors. Margharitone of Arezzo (*c.* 1260) seems to have practised all the arts. Nicola Pisano, who lived about the same time, was eminent as a sculptor and as an architect. He ignored to a great extent the work of his predecessors and took antique forms as his models. His son, Giovanni, relied more directly on nature; but there is little, if any, trace of Gothic inspiration in the work of either. Giotto (1266–1337) is best known as a painter, but he was also the designer of the campanile of Florence Cathedral, which John Ruskin thought 'the loveliest raised on earth under Christian influence'.

Early Gothic Churches. Most of the churches in Italy which bear the closest resemblance to the Gothic of the north and west were built in the first half of the thirteenth century. In some, foreign masons were employed, as at S. Andrea, Vercelli (1219), which is attributed to a Parisian priest who became first abbot of the monastery.[1] The clustered piers and subordinated arches are not Italian, and the plan, with its square east end and apsidal chapels to the transepts, is English rather than French, but the tall octagonal cupola over the crossing shows that the designer, whoever he was, did not depart entirely from local practice. In the arcade the arches are pointed, but elsewhere they are round. Externally all the arches are round, and the structure is in the style of Pisan Romanesque. The octagonal cupola is thoroughly Italian. Another work which is attributed to outside influence is the great double church at Assisi. This is supposed, according to Vasari, to be the work of a German architect—Jacopo d'Allemagnia— but as the Gothic mode had not then (*c.* 1228) reached Germany, it is not likely that the design came from there. The lower church is dark and gloomy, with vast cylindrical piers and no mouldings. The upper church, which is said to have been finished in 1253, is simple and brilliant, with very large bays, and is enriched by the paintings of Giotto and Cimabue; the most exquisite mural paintings in the world. Outside, the semi-circular buttresses are reminiscent of Albi Cathedral, but if the dates given are correct, the Italian church was earlier. Of the other Early Gothic churches, S. Maria sopra Minerva (*c.* 1280) is the only Gothic church in Rome; and in Venice there are only the churches of the Frari and SS. Giovanni e Paolo (both *c.* 1260), but neither is really satisfactory. They are plain and simple, but insipid. The bays seem unnecessarily wide, the columns are mean, and the flat pilasters which carry the vaults are weak and meagre. In the second half of the thirteenth century, however, at Verona, Siena, Orvieto, and Florence, and in the fourteenth century at Lucca

[1] Simpson, and Fergusson in his *History of Architecture in All Countries*, 3rd ed., Vol. 1, p. 610, attributed this building to an Englishman named Brigwithe, but this ascription is not now accepted.

and Milan, cathedrals were built that provide material evidence of the pride of the city states, and show that Italian Gothic architecture, although different from the Gothic of the north and west, at least had distinctive merits. Of these, Siena, Florence, and Milan may be taken as representative of the highest achievements.

Siena Cathedral (Pls. 19, 20). In the cathedral of Siena we find Italian Gothic fully developed, and a complete absence of distinctly foreign details; although even here there is a campanile that harks back to Romanesque precedent. The church was one of the largest undertakings in Italy since the building of the cathedral at Pisa, but no sooner was it completed than the builders decided that its size should be more than doubled by making the present cathedral merely the transept to a much greater church. In 1339 an enormous nave, of which parts still survive, was begun on the south side. The scheme had to be abandoned, however, partly because of more or less constant wars with neighbouring States, but chiefly because of the advent of the Black Death in 1348. The plan of the present church is complicated by the intrusion of the campanile into the south transept, and by the irregular hexagon which forms the base of the dome. The sense of space and the variety of perspective which this hexagon produces is quite remarkable, and much more impressive than the equivalent area at Ely. The columns and the walls are built of layers of black and white marble, giving a startling zebra-like effect. The floor is also of marble and decorated with the celebrated *graffiti*. These consist of designs inlaid in colour and in black-and-white, representing scenes from the Old Testament.

The west front is attributed to Giovanni Pisano, and dates from 1284, although it was not finished until long after his death, and some of the mosaics and carvings are modern. By some this front is considered the most splendid achievement of Italian Gothic. It certainly illustrates very completely the character of the style—its merits and its defects. It is symmetrical and there are three equally important portals, that in the centre coinciding with the axis of the church. The other two are not central with the aisles, and nearly every detail is unrelated to the cathedral behind. There are three great triangular gables, filled with mosaic, but they bear no relation to the shape of the roofs which they screen. The side gables are not on the same axes as the portals of the aisles. The central gable has an enormous circular window which fits into a square compartment wider than the central portal. On either side of this rises a turret, not from the ground but from a strong string course which gives a marked horizontal emphasis to the whole. Everywhere there is sculpture and inlaid marble and mosaic. It is a gorgeous piece of confectionery with no trace of the seriousness and structural reasoning which underlie the work of Central France. Nor is there the overwhelming mystery and up-surge of towering masonry. The spirit which contrived the front of Siena and, say, the front of Amiens, was totally different; but not more than one might expect when one realizes the causes—social, economic, material, and climatic—that distinguish medieval France from medieval Italy.

Florence Cathedral (Pl. 20). S. Maria del Fiore, Florence, is one of the largest cathedrals in the world, and was begun on 8 September 1296 by Arnolfo. It is not known how much of the final design is his, for he died five years later, but he probably left a model of the church. Arnolfo was succeeded by Giotto in 1334, by Andrea Pisano and Tolenti in 1350 and by Brunelleschi who, in 1420, began the construction of the great dome. The lantern was finished in 1462 and the west front was not faced until 1887. The building may therefore be taken as almost contemporary (even to its completion in the last quarter of the nineteenth century) with the cathedral of Cologne, which is about the same in area.

The plan is extraordinary. It consists of a long nave and aisles, culminating in an octagonal space nearly equal in diameter to that of the Pantheon in Rome. From this space three apsidal arms project to the north, east and south, resulting in a trefoil plan almost Byzantine in character. The interior is devoid of decoration, but the outside is entirely panelled in marble and there is a total absence of buttresses or pinnacles, and very little of Gothic character except the dome which, although undertaken by Brunelleschi, the first great Renaissance architect, is constructed of ribs and panels on true medieval principles. On the south side of the cathedral, but detached from it, is the famous campanile which was begun by Giotto only two years before his death. It is square, with octagonal buttresses at the corners, and is of five storeys entirely faced with marble. Giotto's original model included a spire, but this was never built, since the later architects considered it too Germanic and old-fashioned. Opinions vary upon the merits of the campanile, from the extreme praise of

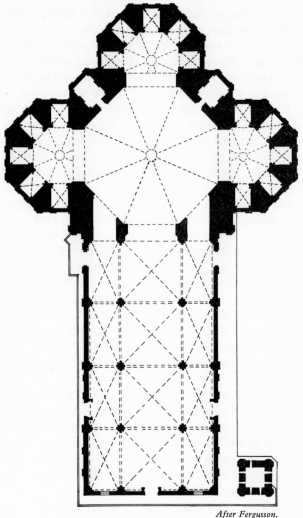

After Fergusson.

Florence Cathedral.
Scale 100 *ft. to* 1 *in.*

Ruskin to complete condemnation;[1] but all agree about its novelty and the merits of the relief sculpture in the lowest storey.

[1] Simpson considered the tower top-heavy, and thought that as Giotto had not finished it he should not be blamed. Fergusson considered it positively ugly; but Lethaby thought it one of the most perfect structures in the world, and T. G. Jackson declared it to be a triumphant work of lovely architecture.

Milan Cathedral (Pl. 21). The cathedral of Milan is the largest of all Italian cathedrals except S. Peter's, Rome, and is beyond doubt the most remarkable. It is a double-aisled church, like Bourges Cathedral in its gradation of the aisles, but it has no triforium storey. It is built all of white marble, even to the tiles of the roof. These are laid to a very low pitch, which accounts for the small amount of wall space between the tops of the arcades and the clerestory in both the nave and the aisles. The clerestory windows are small and insignificant, but the side windows in the outer aisle walls are of great size, rising to a height of 70 feet from the floor, and from these most of the light in the church is obtained. The tracery, especially at the east end, is more fantastic and illogical than any to be found in France or England. One curious fact about Milan Cathedral is that the top line of windows does not light the interior at all, but merely the space between the top of the vault and the tiled roof covering above. This is because the vaulting is very domical transversely. There can be no doubt that if the ridge of the vault had been level and allowed these windows to light the interior, the improvement would have been immense. As it is, this top range of windows is useless from the inside and of very little value outside, since it hardly shows because of the height of the aisle walls and the crowd of pinnacles, flying buttresses and pierced parapets which cover the front.

The outside of Milan Cathedral must be seen to be understood. Full of faults, with detail coarse in the extreme, its mass, its pinnacles and the white glitter of the marble render it a most striking contrast with the quiet simplicity of the Romanesque church of S. Ambrogio. The cathedral is all shout and glitter and finery. The inside is far finer than the outside. The lofty piers are crowned by capitals shaped like fonts and enriched with figures over life size. These capitals are about 20 feet high—as big as a small house. The great width and height of the church, the vistas across it, the dazzling rays of sunlight which, at morning and evening especially, stream through the great aisle windows, all conspire to make it one of the most wondrous interiors in the world. Much has been said in abuse of the painted vaults, but as they deceive no one they ought to displease no one. Nobody who knows anything about vault construction can suppose for a moment that the lines he sees on the vault are structural, that they are anything but painted. It may not be a high form of decoration, but it helps the general effect and certainly does not detract from it.

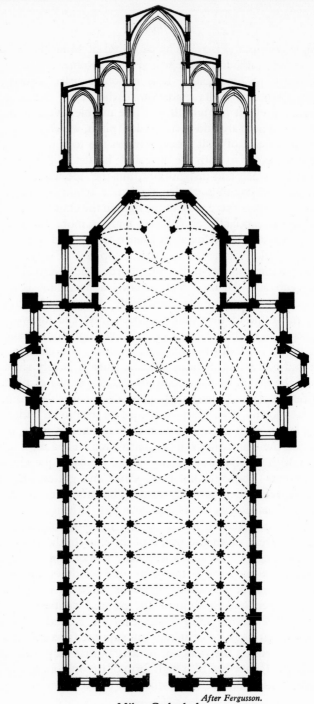

Milan Cathedral.
Scale 100 *ft. to* 1 *in.*

Milan was the last great Gothic building in Italy. It was begun
only in 1385, and the domical vault at the crossing was designed
by Brunelleschi in 1440; the open-work spire was not added until
1750, and the west front was completed, at the command of
Napoleon, early in the nineteenth century. In its way Milan is a
miracle of Gothic architecture, an astonishing culmination of
a style that, having developed a logical construction, ended in a
marble fantasy of fairy-like illogicality.

Interiors. The division of the inside of a church into arcade,
triforium and clerestory, customary in France and England, is
unusual in Italy. The nave of S. Martino, Lucca (*c.* 1340), has a
triforium of commendable size, with a string course above and
below it, but this was a rebuilding. In S. Anastasia, Verona, there
is merely a series of circular openings to mark the middle storey;
and in Como Cathedral there are pairs of openings with surrounding frames which, however, are late in date and Renaissance in
character. In the cathedrals of Florence, Orvieto, and Siena, and
in S. Croce, Florence, corbelled-out galleries run round the naves
immediately above the main arcades. These galleries, like the
entablatures over the architraves in Early Christian churches,
from which they were derived, form strong horizontal lines which
are strangely out of character in the two Florentine churches,
where the arches are sharply pointed. At Orvieto the arches are
semi-circular, but here, as at Siena, the walls and piers are faced
with alternating courses of black and white marble, which in
themselves form horizontal lines, so that the more strongly
marked lines of the galleries are not too pronounced.

In addition to the customary absence of triforiums, there was
little attempt as a rule to give prominence to the clerestories.
Siena is an exception. The windows there are large and have
traceried heads, like those of the churches in France and England.
In Orvieto Cathedral and in S. Croce, Florence, each bay has a
lancet light which, although tall, is very narrow. The most usual
opening is merely a circle, sometimes quite plain, as in Florence
Cathedral, sometimes cusped, as in S. Petronio, Bologna and
S. Anastasia, Verona. It cannot be said that the result in either
case is very satisfactory, but it must be remembered that the
strong light in Italy made large windows unnecessary and that
there seems to have been no desire for stained glass. The effect
inside might have been better, in many cases, if the walls had been
painted (as they are at Assisi and doubtless were originally intended

to be), since the interest would then be the mural decoration and not the architecture, which, it must be admitted, is often uninteresting.

Italian Gothic does not possess that appearance of structural integrity which is a characteristic of the architecture of France and England. It is customary, for instance, to restrain the arches by means of iron tie rods rather than by masonry abutment, but in many churches considerable constructional skill is shown, since the spans of the arches and vaults are far greater than is normal in the Gothic world. The vaults are, as a rule, simple quadripartite, but of great size. Not only are the naves very wide, but the side bays and spacing of supports are equally great. The old Roman plan of approximately square bays was generally adopted in the nave, the oblong form favoured by the Gothic builders of the north being the exception and not the rule, save in the aisles.[1] Here, the bays run lengthwise and not transversely. The result is a great hall with only a few supports, and much of the effect of size is lost. This weakness of scale is increased by the absence of mouldings and by the fact that the Italians seldom adopted the system of subordination which is one of the most important principles of Gothic construction. In S. Anastasia, Verona (*c.* 1280), SS. Giovanni e Paolo, Venice (*c.* 1260), S. Croce, Florence, etc., the columns are cylindrical and the arches un-moulded and with flush soffits. When piers are substituted for columns, as in Florence Cathedral, they are generally merely squares, with only flat pilasters of slight projection at the sides. The typical fourteenth-century Italian capital is perhaps the ugliest ever devised. It consists of two or three tiers of acanthus leaves, placed stiffly one above the other and surmounted by a moulded abacus which, over columns, is generally octagonal in plan.

The treatment of the eastern end is reminiscent of Early Christian basilicas. Transepts are at the extreme east end and there is nothing beyond except chapels. In S. Anastasia, Verona, and SS. Giovanni e Paolo, Venice, there are five chapels with apsidal ends. That at the centre is wider and longer than the others, equalling, in fact, the width of the nave. The fully developed French chevet is unknown in the Gothic churches of Italy. Milan is the nearest approach, but here there is only an ambulatory around an octagonal apse, and there are no chapels.

[1] Milan Cathedral and S. Andrea, Vercelli, are the most important exceptions.

S. Caterina, Pisa;
west front

ena Cathedral; west front

Plate 19

Siena Cathedral; interior

Plate 20

Florence Cathedral; south si

Milan Cathedral;
west front

Plate 21

Palazzo Communale, Siena

Plate 22

Doge's Palace, Venice

Exteriors. In the design of the west front, the Italians paid little attention to the sectional outline of the church, and never adopted the western expedient of masking the aisles by a pair of towers. A wide single gable, as at the Romanesque church of S. Ambrogio, Milan, or else three gables, those at the side being lower and smaller than that at the centre, was the usual arrangement. At Siena and Orvieto the angle of these gables bears no relation to the pitch of the roofs behind. The west fronts are simply screens, rich in carving and sculpture, but beautiful only because of the marble with which they are faced. The sides are often plain brick, but as the churches seldom stand free it matters little. In the vaulted churches the Italians were able to dispense with flying buttresses (except in Milan Cathedral), and where buttresses occur, as, for instance, at S. Anastasia, Verona, they are treated without set-offs and run sheer from the ground to the eaves without a break.

The most interesting contribution was the use of polychrome marbles, either by means of thin slabs applied like a veneer, as can be seen at Venice, or by building the marble into the wall in courses like any other stone. Brickwork was common and gave special character to the Italian style. Cornices were worked with interlacing arches of brick and enriched with brick dentils. It is possible that the use of brick encouraged the continued use of the rounded arch, for it is difficult to make a good junction in brick at the apex of a pointed arch. One expedient was to make the joints of the pointed arch radiate to one, rather than two, points, as may be seen in a palace at Citta della Pieve. Another method was to make the intrados semi-circular and the extrados pointed, as, for instance, at a doorway in Assisi; but here there was no reason why the joints should not radiate from two centres in the usual way, since the construction was in stone.

The Cosmati. The part played by Rome in the development of Gothic architecture was infinitesimal, but mention must be made of one family of architects, sculptors and workers in mosaic whose contribution to art history is of the first importance. Throughout the thirteenth century this family—the Cosmati—were producing all kinds of works in marble and mosaic for pavements, altars, ciboria, ambones, Paschal candlesticks, bishops' thrones, tombs and so forth, for the adornment of the churches of Christendom. Most of their work is to be seen in Rome, but even as far afield as Westminster they designed the pavement in the Sanctuary, the Chapel of S. Edward the Confessor, and the tombs of Henry III, the Princes John and Alphonso and the Princess Katherine. To some, the work of the Cosmati was the true Renaissance, because it was inspired by a direct study of the antique. It was in the Forum of Rome that the Cosmati found, not only their inspiration, but their most precious materials: the porphyry and the *verde antico* columns which they cut to squares, discs and tesserae. Their greatest architectural achievements were the campanili of S. Maria in Cosmedin and S. Pudenziana—both round-arched designs—and the cloisters of S. Giovanni in Lateran and S. Paolo Fuori le Mura. The characteristic feature of Cosmati work is the use of slender marble columns, twisted or straight, richly inlaid with glass mosaic in delicate and brilliant patterns; and of pavements with discs of red or green marble, framework of white bands and intricate infilling of tesserae, which hark back to ancient precedent, to the *opus Alexandrinum* of Early Christian times. The tomb of Henry III at Westminster is in many ways typical of the style. There is nothing Gothic about it; it is Roman, and consists of two great marble chests, one on top of the other. The lower is enriched with squares and rounds of green porphyry, set in an interlacing pattern of mosaic. The upper is constructed of great slabs of purple porphyry, and at the corners are attached twisted columns richly studded with a pattern of gold and coloured tesserae.

Domestic Buildings. Italy, during the Middle Ages, is probably best represented by her contribution to secular architecture. Nearly all the examples are concentrated in the cities, rather than dotted over the countryside like the castles of England or châteaux of France. Early in the twelfth century, as a matter of deliberate policy, the castles of 'those gentlemen who would not be obedient to the city' were destroyed, and the dispossessed lords were forced to come and live within city walls and build for themselves urban palaces. The result was the building, not only of lavish domestic apartments, but also of great towers from which the nobles could defend themselves or annoy their neighbours. In Siena there were twenty-five such towers still standing in the seventeenth century; in San Gimignano thirteen remain today. Most are attractive by the simplicity of their forms, and only a few are dressed with architectural trimmings. The most impressive are those built by the citizens themselves, and of these the finest is probably the tower of the Palazzo Communale at Siena (Pl. 22), which was built in the first half of the fourteenth century. It rises in sheer brickwork, 335 feet, to culminate in a projecting gallery on corbels. W. R. Lethaby considered it one of the three great municipal buildings of the world, the other two being those of Florence and Bruges. He wrote:

> It is of brick, very simple in its parts, and it is difficult to say in what its power consists. The ground storey is formed by a row of pointed arches, then there are two stages of three-light windows, all alike, and a fourth storey in the middle crowned by a fine battlement. The mask-like tower rises at one end. The inside is all glorious with paintings, which cover the walls like tapestry. In the great Council Chamber Simone Martini, from 1315, painted the 'Queen of Siena'. A superbly designed Madonna is enthroned in front of tabernacle work like an altar-piece, beneath a canopy upheld by attendant saints. To her, kneeling angels offer bowls of flowers, and beneath is an inscription in which she says to the citizens that good judgments delight her more than offerings of flowers, and that him who judges wrongfully will she condemn. On the opposite wall is the portrait, larger than life, of the war-leader of Siena, riding alone in a wide, dark landscape spotted over with castles.[1]

Venice. The part played by Venice in the history of architecture is for various reasons quite different from the role of the rest of Italy. Venice, founded on the sea, looked East—to Byzantium, Alexandria, Smyrna and Cyprus. There were no internal wars or struggles comparable with those of the Guelphs and Ghibellines which harrowed the cities of Central Italy. Ever since the Fourth Crusade of 1204, when Venice captured Constantinople and acquired the loot of that fabulously wealthy city, Venice had pursued a series of lucrative conquests all along the Dalmatian coast, taking within her control not only the Adriatic but also the gateway to the Orient. With her maritime supremacy and her particularly fortunate situation amongst the lagoons, Venice had no need for artificial fortifications, for imposing walls and threatening towers. All could be open and gracious and, because of her mercantile supremacy and commercial acumen, opulent as well. So, in Venice, down the Dalmatian coast and in the islands of the Aegean there survive some of the most beautiful examples of civil and domestic architecture in the world. It is Gothic with a curiously Oriental flavour, sensuous, refined and colourful, a mixture of the East with the West.

The building known as the Fondaco dei Turchi is among the

[1] *Medieval Art*, by W. R. Lethaby, revised by D. Talbot Rice, 1949, p. 210.

earliest of these mercantile palaces. It was built in the twelfth or thirteenth century for the Pesari family, and was drastically restored between 1860 and 1869. It is a long, two-storeyed structure flanked by towers, with an open arcade of much-stilted round arches supported on slender columns at ground, or water, level; at the first floor there is a second arcade, with double the number of arches, so that alternate columns rest directly on the tops of the lower arches. The arches are lined with a marble soffit, projecting sufficiently to carry the marble wall facing. There is no crowning cornice, but only a series of pierced triangles to form a parapet.[1]

Fundamentally it is not a great step from the Fondaco dei Turchi to the greatest of all the Venetian medieval buildings: the Doge's Palace (Pl. 22). Again there is the open ground-floor arcade, and above this the quicker rhythm of arches at the first floor. In both cases the columns are baseless, but in the Doge's Palace the arches are pointed, and on the first storey are enriched with cuspings and brought to a level by means of tracery. Above all this is a great mass of masonry arranged in a chequer pattern of pink and white and punctuated by exceptionally wide and squat windows. The whole is finished by a pierced and flimsy cresting.

The Doge's Palace was begun by Pietro Baseggio in 1343, and finished by Giovanni Buon and his son, Bartolommeo, in 1424. It has been the subject of admiration and detestation ever since. Ruskin thought it finer than the Parthenon and above all that was great and beautiful in Greece, Egypt or Gothic Europe. Fergusson considered that it was difficult to judge it calmly, situated as it is, looking on the one hand into the Piazza of S. Mark's and on the other across the water to the churches and palaces that cover the islands. This setting, he thought, spread a halo around the building which furnished an excuse for those who blindly praised its deformities. But while giving credit for its picturesque situation, Fergusson felt compelled wholly to condemn its execution. In 1577 thirteen architects were asked to report on it, and nearly all condemned it. Palladio thought the fault was the planning of a solid storey over an open arcade. Only Jacopo Sansovino and Antonio da Ponte saw its merits. Sansovino said: 'The public palace of Venice is the strongest and finest fabric I have seen in any part of Italy.' Ruskin was especially entranced with the carving

---

[1] A duplicate, with only slight variations, of the Fondaco dei Turchi, built in 1314, exists at Ohrid in Yugoslavia. This, however, is not a palace, but the narthex to the old church of Sancta Sophia.

of the capitals. According to Charles Eastlake, in his *A History of the Gothic Revival*, Ruskin spent month after month studying the capitals of the Ducal Palace and measuring the intercolumniation of the Fondaco dei Turchi.

The sculptures of the Doge's Palace are certainly very wonderful. It is not certain who the sculptor was. John Pope-Hennessy considers that some might be the work of Giovanni Buon himself. The most notable are those over the angle columns, which illustrate The Fall and The Drunkenness of Noah; but below these noble compositions, in the capitals themselves, are a host of little folk, carved within a deeply undercut arrangement of foliage. There is a group illustrating the Judgment of Solomon; there are representations of the Virtues and the Vices; there are figures of philosophers and artists, symbols of the months, and groups depicting the seven deadly sins. All are charmingly contrived within leafy bowers.

The whole of the Doge's Palace is as great as the sum of its parts, even if from the traditional point of view the main parts—the light and airy arcades and the great mass of masonry wall—seem to have been unaccountably reversed. In mid-twentieth century terms, such an arrangement of a great mass supported by slender *piloti* is now acceptable to taste and constructional logic. It is to be seen, for instance, in the Unité d'Habitation at Marseilles. There, Le Corbusier's *piloti* do not, it is true, provide a gallery of sculpture, but they serve much the same function as the arcades of the Doge's Palace by giving an openness at ground level which can be wholly delightful.

Nearly all the palaces of Venice conform to a set arrangement. There is a door to the canal, and a door to the street or piazza behind. The principal front faces the canal, and there is as a rule one large room at the first floor which runs from front to back. On the canal front this room gets the most architectural attention and is furnished outside with the finest tracery and richest marbles. The Ca d'Oro is the most sumptuous of them all. It was built by Giovanni Buon in 1430, and consists of an open loggia on the ground floor, a splendidly rich band of tracery at the first floor, a further but simpler arcade above this, and, finally, a crested battlement. There are no buttresses, no aspiring lines. The Ca d'Oro, with its rich use of marbles and, originally, its added decorations in gold and coloured paints, belongs, as did Venice in her heart, to the East. It is easy to understand why the Ca d'Oro when it was built for Signor Marino Contarini, the Procurator of Venice, was called the Palace of Sancta Sophia. In one sense Byzantium belonged to Venice, for Venice had captured the trade of the Sublime Porte, but in another, Byzantium had captured Venice, for her art, in spite of its pointed arches, was nearer to Byzantium than to Amiens or Beauvais.

CHAPTER XII

SECULAR ARCHITECTURE

THE study of domestic architecture in the Gothic period presents special problems which do not usually apply to religious buildings. These problems are largely dependent less upon period than upon the rank and status of the occupants. They are also regional problems, determined by local building materials and traditional techniques, and often designs are directly affected by special site conditions. The differences between a country house and a town house, and between a lord's mansion and a serf's hovel, are far greater than between a town church and a country church, or even between a cathedral and a chapel. It is proposed in this chapter to consider, first, the building of castles and fortifications in those regions where war encouraged the greatest developments; to follow this with some reference to the greater mansions and manor houses which were built in regions of relative peace, and to conclude with a few details of vernacular architecture, so far as it has survived in town and country.

CASTLES AND FORTIFICATIONS

A castle is first and foremost a functional piece of architecture, directly related to war, conquest and defence. Each development which took place in the design was a logical sequel to every tactical advance which was made in methods of warfare. The one was a direct consequence of the other. At first the castle was purely passive—a secure refuge from a surrounding enemy. It also served as a home for the lord of the demesne, and provided some defence for the town or district in which it was located; for as long as the castle stood intact, conquest could not be complete. Later, the establishment of a castle could become an element of offence, as headquarters for a marauding company in disputed terrain and, if the defences were perfected, as a source of considerable loss to any besieging army. This last factor ultimately led to legislation for wholesale demolition of castles by Cromwell in England and Richelieu in France. The practical history of the castle, however, is limited to the Middle Ages—until, in fact, the effective use of gun-powder, which could demolish its walls from afar.

The Normans had been responsible for two main types of castle: the high rectangular tower of masonry, of which the Tower of London is perhaps the best example; and the shell keep, which usually consisted of a ring of masonry, within which there was room for small subsidiary dwellings, as can be seen at Berkeley, Alnwick and Windsor. Reliance was placed by the designers simply on the strength and solidity of the structure. The walls had to be thick enough to withstand the battering-ram, and well enough built to make undermining a hopeless task because of the time and labour involved.

At this stage, when Romanesque architecture was changing towards Gothic, the Crusades, with the consequent opportunities for studying the fortifications of the Byzantine Empire, led to a revolution in the art of castle building. The first new requirement was that a second line of defence should be built within the main enceinte, and possibly a third within that. The second require-ment was that these lines should be flanked by projecting towers. In the West the donjon, or keep, had been regarded as the fortress, and any outer walls as merely additional defences. In the East, each envelope was thought of as a fortress in itself, and the keep only as the final stronghold, to be used after each surrounding fortress had fallen. The keep in the West, in fact, became less and less important and rarely functioned as the ultimate refuge. It was often no more than a strong tower amongst other towers in the innermost ward.

Certain fundamental features dominated the design of castles throughout the Middle Ages. The first was that the walls should be sufficiently high to prevent escalade; the second, that they should be thick enough at the top to provide an adequate platform for the defenders; and the third was that the walls should be protected by projecting towers from which fire could be directed on an attacker. The methods of attack varied according to circumstances. The most obvious was escalade, but if the walls were too high to scale, then recourse was made to the battering-ram, or to the undermining of the walls. To a large extent, these techniques were countered by the castle builders, and made ineffective either by building the wall above a steep precipice of rock or by surrounding the wall with a moat. If the terrain was relatively easy, the attacker might construct siege towers as high, if not higher, than the castle wall, and provide them with bridges by means of which a storming party might overwhelm the defenders when the towers were wheeled alongside. Lastly, there was the use of engines which could throw missiles from afar in the hope of ultimately battering down the wall. The missile engines could throw stones up to six hundred pounds' weight for distances of over six hundred yards; but they were expensive, and difficult to manœuvre. Throughout the Middle Ages methods of attack proved to be inferior to those of defence. The real dangers were treachery, famine and disease, against which the finest architecture was powerless.

Crusader Castles. The development of the art of fortification received its most powerful impetus as a result of the Crusades. For two hundred years following the conquest of Jerusalem in 1099, the Crusaders endeavoured to maintain a Latin Kingdom in the Levant. Their territory consisted of a narrow coastal strip, about fifty miles across, stretching for over six hundred miles from Antioch in the north to the Gulf of Aqaba in the south. The conquest in the first instance had been relatively easy, because of the superior strength of the heavily armoured knights, with their lances, swords, maces and bucklers. The Crusader soon found himself master in the field, though by no means secure. 'But', wrote Robin Fedden, 'he could not always be in the field. When he drew off his heavy mail he needed a shell into which, tortoise like, he could withdraw.'[1] If the territory was to be held permanently by comparatively small numbers, a system of strong-points had to be established throughout the elongated Kingdom, from which control could be regained after each offensive foray.

The earliest of the Crusader castles seem to have followed western precedents, except that because of the shortage of timber for floors, they were lower than the keeps of France and England. They were purely passive, and depended entirely upon the relative indestructibility of their walls. By the thirteenth century far more complete systems of fortification were being evolved, which were obviously the result of much thought by military architects and engineers. Their design was fundamentally different and was certainly based upon Byzantine inspiration. The form of the castle was now dependent upon the configuration of the ground and upon a sound knowledge of military tactics. No longer were castles as like to each other as, say, Rochester, Hedingham and Newcastle. They were designed to take advantage of every natural feature, and the builders even, on occasion, by means of deep cuttings in

[1] Robin Fedden and John Thomson: *Crusader Castles*, 1957.

the rock, contrived moats indestructible by any weapon of the time. The curtain walls, which usually conformed to the contours, followed the pattern of Constantinople by having at regular intervals projecting towers. At first these were square, as at Saône (early twelfth century) and of only slight projection; but later they were round, and protruded well beyond the curtain wall. This had the double advantage of making attack by the ram more difficult, and of ensuring the most effective cross fire against the enemy.

Two features which were probably original inventions of the Crusaders were the portcullis and the bent entrance. The Byzantines, and the Romans before them, had usually provided a straight and direct approach to their forts. Now the gates were placed at a side of a tower, preferably opposite another tower so that the approaching attacker would be under direct fire from behind. Inside there would be a covered passageway, if possible running uphill, and all along would be loopholes so that the garrison could shoot the enemy in the passage; and at the end the invaders would face another barrage of fire and another turn before they could hope to reach the gateway to the courtyard.

Not all the Crusader castles were merely passive. Some were so placed that they could control a pass and prohibit the entrance of an invading force, and could house a garrison sufficiently strong to make practicable marauding adventures into enemy territory. They were formidable enough in isolation, but acquired even greater strength by being linked to others, with a system of communications by signalling and carrier pigeon, the former learned from the Arabs and the latter from the Byzantines. In the Holy Land the art of medieval warfare was perfected.

Out of the wealth of material which has survived, it is difficult to select one example to illustrate the character of the Crusader castles. Each differs according to its site. Saône is remarkable for its deeply cut ditch, 426 feet long, 63 feet wide and 92 feet deep, which made approach to the citadel well-nigh impossible except across the great drawbridge which was supported on a central pillar of natural rock. Castrum Peregrinorum, which became better known as Chastel Pèlerin, was built on a rocky promontory near modern Haifa and provided with a series of formidable landward defences. First there was a wall, and a moat 80 feet wide and 20 feet deep, which could be flooded when required. Then came the curtain wall, strengthened by towers. Behind this was a second wall, similarly reinforced by towers, which still stands to a height of

110 feet.[1] Finally, there are the residential quarters, where the Queen of France, the wife of St. Louis, lodged. This castle never fell. When the Latin Kingdom had collapsed it no longer had a *raison d'être*, and the Knights Templar evacuated the castle and sailed to the last stronghold of Cyprus.

The most powerful and imposing of all the Crusader castles is the Krak des Chevaliers (Pl. 23). It is situated in the mountainous district

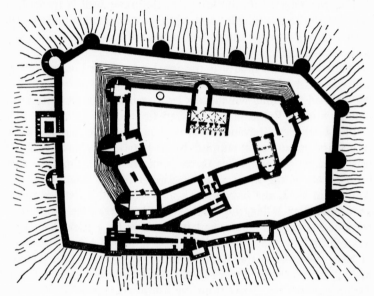

After Toy.

Krak des Chevaliers.
Scale 200 ft. to 1 in.

west of Homs, at a point which controlled the only practical line of communication between the Tripoli coast and the valley of the Orontes. The castle, when completed, stuck, according to a Muslim writer, like a bone in the throat of the Saracens. In 1142 the castle was in the charge of the Knights Hospitaller, and from here they made regular expeditions into Muslim territory. All the outer walls, with the exception of the square tower on the south side, are their work. The castle stands high on a hill dominating the landscape, with steep falls on all but the south side, which is the only possible line of approach. The entrance, however, is contrived on the east side, at a point so far along that the enemy must pass,

[1] According to Fedden, op. cit.

under fire all the way, two-thirds of the length of the fortress before he reaches it. And then he is confronted with a rising serpentine vaulted passage and must overcome four successive gates, each reinforced from above by massive machicolations, before reaching the upper and most heavily fortified gate of all. It is not surprising that the great Saladin, after examining the defences, decided to withdraw rather than even attempt a siege.

The character of the buildings in the inner wall is in distinct contrast to the formidable shell. Here is a noble banqueting hall, with vaulted portico; a chapel with a pointed barrel vault, complete with semi-circular apse and lancet windows; and finally, a donjon on the south side which was the residence of the Grand Master and was richly decorated with all the delicate mouldings, tracery and ribbed vaulting which can be paralleled in contemporary church work at Reims and Ste. Chapelle.

The Krak des Chevaliers was well provisioned. It had ample reservoirs and sufficient supplies for its garrison for three years. It was shortage of manpower throughout the Latin Kingdom that brought about the final collapse. Saphet fell in 1266, Jaffa and Antioch in 1268, and only a few points along the coast remained. In 1271, after a lengthy siege, still the Krak des Chevaliers remained largely inviolate, and it was only by a trick that entry was effected by the attacking Beibars. A forged letter, supposed to have come from the Grand Master and stating that Tripoli had fallen and that therefore further resistance was useless, led to the final surrender. Apart from the south-west tower in the outer curtain, which was successfully mined during the siege, the castle remains intact. Like war itself, its style is international. Its external character stems largely from Constantinople, its internal architecture belongs to France, and its siting and landscape belong to the Holy Land.

Castles in France. The Crusades had immediate effects upon castle building in the West. The Crusaders had learned the devastating effects of siege engines and of mining. Now they chose sites upon precipitous hillsides, placing their inner citadel at the cliff edge and protecting the approach by a series of defence works. The Château Gaillard and the English castles of Pembroke and Beeston all followed this plan. Other older castles, like Corfe and Chepstow, were reinforced by the building of advance works. The Château Gaillard, which was built (1196–8) by Richard Lionheart, is the most dramatic. His famous exclamation: '*Ecce!*

Quam pulchra filia unius anni' (Behold! What a beautiful daughter of one year) is unfortunately based on a false chronicle of 1436, as is proved by the Exchequer Rolls, which show that the construction took some three years. No architect is mentioned, and it is generally agreed that Richard, with his wide experience in the Holy Land, personally supervised its erection. The plan consists of three bays, or courtyards, arranged in a line. The last, that is, the inner bailey, is on the cliff edge and farthest from the approach which any attacker, because of the nature of the site, was forced to follow. Apart from the massiveness of the ditches and escarpments which had to be carved out of the solid rock, there are two

After Viollet-le-Duc.

Château Gaillard. Donjon.

interesting and important features. The first is the waved face of the inner or main wall, which gave reinforcement and a divergent fire over the front, and the other is the masonry construction of the machicolations on the top of the donjon, built at a time when wooden projecting hoardings were customary. Timber structures, erected on the outside of parapets to protect the bases of walls and towers, seem to have been employed since the earliest times. They were usually provided with holes in the floor through which heavy objects could be dropped on anyone below, and were protected by a screen and covered with a roof. They were, of course, very vulnerable, for they would be relatively easy

Machicolations.

to set alight by burning missiles, and the introduction of some form of stone construction in their place was an obvious improvement. At the Château Gaillard the machicolations were supported by great buttresses springing from the splayed base. It is probably the earliest example in western Europe of this formidable method of defence.

A simpler technique was adopted at Coucy (*c.* 1240), where rows of stone corbels were built to carry the parapet. The donjon at Coucy was the last of the great keeps. It stood some 200 feet above the rocks and was isolated from other buildings in the bailey by its own moat. It was a great cylinder of masonry, almost windowless, built in three great storeys, each magnificently vaulted and lit by means of a large circular eye in each centre. Unfortunately, it was completely destroyed by the Germans in their retreat of 1917. The plan of the fortress was essentially different from that of the Château Gaillard. It was linked to a lower bailey, equipped with a well and a chapel, which was probably provided to give shelter to the neighbouring town. The castle proper, reached by a heavily fortified bridge, was of an irregular quadrilateral shape and was reinforced at each corner by nearly independent circular towers, which must have provided the maximum possible range for a defending bowman. All along the inside of the curtain wall were two-storey buildings, including two great halls and a chapel, which were the living quarters of the lord and his garrison.

As the Middle Ages developed, and in spite of the interruption of the Hundred Years War (1339–1453), the general tendency was towards the establishment of strongly fortified residences rather than castles. Within the powerful enveloping walls there was more and more concern with the building of comfortable, even sumptuous, residential quarters. Elaborate staircases linked whole series of apartments, which were furnished with tapestry hangings and panelled walls, hooded fireplaces and intricate plaster relief and painted ceilings. While considerations of defence remained of prime importance, so far as the siting and the disposition of the bastion walls were concerned, the noblemen of France were not prepared to forego a reasonable degree of elegance within the enceinte.

The castle of Pierrefonds (Pl. 23), which was built between 1390 and 1420 by Louis of Orleans, a brother of the king, was the last great fortified castle to be built before peace came back to France. Now the residential quarters are all ranged round the courtyard, against a strong inner curtain which is reinforced by round bastions at each corner and at the middle of each side. The approach is made as complicated as possible. It is by means of a ramp on the west side, which leads to a gate and a bent entrance into the outer enceinte at the south-west corner. Then one must traverse the west, north and east sides of the main fortress, all the time subject to direct attack, before reaching the barbican and crossing the

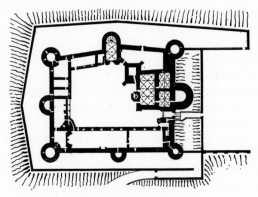

Castle of Pierrefonds.
Scale 200 ft. to 1 in.

bridge to the drawbridge which gives access to the inner courtyard. This castle, like so many others, was dismantled at the command of Richelieu, but was all too thoroughly 'restored' by Viollet-le-Duc between 1857 and 1870, so that it was made sufficiently comfortable to serve as a residence for Napoleon III.

From afar, two important features predominate. They are the stupendous circular bastions and the complicated skyline. Both features were to persist as the norm of French aristocratic architecture long after the Middle Ages had passed. Indeed, the great Renaissance châteaux of Chambord, Azay-le-Rideau, and Chaumont, all built well into the sixteenth century, preserve great circular turrets crowned with machicolations, steep conical roofs, pinnacled gables and spires. They belong, however, to a romantic revival, and have nothing in common with the stern realities of medieval warfare. Where the medievalist would have had a formidable moat, the Renaissance courtier provided ornamental waters for fountains and reflections; where the fortress had a marshalling yard, the courtier provided grounds for a fashion parade. In place of a plot of herbs for seasoning the meat, there would be extensive formal gardens, and in place of look-out points for the guard there were windows for the view.

Castles in England. The reign of Edward I (1272–1307) was the most brilliant period of military architecture in this country. Edward returned from the Crusades in 1274. Two years later he began his conquest of Wales, and followed this by attacks on Scotland which lasted practically to the end of his reign. Both military adventures resulted in major developments in the art of fortification. The wars in Wales were concluded in 1283, and the subjection was completed by the establishment of a strong line of castles and fortified towns. Edward was, in effect, repeating a policy, which he had learned so successfully in Gascony, of setting up *bastides*, or *villes anglaises*, to serve the same purpose of protection and defence and to spread commerce and civilization. The new towns were to accommodate English settlers—soldiers and traders—and the adjoining castles were to protect them from the Welsh.

Here the most extraordinary development in castle design was the multiplication of gateways. The gateway, which had originally been a weak point simply because it was the entrance, was now, because of the complexity of machicolations, crenellations and loopholes, the strongest part. It was the one point which an enemy would not dream of attacking; it was also the one point which a besieger would guard, for the king or nobleman, secure behind his walls, was doomed ultimately to starvation unless he could effectively maintain supplies for the garrison. In the new castles, therefore, more gateways were introduced that could, in an emergency, provide an exit and a means of communication with the world outside. Caerphilly, Caernarvon, Conway, and Harlech are each supplied with two powerful entrances as well as supplementary postern gates.

The Marches of South Wales had already been secured by the building of Caerphilly (1267). Edward's principal works were concentrated along the northern coast. Flint (1277–80), Rhuddlan (1280), Conway (1283–7), Caernarvon (1285–1322), Harlech (1285–90), and Beaumaris (1295–1320), constitute as impressive a series of fortifications as any in the Holy Land. The plans vary. At Flint the conception of the keep isolated at one corner persists, but this is strangely built of two concentric shells of masonry, separated by a circular vaulted passage in a manner which Sidney

Krak des Chevaliers

Plate 23

Château du Pierrefonds

Harlech Castle

Plate 24

Moreton Old Hall

Toy says is reminiscent of the huge round towers of old Cairo.[1]
Conway and Caernarvon have long, narrow plans, the former
reinforced by round and the latter by octagonal towers. Both
incorporate domestic buildings within the walls, at Caernarvon
on a palatial scale. Harlech and Beaumaris illustrate better the
perfected Edwardian scheme. They belong to the type known as
concentric, the inner fortress being completely enclosed by a ring
of fortifications. At Beaumaris this was further reinforced in

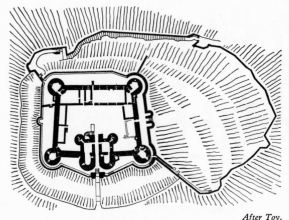

After Toy.

Harlech Castle.
Scale 200 ft. to 1 in.

1316–20 by a moat all round, and at Harlech there is also a wide
moat on the south and east and an outer walled bailey on the steep,
rocky slopes to the north and west.

   Harlech (Pl. 24) is a rectangular fortress defined by two concentric
rings of walls, forming the inner and middle wards. There are
postern gates to the north and west, the latter providing a direct
escape from the great hall. The main gatehouse on the east side
is the stronghold of the castle. This was the most vulnerable side.
It was defended by two drawbridges, one at either end of the bridge
across the moat. There were two gateways, three portcullises and,
above, a formidable series of machicolations. Anyone who dared
to attack at this point would have been under fire from the walls
and towers in front as well as from a wide wall walk which divided
the outer ward from the moat.

[1] *The Castles of Great Britain*, 1953.

15

Beaumaris was the last and the most regular of all the Edwardian castles. It represents the most elaborate and the most perfect degree of impregnability which the medieval architects reached. The site on the seashore of Anglesey is level, and is therefore very different from that of Harlech, but the building resembles Harlech in having two lines of fortifications, one inside

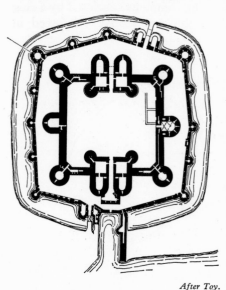

After Toy.

Beaumaris Castle.
Scale 200 *ft. to* 1 *in.*

the other and forming inner and outer wards or baileys. The surrounding moat is broken at one point on the south, where the sea enters to form a small dock. The inner wall is square, and defended by half-a-dozen bastions and two formidable gatehouses on opposite sides, each equipped with portcullises and machicolations, as at Harlech. The outer curtain was added later, and has gateways which are placed off centre, so that an enemy approaching one of the citadel entrances would be under flanking fire from the principal bastions.

After Beaumaris the history of fortifications in England can no longer be regarded as belonging to the purely functional tradition. In place of a fortress accommodating a dwelling, we have a dwelling decked out to look like a fortress. The artillery of the fifteenth century could have made nonsense of the castellations of such architecture as Tattersall and Hurstmonceaux, with their thin brick walls and turrets. The arrow-slits, crenellations and machicolations are meaningless in terms of practical defence. They are there only as symbols of nobility and romantic reminiscence.

Castles in Scotland. The castellated architecture of Scotland has a number of curious features which make it worthy of special study, and it is surprising, in view of the strong sentimental associations which the Scottish castle evokes, that only monographical studies have been undertaken since 1888, when McGibbon and Ross produced their now classic work, *The Castellated and Domestic Architecture of Scotland.* Historically, Scotland's contribution came late. Nothing survives of Norman times, although there is ample literary evidence that many castles were constructed in the twelfth and thirteenth centuries. The invasion of Edward I in 1296, clan feuds and wars of independence seem to have destroyed much of what there was. Throughout the fourteenth century the country was in a state of more or less complete exhaustion, and in no condition to undertake expensive building operations. In any case, Robert Bruce was opposed to large castle building. He was an early believer in a scorched earth policy, destroying everything rather than allowing the possibility of the capture of a castle by the English, which would give them a secure footing in the country. There is, therefore, nothing much before the end of the fourteenth century, and even then the castles are not royal constructions, but the work of local magnates who found it necessary to protect their lands against private enemies and border invaders rather than against national forces.

These early castles were like Norman keeps. They were square or oblong towers with thick stone walls, and defended by a parapet walk at roof level. In place of the great bastioned corners of contemporary castles elsewhere, a more economical practice was adopted by projecting on corbels a corner turret, sometimes equipped with open machicolations. These turrets were not placed at all four corners, however, but only at two, diagonally opposite, it being assumed that from one turret two of the walls could be adequately defended. The ground floor, which was chiefly a store, was invariably vaulted and had no connection with the upper floors except by a hatch in the vault. The main entrance was at the first, or even second, floor level, by means of a ladder or removable wooden stair. The private apartments were located on the top floors. This was the usual Norman pattern, and persisted in Scotland almost to the seventeenth century. The roof was generally constructed of stone slabs, well dressed and grooved into each other. The gutter was also of stone construction and provided at frequent intervals with a drain across the parapet walk, leading to a projecting gargoyle. Chimneys were carried up on the inside to allow a free way all round.

Hundreds of these tower castles survive, especially on the border lands. They were not disposed systematically to defend a frontier or a zone of occupation, like the Crusader castles or Edward's fortified chain along the north of Wales, or even like the Martello towers of a later age. In a region so liable to foray and feud, they were simply dwellings with a very narrow frontage, built strongly enough not to be set on fire or to suffer from attack by a small number. They were the homes of the Scottish lairds.

The extent to which Scottish architecture is in debt to England or to France is a controversial matter. McGibbon and Ross believed that it was largely of native growth, although they recognized its long antecedents. They admitted also certain remarkable affinities with France. The Tour du Pont at Villeneuve, for instance, which was erected in 1307 by Philip the Fair, is extremely like the fifteenth-century tower of Clackmannan, and the Château de Monsabert on the Loire, which is of the fifteenth century, resembles in form, and even in its purely ornamental machicolations, Fyfie Castle in Aberdeenshire, which was not built until the beginning of the seventeenth century. But apart from occasional similarities, which are especially marked in later buildings, as, for instance, Falkland Palace, with its great rounded bastions, and Charles II's rebuilding of Holyrood Palace, Scottish architecture certainly evolved some novel features. During the more prosperous fifteenth century it became common to add a small wing at one corner, giving an L-shaped plan. This gave at least one additional room at each floor, sometimes more, if the rooms in the wing had lower ceilings. A spiral staircase would be fitted into the angle, and if the upper floor walls were not thick enough to accommodate this it would be corbelled out, like a turret, to run from the first floor to the roof.

The affinity of Scottish castellated architecture with its counterpart in France is most obvious in the greater castles and palaces which were built in Scotland during the fifteenth and sixteenth centuries. Of these the most notable are Edinburgh, Stirling, Linlithgow, Falkland, and Dunfermline. They were royal palaces, built not only for strength but also for a more elegant and cultured life.

Linlithgow Palace may be taken to illustrate the character of this more refined architecture. It is conveniently situated midway between Edinburgh and Stirling, and is intimately associated with the private history of the Scottish royal family. Here were born James V and his daughter Mary, Queen of Scots. It was designed in the form of a mansion surrounding a paved courtyard. The entrance was defended by three gates, a drawbridge and a portcullis. This was reinforced by round towers with loopholes, which were small and thin by Edwardian or French standards. The principal apartments are all on the first floor. Here are the great hall, 100 feet long by 30 feet wide, the chapel and various smaller but by no means insignificant rooms. A new feature occurs in the provision of access galleries on the courtyard side, and in the regular system of fenestration. The courtyard walls, with their symmetrical disposition of turret stairways, in fact mark a break with the Middle Ages and herald the Renaissance. Considering that Linlithgow was virtually complete by 1496, that is, twenty years before the principal works at the château of Blois, it is not surprising that the bride of James V, Mary of Guise, should have declared that she 'had never seen a more princely palace'.

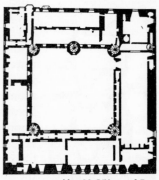

After McGibbon and Ross.
Linlithgow Palace.
Scale 100 *ft. to* 1 *in.*

In 1603 James VI of Scotland succeeded to the throne of England, and this date may conveniently be taken to mark the advent of the final and most extraordinary development of Scottish architecture. The use of artillery meant that the formidable walls, with their crenellations, machicolations and bastions, were no longer effective deterrents; nor was there any point in maintaining a garrison of retainers within the castle, with the result that the great hall was less important than the private apartments. The best sites were no longer those which dominated the horizon, but rather those that provided shelter from the elements and a pleasant environment. The castle as an architectural form remained, however, as a symbol of the nobleman's dwelling. For this reason, the medieval stylisms persisted. The Scotsman's home, even more than the Englishman's, was his castle. Towers and battlements, moats, drawbridges, and all the trimmings of the past were applied to buildings whose internal economy had become purely domestic and residential, and they were applied in extraordinary profusion. The castles of the seventeenth and eighteenth centuries are mansions decked out with picturesque turrets, corbelled at every angle. The parapets are false and broken with ornamental dormers. The roofs are high-pitched and have fanciful chimneys and crow-stepped gables. Turrets, staircases and parapets are all corbelled, and the principal towers are often changed from a circular lower floor to a square upper floor, without any purpose or meaning other than to achieve a picturesque effect.

Claypotts.
Scale 50 ft. to 1 in.

Claypotts, which lies in a fertile plain only three miles east of Dundee, is typical of the new style. It is dated, on the northern tower, 1588, and shows a decided advance in domestic planning. The small square rooms in the turrets are not, it is true, luxurious bedrooms, but they are a vast improvement on the wall chambers of earlier keeps. The ground floor is still vaulted, and lit by shot-holes rather than windows, but the so-called battlement walks on the top floor are no more than pleasant terraces opening off the principal bedroom, from one of which there is a panoramic view across the estuary of the Tay.

With the union of the crowns, the castle became a symbol of romance, an aristocratic conceit. Its associations with warfare were lost in an image of fantasy and heraldic charade. What followed in the nineteenth century, under the stimulus of Walter Scott at Abbotsford and the Prince Consort at Balmoral, belongs, with the tartans and the sentimentality, not to the Gothic age but to the Gothic Revival.

THE MANOR HOUSE

The word manor, which occurs in the Domesday Book, meant the place where a man of some local consequence lived. It was a small estate closely linked to a village community and to the rural economy of the Middle Ages. It was by no means an exclusively English institution, but occurred in every country where feudalism reigned. The English manor house has its equivalent in the French *manoir* and the German *hof*. All were the houses of the landed gentry, as the castles were the houses of the barons. All were, in effect, the administrative centres of agricultural life. Their function was passive and productive, as opposed to the castles, whose purpose was military and defensive. They were homes for farmers rather than for soldiers. Nevertheless, local violence had to be guarded against, and many of the manor houses which were built in the peaceful South and Midlands of England, if not completely castellated, were provided with loopholes, a moat and a draw-bridge.

The feature which really distinguishes the castle from the manor house is not the amount of fortification but the arrangement of the

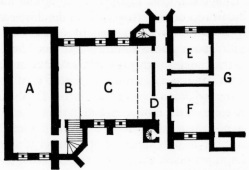

After Nathaniel Lloyd.

Penshurst Place: (*a*) Cellar, solar above; (*b*) Dais;
(*c*) Great Hall; (*d*) Screens, gallery over; (*e*)
Buttery; (*f*) Pantry; (*g*) Kitchen.

Scale 50 ft. to 1 in.

plan. As a general rule, the rooms in a castle were piled one on top of another, while in a manor house they were arranged alongside each other. The most important room was the hall, where most of the household ate, slept and spent their leisure. Sometimes, as at Aydon, Northumberland, this might be at first-floor level, reached by an outside stair; but more commonly, as at Penshurst Place, Kent, and Haddon Hall, Derbyshire, it was entered at ground level. The entry was a passage extending along one end of the hall and cut off by screens, through which two doorways gave access. Over this entry there was a gallery (the minstrel gallery), reached by a small staircase or step-ladder, which led to the servants' quarters. From the entry, at hall level, doors communicated with the kitchen, buttery and pantry. At the opposite end of the hall was the dais, only a few inches above floor level, and possibly a door leading to the 'bour' (bower), chamber or parlour, if one were provided for the women of the household. From the dais a stairway would take one to a room above the parlour, called the solar. This was a private apartment in the roof space.

The hall was usually open to the roof timbers, and sometimes was equipped with an open fireplace and chimney, but more often with only a central hearth on the floor, and an opening in the roof covered with louvres through which the smoke escaped. It is difficult to imagine any high degree of comfort, and the records embodied in the Liberate and Close Rolls indicate constant efforts to improve living conditions. Instructions regarding the provision of glazed windows occur most frequently in the thirteenth century. Before then, the openings were closed by shutters. At the Royal Palace at Westminster a glazed window was ordered for the Queen's wardrobe, 'so that the chamber may not be so windy as it used to be'. At Winchester there was a determined effort to keep out draughts by an order 'everywhere to repair the crevices'. Double doors were introduced to close off the lavatories, and in the Close Rolls of 1246 there is a record which reads: 'King to Edward Fitz-Otho. Since the privy chamber in our wardrobe at London is situated in an undue and improper place, wherefor it smells badly, we command you on the faith and love by which you are bound unto us, that you in no wise omit to cause another privy chamber to be made in the same wardrobe in such more fitting and proper place as you may select there, even though it should cost a hundred pounds.'[1]

Alterations, additions and improvements were made to manor houses throughout the Middle Ages. They do not follow any set pattern, but the basic disposition of rooms so that the hall formed the nucleus, with the family accommodation at one end and the kitchen quarters at the other, remained constant for three hundred years, that is, to the time of Elizabeth. Privacy did not exist. The only comfort was a sense of security from attack, of warmth when the shutters were fixed, and possibly of abundance of food, wine and company. No effort was made at symmetry of design, as, for instance, at Beaumaris and Bodiam castles. The attraction of the manor house depends largely upon picturesque grouping and the dignity and impressiveness of the hall, with its dais, its panelled screen, its painted walls and great trussed roof.

Of all the halls, the most magnificent is Westminster, which was remodelled at the command of Richard II between 1394 and 1402. The mason was Henry Yevele, and the carpenter Hugh Herland.

[1] Quoted by Nathaniel Lloyd: *A History of the English House*, 1931, p. 32.

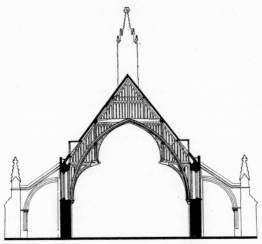

Westminster Hall, cross section.
Scale 50 ft. to 1 in.

The roof, which spans nearly 70 feet, has no parallel in Europe. It is of the hammer beam type, but with an additional arched brace which passes through the hammer beams and hammer posts. Tracery is used to fill the spandrels everywhere, and there is a system of arches along the length of the hall, bracing each truss to the next. The sections of the timbers are proportionately great. The hammer posts, that is, the vertical members which rise from the hammer beams, for instance, measure 39 inches by 25 inches and are some 21 feet long.

Considerable attention was paid to interior decoration. The walls were usually rendered with plaster, and this might be painted or lined with wainscote, consisting of plain boarding. The Queen's Chamber in the Tower of London in the thirteenth century was ordered to be 'whitewashed and pointed and within those pointings to be painted with flowers', and in the following year to be 'thoroughly whitened internally and newly painted with roses'. Tapestry hangings were common from the end of the thirteenth century, but if this were too expensive painted canvas was applied to the walls. Towards the end of the fifteenth century leather, stamped with decorative designs, was usual, and sometimes the walls were panelled. Sanitary accommodation was still of the most primitive sort. At Bodiam there were some twenty garderobes, and the outlets passed simply through the thickness of the wall to discharge into the moat. Where there was no convenient wet ditch, the soil just dropped into a barrel below, which could be emptied from time to time. Unless there were a fast-running stream alongside the house, no satisfactory answer to this problem was found. It was not solved, in fact, until 1596, when Sir John Harington invented the water closet, which he introduced into his house at Kelston, near Bath, and later into the Queen's palace at Richmond.

In the fourteenth century we read of a new architectural feature: the oriole. This would seem to have been a recess opening off the hall, either for a chapel or to accommodate the reader's pulpit. In the fifteenth century it became an oriel window, usually on the first floor, and because it so frequently occurs over gateways some antiquaries consider that it was most probably a development of machicolations or bartizans of military architecture which, when covered in and glazed in more peaceful times, assumed its commonly understood form. Whatever its origin, it became one of the most striking features of many domestic buildings, and one which has persisted to this day, in the form of bay windows, as a normal excrescence to the suburban parlour. Examples are to be found abroad in Germany and in France, but it was in England that it was most attractively developed. The grandest example is probably in the Great Hall at Hampton Court (1532–36), where it provides the principal lighting to the dais.

Henry VII's extensions to Wolsey's Hampton Court mark the climax of medieval domestic architecture. The gallery and screens remain at the lower end of the hall, with stairways up to the principal entrance and down to the kitchens and offices. The walls are hung with tapestry, fragments of which are original, and the roof, of hammer beam construction, is one of the richest of its kind. It is only in minor ornamental details, especially in the spandrels of the lower arch braces and the pendants with their cupids, that one can trace the beginnings of the Renaissance. The style and the plan are still medieval, even if the arches are very flat and the mouldings thin. Already, under Wolsey, there were Italian craftsmen at work in Hampton Court. In the courtyard the sculptor Majano was introducing terracotta medallions of Roman emperors, and the gatehouse, with its octagonal turreted corners, indicated a new predilection for symmetry. The transition from Gothic had begun. Soon the hall in domestic architecture was to change in character completely. Gradually it diminished in importance, as the family retired to their own rooms at one end and the servants to theirs at the other, until it became, by the eighteenth century, little more than an entrance vestibule with a communicating stair.

THE VERNACULAR DWELLING

Houses of permanent construction were built throughout the Middle Ages, but very few survive today. The use of lasting materials was largely restricted to the wealthier classes, while the great mass of the people had to depend on some system of wattle framing with a covering of skins, reeds or heather. For many centuries after the Norman Conquest, the great majority of houses were built in this way, and little or nothing survives to give us a clear idea of their architecture. It is not, in fact, until the fifteenth century that we get any appreciable number of smaller houses built in such a permanent manner that they have survived to the present day. These early houses were rarely built with masonry walls, except perhaps in a few uplands areas where outcrop stone was readily available and timber was scarce. Elsewhere, for the most part, timber seems to have been the most popular material for this class of dwelling, and in the British Isles, at least, two distinct practices emerge. In the northern and western regions, houses were built by a system of timber crucks or trusses, usually of oak, set in pairs across the width of the house to carry the roof. The space between each pair was termed a 'bay', and houses were commonly built with one, two or three such bays, depending on the needs and, no doubt, the means of the individual family. The bay was generally about 16 feet square, and this served as a medieval standard of measurement (a rod, pole or perch). It seems to have been determined in very early times by the space required for two pairs of oxen. The trusses were formed by pairs of heavy timbers, about 7 to 8 inches thick and up to 21 inches across the knee, or widest point, each pair of timbers being split halves of the same branch. These were set in the ground, or raised on stone pads, joined at the apex and linked to each other by a heavy timber ridge tree. One or two purlins, or side trees as they were called, were fixed to each side, and this completed the framing of the roof structure.

In a single bay house, the trusses were elaborated by the inclusion of a tie beam, which joined the two 'blades' of each truss. These ties, like the rest, were of heavy section and joined by a deep housing

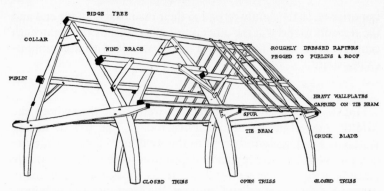

A typical two-bay cruck-trussed structure, showing two end trusses with
tie beams and a middle truss, with cruck spurs, used in order to produce
uninterrupted headroom within the building.

into the face of each blade and pinned with one or two oak pegs.
They generally projected beyond the back of each blade, where they
gave support to a wall plate. Roughly wrought rafters were then
laid across the roof timbers to carry the covering, which was usually
of thatch.

The walls of the gable ends and the sides of the house were often
formed by vertical studs, or posts, made with split lengths of
timber, jointed at each end and sprung into mortice holes, which
were drilled into a wooden sill at the floor level and into the under
side of the wall plate at the top. The posts were set close together,
and additional support was often given to the wall plate by the
insertion of heavier sections of roughly squared timbers, which
framed the wall into panels. The framework was then filled with a
thick coating of 'daub', that is, a mixture of mud and clay with
chopped straw; and finished with a coating of limewash, leaving
the main timbers exposed. In this way the characteristic 'black-
and-white' appearance of these buildings was obtained. It was of
the essence of this system of building that the roof should be
supported quite independently of the walls, and indeed it is
probable that the latter were not inserted until the roof was
completed.

The house of two or three bays usually varied from the single-
bay houses in that the intermediate trusses did not have tie beams,
which might have caused an obstruction, but were fitted with an
ingenious bracket, or 'spur', which permitted the vertical load
from the wall plate to be carried by the cruck blade. There were

many variations in detail of construction between one district and another. In some places it was usual to join the blades at the apex with a halved joint, so that the overlapping blades formed a cradle to carry the ridge tree. In other locations the blades did not intersect, but were cut short and linked by a collar so that their butt ends formed the cradle. In some areas the whole roof was stiffened by the use of diagonal braces, set between the trusses and the purlins. This made it possible to use slighter sections of timber for the structure generally.

The yeomanry of England in the fifteenth and sixteenth centuries, like the middle income group of the early twentieth century, lived in houses of a 'universal' plan. The general arrangement consisted of a through passage entry (corresponding with the screens passage in the manor house), with a door at each end. From this passage a door opened into the hall, the principal family room, which had a chamber, or parlour (often called the bower), beyond it in the second bay. Sometimes this second bay was subdivided to provide a buttery, where the household posses-

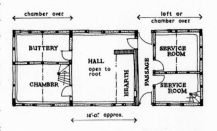

sions and cooking utensils were kept. At the opposite end of the cross passage lay the service room, a kind of inferior kitchen where the brewing and baking and other household duties were performed. In Westmorland this was called the 'downhouse', a term which was derived from the common practice of building the house on sloping ground, with the best rooms at the

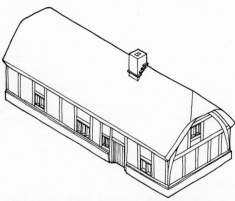

A typical three-bay cruck trussed dwelling of the sixteenth century in North-west Lancashire. The principal room—the 'house' or 'house part', as it was sometimes called—was open to the roof, the two end bays having attics above them occupying the roof space.

higher end and one or more steps at each change of level. In houses of only two bays the cross passage and service room were lacking, and the house was usually entered from the gable end.

At first, the whole of the accommodation in these houses was provided at ground level, but in due course extra room was found by the insertion of a loft, or attic, over the chamber, which could be reached by a ladder or primitive type of wooden stair. Another similar loft, with its own stair, would be contrived over the service room, to provide a sleeping apartment for the servants and hired labourers of the household.

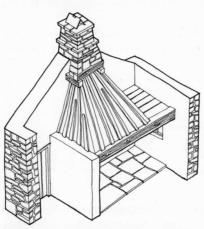

The open hearth fireplace, with a lath-and-plaster chimney, shown in the farmhouse at Saltcoats in the Fylde District of West Lancashire.

The hall remained a lofty room, open to the roof, until the middle of the seventeenth century, and later still in some remote parts of the countryside. It was in this that the open hearth was first provided. Built against a cross wall adjoining the entry, it superseded the open central fire in the late fifteenth and early sixteenth centuries. The fire was set upon a stone hearth and screened from the entry by a projecting partition, called the spere. The heavy oak bressemer spanned across the front of the hearth to form a space about 10 feet wide by 6 to 7 feet deep, within which the family could sit on benches. Above the bressemer a tapered hood was formed of lath and plaster, to gather the smoke from the fire and convey it to a narrower flue. Within this conical smoke hood the meats were dried for winter use. A number of primitive chimneys of this type have survived in old farmhouses in the country.

Contemporaneously with this north-western cruck tradition of timber framing an alternative system evolved and was widely used in the southern and eastern counties of England. This practice was distinguished by the fact that the roof was carried by the walls, which were framed into a series of bays or boxes, outlined by vertical posts and horizontal and transverse upper members. The roof was independent of the frame, and in this respect was similar to the modern method of building with load-bearing masonry walls. Usually the timbers forming the box frame walls were of very heavy section, while those employed in the roof structure were slender by contrast. Sometimes the rafters were joined by a collar near the apex, and frequently they lacked the ridge tree which was such an important element in the northern tradition.

During the fifteenth and sixteenth centuries, two and even three-storey dwellings began to be erected, especially in towns, which were of a different form. They were complete timber framed buildings, in which the construction of the walls was just as important as that of the roof. First, horizontal baulks of timber, or

Box-framed house with jettied upper storey.

sills, were laid on low foundation walls of brick or stone. Into these a series of upright posts was set, morticed and tenoned into the sill. On to these posts a wall plate would be laid to carry the first-floor joists. It was a common practice to allow these joists to project about 18 inches beyond the wall and to place at the edge the sill to carry the uprights of the next storey. Various reasons have been put forward to account for this projection: that it gave more room upstairs, that it protected the wall beneath, and that it gave greater stability to the whole building, because the joists were usually laid flat and were naturally inclined to sag. By projecting them, cantilever fashion, beyond the wall below, and loading them with the first floor wall, greater rigidity would result; but when the upper storey projected on all sides, a special problem arose at the corners. In many cases a large corner post, cut from the bole of a tree, was erected upside down so that the outward curve of the roots could support the projection and the diagonal, or dragon beams, which were inserted at this point. It was an ingenious and extravagant system which seems difficult to justify on practical, or even aesthetic, grounds.

The methods of wall finish varied according to the region. 'Wattle and daub' was general throughout the Midlands of England. In Hertfordshire and Hampshire brick nogging was used for infilling panels, and in Kent and Surrey weather-board and tile-hanging were commonly applied as a facing. In all these cases a timber framework formed the basis. The use of stone or brick as load-bearing walling material in the ordinary cottage seems to be relatively modern, even in districts well provided with good building stone. An exception was the Cotswold Grazings, where at the close of the Middle Ages the wealth accruing from the wool trade made possible higher standards of living and therefore of building.

Wattle-work, or basket-work, covered with clay, is as old as the Roman occupation. It consisted basically of an interweaving, vertically and horizontally, of hazel or ash twigs, nailed or wedged between timber uprights. Two men, one on each side, would daub a mixture of clay and straw into the wattle until the required thickness was reached. The outside would then be combed to provide a key for rough-cast plastering, and in some eastern counties this might be developed decoratively as pargetting, in which the plasterer might introduce mouldings and ornaments in sculptured relief.

The proportion of timber to infilling, and the sizes of the baulks used, were very extravagant. In the earliest works (known as post and pan), the posts were placed at intervals equal to their own width, and were usually straight and obviously carefully selected. As the oak forests became denuded in Elizabethan times, with the continuous demand for fine timber for the growing navy, the posts were placed at much wider intervals, so that the infilling panels were approximately square. The poorer dwellings had to rely more and more on smaller and less regular baulks, while the wealthier establishments were contrived also with shorter lengths, but with panels which were often enriched by quadrant corners, cuspings and quarterings, usually formed of crooked boughs that were of no use for shipbuilding. This elaboration reached extra-ordinary limits in Cheshire (pl. 24) and along the Welsh borders. It resulted in an architecture altogether romantic and surpassing anything on the Continent. Nevertheless, the same principles of construction seem to have been followed in most western countries. In Germany, on the borders of the Rhine, and in France at Rouen, Beauvais, and Bayeux, there are half-timbered houses several storeys high which are incredibly picturesque. They are not great architecture; there is something too fussy about them to attract modern taste; but they form the backcloth, as it were, to the greater medieval architectural drama.

REFERENCES

The following list of books indicates the principal works referred to and the sources of many of the illustrations.

GENERAL

ARNOLD, HUGH. *Stained Glass of the Middle Ages*. 1913.
DAVIS, H. W. C. *Medieval Europe*. 1948.
FERGUSSON, J. *A History of Architecture of All Countries*. 3rd edition, edited by R. Phéné Spiers. 1893.
FLETCHER, SIR BANISTER. *A History of Architecture on the Comparative Method*. 8th edition, 1928.
HARVEY, J. H. *The Gothic World*. 1950.
JACKSON, SIR T. G. *Gothic Architecture in France, England and Italy*. 2 vols. 1915.
LETHABY, W. R. *Medieval Art*. Revised and edited by D. Talbot Rice. 1949.
PEVSNER, NIKOLAUS. *An Outline of European Architecture*. 1948.
PORTER, A. KINGSLEY. *Medieval Architecture, its Origins and Development*. 1909.
POWER, EILEEN. *Medieval People*. 1924.
SIMSON, OTTO VON. *The Gothic Cathedral*. 1956.
STURGIS, R. and FROTHINGHAM, A. L. *A History of Architecture*. 4 vols. 1917.
TOUT, T. F. *Medieval Town Planning*. 1934.

FRANCE

ENLART, C. *Manuel d'Archéologie Française*. 2 vols. 1902–4.
LAVEDAN, P. *French Architecture*. English edition. 1956.
SAINT-PAUL, ANTHYME. *Histoire Monumentale de la France*. 1884.
VIOLLET-LE-DUC, E. E. *Dictionnaire Raisonée de l'Architecture Française*. 1859.

ENGLAND

BOND, F. *Gothic Architecture in England*. 1906.
    An Introduction to English Church Architecture. 1913.
BRANDON, J. R. and J. A. *Open Timber Roofs of the Middle Ages*. 1899.
COOK, G. H. *Portrait of Salisbury Cathedral*. 1949.
COX, J. C. *The English Parish Church*. 1914.

GARDNER, S. *A Guide to English Gothic Architecture.* 1922.
HARVEY, J. H. *Gothic England.* 1947.
HARVEY, J. H. and FELTON, H. *The English Cathedrals.* 1950.
PEVSNER, NIKOLAUS. *The Leaves of Southwell.* 1945.
POWER, C. E. *English Medieval Architecture.* 2nd ed. 3 vols. 1923.
PRIOR, E. S. *History of Gothic Art in England.* 1900.
RICKMAN, T. *An Attempt to Discriminate the Styles of English Architecture.* 1817.
SCOTT, G. G. *An Essay on the History of English Church Architecture.* 1881.
SHARPE, E. *Architectural Parallels in the Twelfth and Thirteenth Centuries, Selected from Abbey Churches.* 1848.
WEBB, G. F. *Gothic Architecture in England.* 1951.
   Architecture in Britain: The Middle Ages. 1956.

GERMANY

DEHIO, G. *Geschichte der Deutschen Kunst.* 6 vols. 1921–31.
DEHIO, G. and BEZOLD, G. V. *Die Kirchliche Baukunst des Abendlandes.* 1884.
LÜBKE, W. *Ecclesiastical Art in Germany.* 1873.

SPAIN

BEVAN, B. *A History of Spanish Architecture.* 1938.
HARVEY, J. H. *Cathedrals of Spain.* 1957.
STREET, G. E. *Some Account of Gothic Architecture in Spain.* 1914.

ITALY

CUMMINGS, C. A. *A History of Italian Architecture.* 1901.
RUSKIN, J. *Stones of Venice.* 1886.
STREET, G. E. *Brick and Marble Architecture in North Italy.* 1874.

SECULAR ARCHITECTURE

BROWN, R. Allen, *English Medieval Castles.* 1954.
FEDDEN, R. and THOMSON, J. *Crusader Castles.* 1957.
LLOYD, N. *A History of the English House.* 1931.
McGIBBON, J. and ROSS, T. *The Castellated and Domestic Architecture of Scotland.* 5 vols. 1888.
TOY, S. *The Castles of Great Britain.* 1953.
   A History of Fortifications from 3000 B.C. to A.D. 1700. 1955.

ARCHITECTURAL GLOSSARY

Note: This glossary is limited to words and terms used in this volume only.

Abacus. The top member of the capital of a column, in Gothic work usually moulded. In England it is commonly circular or octagonal in plan, whereas in France the square form is occasionally found.

Abbey. A religious establishment governed by an abbot.

Acanthus. A stylized leaf form which is commonly associated with carving in a Corinthian capital, but which also occurs in a debased form in Gothic work.

Aedicule. A small niched setting designed to accommodate a statue.

Aisles. The parts on either side of the nave of a church whose interior is divided by columns or piers; generally lower and narrower than the nave.

Ambulatory. The aisle which surrounds the apse of a church at the eastern end.

Annulet. A ring round the shaft of a column.

Apse. A semi-circular or multangular termination of the chancel.

Arcade. A series of arches carried on columns or piers, either attached to or independent of a wall.

Arched Braced Roof. A form of roof truss spaced at intervals and incorporating curved members, or arched braces, to support purlins (see p. 156).

Architrave. The lowest division of the entablature (*q.v.*) spanning horizontally between columns.

Archivolt. The moulded face of an arch.

Arris. The sharp edge formed at the meeting of two surfaces.

Ashlar. Stone walling, the exposed face of which is squared and finished construction.

Bailey. The fortified open courtyard of a feudal castle.

Ball-flower. A carved ornament consisting of three leaves enclosing a small ball. A common repeating ornament in English Decorated architecture of the fourteenth century (see p. 70).

Barbican. An outwork defending the entrance to a castle.

Barrel Vault. See Vaulting.

Bar Tracery. Intersecting framework of slender shafts continuing the lines of the mullions and forming a decorative network at the head of a window.

Bastide. A medieval planned town, usually arranged on a grid pattern (see pp. 17–18.)

Bastion. A projecting tower in a system of fortifications.

Batter. The slightly inclined face of a wall.

Bay. One of a series of compartments of a building, defined by walls, buttresses, or columns.

Boss. A projecting stone, ornamentally carved, which occurs at the intersection of vaulting ribs.

Bowtell. A convex moulding, three-quarters round in section.

Broach Spire. An octagonal spire rising without a parapet from a square tower, with inclined half-pyramidal forms at the corners (see p. 161).

Buttress. A mass of masonry built to resist the pressure of an arch or vault. See also Flying Buttress.

Campanile. An Italian name for a bell-tower. Often detached from the main building.

Capital. The top feature of a column or pier, usually carved.

Castellation. Parapet having a series of openings or embrasures. Also called Crenellation.

Cathedral. A church which accommodates a Bishop's Throne, or Cathedra.

Chamfer. The diagonal plane formed by cutting the square angle of a block of stone or wood to a splay.

Chancel. The portion of a church, usually at the eastern end, which accommodates clergy and choir.

Chantry Chapel. A chapel, usually in a church, which is endowed for the saying of Masses for the soul of the founder.

Chapter House. One of the rooms in a monastery, usually entered off the cloisters, in which the business of the establishment was transacted.

Chevet. The rounded eastern termination of a church, which includes the chancel, the ambulatory and radiating chapels.

Chevron. A zigzag ornamental moulding, especially common in Norman work (see p. 70).

Choir. The eastern portion of a church which accommodates the singers.

Cimborio. A Spanish term for the cupola or lantern which rises immediately above the crossing.

Cinquefoil. In tracery, a panel divided into five leaf-shaped openings by cusps.

Clerestory. The portion of the nave of a church which rises above the aisle roof and is pierced by windows.

Cloister. A covered walkway round an open square, connecting the church to the chapter house, refectory, and other parts of the monastery.

Clustered Pier. A mass of masonry composed of a series of column shafts.

Collar Beam. A tie beam connecting the two slopes of a roof, usually about half-way up, to prevent spreading.

Coping. The capping or covering member of a wall.

Corbel. A projecting block of stone, often carved, and generally used to support a beam.

Cornice. The crowning member of an entablature (*q.v.*).

Crenellation. See Castellation.

Crockets. Projecting spurs of stone, carved with foliage, placed at intervals to decorate the raking sides of spires, pinnacles, gables, etc; occasionally also in wood carving, as, for instance, in the canopies of choir stalls (see p. 70).

Cross Vault. See Vaulting.

Crypt. Underground space, usually beneath the chancel, and used for burial.

Curtain Wall. The wall between towers or bastions in defensive works.

Curved Braces. Curved timbers inserted to strengthen others in roof construction.

Curvilinear. Tracery of the Decorated period of English architecture, distinguished by its flowing lines (see p. 56).

Cusp. A small pointed member between the lobes or foils in Gothic tracery (see p. 58).

Dentils. Cube-like decoration, commonly found in the cornice of the Ionic and Corinthian Orders.

Diaper. Decoration of square or diamond shapes (see p. 70).

Dog-tooth. A geometric ornament consisting of a series of four-cornered stars raised as pyramids. Especially common in Early English Gothic (see p. 70).

Eaves. The underside of an overhanging roof.

Encaustic Tiles. Glazed earthenware tiles, often decorated and used for paving.

Enceinte. The outer line or enclosure of a fortress.

Entablature. The upper horizontal parts of a Classical Order of architecture, comprising architrave, frieze, and cornice.

Extrados. The outer curve or boundary of the face of an arch.

Fan Vault. See vaulting.

Fillet. A narrow projecting, or sunken, flat band, running down a shaft or along a roll moulding.

Finial. The top of a pinnacle, gable, or other architectural feature.

Flamboyant. The last phase of French Gothic architecture, identifiable by the flowing, flame-like character of the window tracery.

Flèche. A slender spire, usually of wood covered with lead or copper, rising from the ridge of the roof.

Flying Buttress. A structure of masonry, usually consisting of a quadrant arch springing from an independent pier to the wall of the nave of a church to resist the thrust of the nave vault.

Fresco. Properly applied to painting on wet plaster, but often for any wall painting other than oil painting.

Frieze. The horizontal division of an entablature (*q.v.*) between the architrave and the cornice. Also used to refer to any long horizontal decoration at a high level.

Gargoyle. A waterspout projecting from a parapet and carved into some animal or human form.

Geometric. Tracery of the Early English period, consisting chiefly of circles or foiled circles.

Grisaille. A kind of stained-glass window, basically white but with an irregular studding of coloured pieces and occasionally a border.

Groined Vault. See Vaulting.

Hammer Beam. A timber cantilever projecting from the top of the wall to carry arch timbers and struts (see p. 157).

Haunch. That portion of an arch or vault immediately above the springing.

Helm Roof. A pyramidal type of roof to a square tower, in which the four faces rest diagonally between the gables.

Hip. The sloped end of a roof.

Hood Mould. A projecting moulding over the head of an opening to throw off rain. Sometimes called a dripstone, and when rectangular, a label.

Infilling. The masonry of the vault between the ribs.

Intersecting Vault. See Vaulting.

Intrados. The soffit or underside of an arch.

Jambs. The upright sides of a door or window opening.

Keep. The strongest part of a castle, sometimes detached from, but surrounded by, other defences.

King post. The upright member in a roof truss which unites the ridge beam with the tie beam or collar beam.

Label. See Hood Mould.

Lady Chapel. A chapel dedicated to the Virgin Mary, usually constructed at the extreme east end of greater churches.

Lancet Arch. A sharply pointed arch, commonly found in the early period of Gothic architecture.

Lantern. A turret with windows, crowned by a roof.

Lierne Rib or Vault. See Vaulting.

Lintel. A horizontal beam bridging an opening.

Lucarne. A roof window.

Machicolation. Stonework forming a projecting parapet, supported on corbels between which missiles could be dropped on an enemy (see p. 205).

Misericord. The bracketed underside of a hinged seat which provides some support while standing and is frequently grotesquely carved.

Moat. A ditch, not necessarily filled with water, which was dug around fortified works.

Mullion. Vertical member dividing a window into two or more lights.

Nave. The central and chief division of a church.

Niche. An arched recess in a wall.

Ogee. A moulding made up of a convex and a concave curve. Also applied to arches of similar shape.

Order. In Classical architecture, signifies a column with base and capital, together with the entablature. In Gothic architecture, each ring of voussoirs in an arch consisting of several rings.

Oriel. A projecting bow window, usually on an upper floor.

Parapet. The portion of wall above the roof gutter, sometimes battlemented.

Pendant Vault. See Vaulting.

Pier. Any more or less isolated mass of masonry from which arches spring in an arcade.

Pilaster. A shallow engaged pier, usually with a flat face.

Pinnacle. The small spired termination on the top of buttresses and parapets, frequently ornamented with crockets or carved foliage.

Piscina. A stone basin near the altar, in which the priest washes the chalice.

Plate Tracery. An early form of tracery, where decoratively shaped openings are cut through the infilling panel of masonry under the head of an arch.

Plinth. The projecting base of a building or pier.

Portcullis. The gate of a castle, constructed to rise and fall in vertical grooves.

Postern. A secondary gateway to a castle.

Presbytery. The eastern, or sanctuary, end of a church, usually reserved for the clergy.

Pulpitum. A rood screen.

Purlin. A timber member laid horizontally, and parallel with wall plate, between roof trusses to carry rafters.

Quadripartite Vault. See Vaulting.

Quatrefoil. In tracery, a panel divided into four leaf-shaped openings by cusps.

Queen posts. Two vertical struts in a roof truss which link the principal rafters with the tie beam.

Rafters. The sloping timbers which run from the top of the wall to the ridge in a roof.

Reredos. The screen behind the altar.

Rere Vault. The arched surface between the window arch and the inner arch in a specially thick wall.

Retrochoir. The part of a chancel which lies behind the high altar.

Ribbed Vault. See Vaulting.

Ridge. The apex to a roof, and also, in Gothic vaulting, the horizontal rib at the crown of a vault.

Rood Screen. A screen dividing the chancel from the nave and surmounted by a large cross.

Rose Window. A circular window filled with patterned tracery (see p. 60).

Rubble. Walling of stones of irregular shapes and sizes.

Sanctuary. The place which accommodates the principal altar of a church.

Scoinson Arch. The inner arch, as opposed to the window arch, in a specially thick wall (see p. 58).

Set-off or Weathering. Sloping surface on sills, buttresses, etc., to throw off water.

Sexpartite Vault. See Vaulting.

Shaft. The portion of a column between the base and the capital.

Sill. The lower horizontal member of a window.

Soffit. The under-surface of a lintel or arch.

Solar. The upper drawing-room of a medieval house.

Spandrel. The roughly triangular space between two adjoining arches.

Spire. A steep, conical structure, usually octagonal on plan, which is built on top of a tower.

Springing. The horizontal level from which an arch or vault rises.

Steeple. A tower capped by a spire.

Stellar Vault. See Vaulting (lierne).

Stilt. A term applied when the springing of an arch is raised higher than is normal.

String Course. A projecting horizontal moulding running along the face of a wall.

Stucco. Ornamental plaster work.

Tas-de-charge. The lowest course of a ribbed vault laid with horizontal, rather than radiating, joints, on which the rib mouldings are mitred and carved (see p. 41).

Tempera. A form of wall painting applied to a dry wall surface, in which the medium is commonly yolk of egg.

Tesserae. Small cubes of stone, marble, or glass, used in mosaic decoration.

Tie Beam. The timber member connecting the two slopes of a roof and usually laid at the level of the wall plate to prevent the roof from spreading.

Tierceron Rib or Vault. See Vaulting.

Tracery. Ornamental stonework at the heads of window openings.

Transept. Part of a cruciform church projecting at right angles to the main building.

Transom. A horizontal bar across a window opening.

Transverse Arch. An arch spanning at right angles to the main walls of a church.

Trefoil. In tracery, a panel divided into three leaf-shaped openings by cusps.

Triforium. In Gothic architecture, the area between the top of the arcade and the clerestory.

Truss. A triangular arrangement of timbers placed at intervals to carry purlins, which in their turn carry roof rafters.

Tympanum. In Gothic architecture, a slab or piece of walling which fills the space enclosed by an arch over the lintel of a doorway.

Vaulting. Arched covering in stone or brick.

    Barrel Vault. The simplest type of vault, usually of semi-circular section, covering a rectangular space.

    Cross or Groined Vault also called **Intersecting Vault.** Generally used over square bays, and formed by the intersection of two equal barrel vaults at right angles.

    Fan Vault. A vault in which all the ribs, and there are usually many, are of the same length and curvature, forming conoids. In such a vault, the infilling is reduced to a minimum, and in many cases the infilling and rib are cut from the same stone (see p. 44).

    Lierne Vault. A ribbed vault, having tertiary ribs which do not rise from the springing but link, more or less obliquely, one rib to another. When used to make star-like patterns, referred to as *Stellar Vaulting* (see p. 42).

    Pendant Vault. A vault incorporating in its construction elongated voussoirs, from which vaulting ribs may spring (see p. 46).

    Quadripartite Vault. A vault divided into four parts (see p. 38).

    Ribbed Vault. A vault framed with ribs which carry light panel infilling.

    Sexpartite Vault. A vault which is divided into six parts by means of an additional transverse rib.

    Tierceron Vault. A ribbed vault, having secondary ribs which rise from the springing to the ridge and thus reduce the span of the infilling (see p. 40).

Volute. A scroll or spiral ornament.

Voussoir. One of the wedge-shaped stones used in the structure of an arch.

Wall Plate. A length of timber laid along the top of a wall to receive the rafters or members of a roof truss.

Web. The infilling panel of light masonry constructed between the ribs in a vault.

Wheel Window. A circular window with radiating mullions in the pattern of a wheel.

INDEX OF BUILDINGS AND PLACES

Illustrations in heavy type